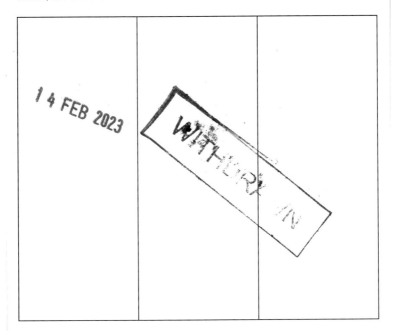

MURDER, WITCHCRAFT AND THE KILLING OF WILDLIFE

MEMOIRS OF A POLICE OFFICER IN THE HEART OF AFRICA

This book is dedicated to all those police officers, friends and colleagues who served in the elite Northern Rhodesia Police, irrespective of colour or creed, and to those who lost their lives or suffered life-changing injuries through their devotion, commitment and courage in safeguarding the country and its people through to Independence.

And to the ever-bright memory of Graf Von Schwarzwald, aka my boy Alex, the magnificent Doberman, born 12 May 1961, who was my most trusted and loyal friend, imbued with inestimable courage and who was frequently prepared to lay down his life for me and his family, and who saved my life on several occasions.

I told them we had buried my boy Alex in his favourite summer spot,
with his ball and his bowl, but this was not the complete truth,
for he lies forever within my heart.

Stephen R. Matthews

MURDER, WITCHCRAFT AND THE KILLING OF WILDLIFE

MEMOIRS OF A POLICE OFFICER IN THE HEART OF AFRICA

STEPHEN R. MATTHEWS

PEN & SWORD
HISTORY

AN IMPRINT OF PEN & SWORD BOOKS LTD.
YORKSHIRE – PHILADELPHIA

First published in Great Britain in 2019 by
PEN AND SWORD HISTORY
An imprint of
Pen & Sword Books Ltd
Yorkshire – Philadelphia

Paperback ISBN: 978 1 52676 411 9
Hardback ISBN: 978 1 52676 407 2

Typeset in Times New Roman 11.5/14 by
Aura Technology and Software Services, India
Printed and bound in the UK by TJ International

Pen & Sword Books Limited incorporates the imprints of Atlas, Archaeology,
Aviation, Discovery, Family History, Fiction, History, Maritime, Military, Military
Classics, Politics, Select, Transport, True Crime, Air World, Frontline Publishing,
Leo Cooper, Remember When, Seaforth Publishing, The Praetorian Press,
Wharncliffe Local History, Wharncliffe Transport, Wharncliffe True Crime and
White Owl.

For a complete list of Pen & Sword titles please contact
PEN & SWORD BOOKS LIMITED
47 Church Street, Barnsley, South Yorkshire, S70 2AS, England
E-mail: enquiries@pen-and-sword.co.uk
Website: www.pen-and-sword.co.uk

Or
PEN AND SWORD BOOKS
1950 Lawrence Rd, Havertown, PA 19083, USA
E-mail: Uspen-and-sword@casematepublishers.com
Website: www.penandswordbooks.com

Contents

Acknowledgements

It is an impossibility to name everyone who has given their time to ensure the book was published but it does provide me with an opportunity to record my deep appreciation for the help and support of the following:

Lee Durrell MBE PhD, For her Message of Hope and her kind permission to use the evocative poem written by her late husband Gerald Durrell OBE. Lee is an American naturalist, author, and TV presenter.

Peter le Vasseur, International Wildlife Artist, Naturalist and Ecologist and fellow Guernseyman, for his gracious permission to use reproductions of his extraordinary and thought provoking wildlife paintings.

Sharon Lewis, Widow of my friend, ex-Police colleague and award winning poet David Lewis for consenting to my using David's inspiring 'Africa' Poem in this book.

The Message of Hope

My late husband, Gerald Durrell, wrote the inspiring words below more than 30 years ago, after nearly a lifetime trying to make sure they would come true. Although much has been accomplished in nature conservation since then, the struggle to protect biodiversity is escalating as situations worsen on many fronts. For example, the international illegal trade in wildlife (and wildlife parts) is one of the major factors in driving species towards extinction.

Stephen Matthews's book reminds us that wildlife crime has been around a long time. Today's challenges are simply new faces of the same lawlessness. But there is something different about today – the widespread public awareness of the intrinsic value of the wildlife with which we share this beautiful planet. Can that awareness be converted to action to stop the plunder of the natural world? Dare we hope that Gerry's efforts to ensure there will still be "extraordinary varieties of creatures sharing the land of the planet" have not been wasted?

Lee Durrell MBE PhD widow of the famous
author and conservationist Gerald Durrell OBE.

These evocative and heartfelt words were penned by the late Gerald Durrell OBE, and buried in a time-capsule at Jersey Zoo, Channel Islands in 1988.

'We hope that there will be fireflies and glow-worms at
night to guide you and butterflies in hedges and forests
to greet you.

We hope that your dawns will have an orchestra of bird
song and that the sound of their wings and the opalescence
of their colouring will dazzle you.

MURDER, WITCHCRAFT AND THE KILLING OF WILDLIFE

We hope that there will still be the extraordinary varieties of creatures sharing the land of the planet with you to enchant you and enrich your lives as they have done for us.

We hope that you will be grateful for having been born into such a magical world.'

The African Leopard
From a painting by Peter Le Vasseur.

Glossary

Bwana	Boss
Braaivleis	South African BBQ
Boerewors	South African spicy sausages
Bantu	African people from Central or Southern Africa
Biltong	Sun dried, spicy meat
Boma	Government offices/ Administration
Bundu	Bush country/ a wild region
Bushbuck	A type of antelope
Cabwino	Okay. Alright
Chitimukulu	Paramount Chief of Bemba tribe
CID.	Criminal Investigation Department
Compol	Abbreviation for Commissioner of Police
Dagga	Form of Cannabis
Dambo	Small pool or reservoir/ watery marsh
Donna	Housewife/ lady of house
Duiker	Small antelope
Inde	Yes, indeed
Katundu	Baggage/ belongings/ luggage
Kachasu/ kacasu	Alcoholic spirit
Knobkerrie	Zulu war weapon/ wooden stave
Kraal	Afrikaans word for a cattle enclosure
Medami	Madame, Mrs
Mealie-Meal	A coarse flour made from maize
Mfiti	Sorcerer, witch, wizard
Mowa	Opaque Beer made from Maize
Mzungu	White-man/ European
Nyama	Game meat/ red meat
Nkhwazi	Fish Eagle, and badge of Northern Rhodesia Police also national bird of Zambia

Ndaba	Sheltered tree used as a meeting point to discuss problems.
Ops	Operations Room
Phiri	Hill or mountain
Piccanin Kaya	Toilet
Simba	Lion
Situpa(s)	Identity Card
Shebeen	Den of vice and illegal drinking lair
Zikomo	Thank you! Please

Preface

I was once told by an editor, that the best place for the boring fragments of a book should be tucked away safely in the Preface because in his inestimable opinion no-one would ever read it!

On 3 February 1960, Britain's Prime Minister, Harold Macmillan, who had spent over a month travelling throughout Africa, gave a speech to the South African Parliament in Cape Town, in which he stated it was his intention of granting full independence to many African territories. He went on to say that 'The wind of change is blowing through this continent, and whether we like it or not, this growth of natural consciousness is a political fact.'

The British Colonial Secretary at this critical period of Britain and Africa's history was Iain Macleod and on 1 April 1960, just as I landed in Northern Rhodesia, he released Dr Hastings Banda of Nyasaland (now Malawi) from detention. Then, on 16 June 1960, he followed this up by lifting the State of Emergency in the territories. Iain Macleod had been appointed by Macmillan and he went on to oversee the independence of many African countries from under British rule. He earned the enmity of many British politicians, who branded him as being simply too clever by half! He was also described by many senior government officials and administrators in those African countries as being gratuitously and grossly offensive.

Later that year, it was followed by a commission conducted by Walter Monckton, 1st Viscount Monckton of Brenchley, in order to make proposals for the future of the Federation of Rhodesia and Nyasaland. His report concluded that the Federation could not be sustained except by force, or through massive changes in racial legislation. Monckton's report was released in October 1960, just as I was about to take up my new posting in Chingola, in Northern Rhodesia. It advocated sweeping changes to the Federal structure; nevertheless, the Federal Prime

Minister, Sir Roy Welensky was outraged over the content of the report, though the British government of that time broadly accepted the written document.

It was against this disturbing backdrop that I had travelled to Northern Rhodesia and was inducted into their elite Police Force as an Assistant Inspector, where I was soon to be catapulted into a world of political unrest, with the serious undercurrents of witchcraft, murder and the continuous onslaught against the country's precious wildlife, which unfortunately still carries on to the present day. In late 1964, Northern Rhodesia became the proud and peaceful nation of Zambia under their new elected leader Dr Kenneth Kaunda.

Introduction

I started writing this book, oft-times on the edge of the Pearl River Delta in the midst of a gentle and peaceful classical Chinese garden, created by the first Nationalist Prime Minister of China, where I was surrounded by colourful azalea and rhododendron bushes and where I could look right down into the South China Seas. In this serene and spiritual setting, it is easy to imagine those of my friends and colleagues, who served with me in the police in Northern Rhodesia (now Zambia) and who have gone on ahead in spirit. Their vibrant energy and dedication is still all-pervading and I can visualise them in my mind's eye, just as they were all those decades ago.

With the bright green and shimmering bamboos rustling in the light summer breeze, I almost expected them to emerge into the bright sunlight with their bronzed and smiling faces. 'We few, we happy few, we band of brothers.' Brothers in arms, we were, who will never die as long as our story is told, and this then is their amazing and true narrative.

I have endeavoured to provide a distant glimpse of life and events from a different era, once vibrant and resonating with energy and purpose, then overcome with turbulent political unrest and overtones of diabolical witchcraft and the abhorrent slaughter of wildlife, all now largely consigned to a mere historical footnote in dusty and forgotten volumes. The time for writing seems apposite just now, whilst my memory remains reasonably clear and stable for even as I write, these images previously set in my mind in clear and vivid colours are already beginning to fade.

Zambia is a land-locked country in the southern part of Central Africa, covering some 290,585 square miles and it is made up of a high plateau of savannah country with sweeping hills and mountains. To put it in perspective, the United Kingdom including Northern Ireland is less than a third of the size, and one of Zambia's most outstanding features is the majestic Victoria Falls first seen by the intrepid explorer David Livingstone. I found the subtropical climate a sheer delight, mainly because of such a high elevated position (up to 5,000 feet above sea level). The mighty Zambezi river cuts through the land and is joined midway along its length by the surging Kafue River which rises in the copper-rich bush country near the Congo border.

This is the story of success and failures, of my fears and happiness and while my elders and betters in the form of senior officers were all grappling with the enormous difficulties of trying to steer the great Ship of State towards independence, I was down at the sharp end with many of my compatriots, mired in a constant mess of trial and tribulation for which I am ever grateful! This period also revealed the courage and dedication of both my European and African colleagues, who I am proud to have served alongside during those stirring times. I think it is true to say we went out to Africa as mere boys and returned later as much wiser young men.

Some names, places and identifying details have been changed in order that the privacy of certain individuals mentioned within the book may be protected. I have also made every attempt to contact the relevant copyright-holders, where appropriate, but some were either unobtainable or did not reply. I would, therefore, be grateful if the appropriate people would contact me through the publishers.

Stephen Matthews, 2019

Chapter 1

Death Stalks the Township

Mid-autumn in Brittany and the old man, sitting in front of the large picture window, is watching the spectacular golden and russet leaves gently spiralling down from the woodland trees and yet he really doesn't see them, for his mind is firmly fixed on events that occurred nearly sixty years ago, in the subtropical heat of an African plateau. He is thinking too, about the swift passing of the years and the dispiriting fact that in spite of everyone's best efforts, nothing seems to have changed under the hot African sun. People were still being slaughtered in their droves and terrorised in malignant bouts of ethnic cleansing. In the intervening years, over six million human beings have been exterminated in the Democratic Republic of Congo and migrants are constantly fleeing porous borders to seek sanctuary in neighbouring countries, just as they did all those years ago. The precious animals and wildlife continue to be decimated, to the point of eradication, unbelievably aided by politicians in many countries who actively encourage trophy hunting. Six decades before, the old, man had tried his best to help stop the killing, but he now realised, in this one moment, he had failed. He had endeavoured to help the courageous African people, but the real question was should he have done more, and could he have done more?

I am that grey-haired old man, and I have always valued my police service in Africa, but what brought everything into sharp focus on that day was the atrocious statistics that fifty-five elephants are still being massacred every day, solely for their highly prized ivory tusks. With 20,000 elephants being relentlessly killed each year, it will be only a few

1

more decades before they become extinct. Additionally, in these modern times, one rhinoceros is butchered every eight hours by criminal gangs, to feed a supposed cancer cure. Where did I and my colleagues fail, and should the world shoulder a greater measure of responsibility?

Since time immemorial, Zambia always had a torrid history, cloaked in what has been termed pagan darkness. Tribe fought tribe and rigid tribal laws dealt out a terrible justice backed up with assegais and pangas. Victims were often sold into slavery by local chiefs who held sway over vast tracts of land, and communities were ruled by fear, superstition and witchcraft. This darkest part of Africa was a country where mercy and generosity were unknown and in early 1960, when I arrived, it seemed to me in that time very little had changed. The name of Rhodesia had emanated from Cecil John Rhodes, a British capitalist and empire builder. Rhodes pushed hard for British influence in the region and obtained mineral rights from local chiefs, albeit under very dubious circumstances. The most important development in Northern Rhodesia was the discovery and development of copper, through extensive mining on the Copperbelt, where I was to be stationed for some time.

The year was now 1960, and the country, Northern Rhodesia, a British Protectorate, soon to become the sovereign state of Zambia. I had joined the force in order to help in the Africanisation of the police prior to the anticipated independence of that country. After six months of intensive training in weapons, law and African languages, the garden town of Chingola, one of the major Copperbelt towns, had been my very first posting as an Assistant Inspector of Police, a euphoric period, when I had been warmly welcomed. Police colleagues invariably remained friends for life, from Assistant Superintendent Roy Coppard, who ran his station like a well-oiled machine, to Assistant Inspector David Lewis, who was the farm-patrol officer. David had a great love for Africa and its peoples and always relished the opportunity to visit African villages, or to seek out and photograph both animals and some of the more exotic local scenery. Sometimes, both of us would drive out to isolated farmsteads, or down to the riverside, for some fishing. Today, I treasure some of his poems and I well remember him sitting on the banks of the swiftly flowing Kafue River with his fishing rod and line dangling in the water, writing some of his award-winning compositions.

A few months before, I had married Wendy a very beautiful girl from my home island of Guernsey in a moving ceremony in the United Reform

Church in Chingola, conducted by the Reverend Charles Catto, who had once been the Christian spiritual leader of several Native American peoples in America and Canada. A guard of honour in full dress uniform had been provided by a few of my colleagues and with an old school friend Ted Osmond-Jones acting as my best man. The bride had been given away by another old boy from my college in Guernsey, Assistant Superintendent Chris Thorne; who would also remain a true and lifelong friend. My new wife and I then embarked on a carefree honeymoon at the awe-inspiring Victoria Falls, visiting various game parks and the flooding plains of the newly constructed Kariba Dam. Then it was back to my new posting amidst the maelstrom of political agitation, where we desperately tried to stop the violence aimed at their opponents in the various townships, while criminal gangs operated with a measure of impunity.

In the meantime, I started out as leader of my inaugural shift and the very first friendly face was that of my second in command, Head Constable Kaunda, although he much preferred to be called Sergeant Major. Kaunda was a hearty, jovial man, totally dedicated to the police force and especially to the young men in his charge. The beds in our old bungalow were single ones, at varying heights, which did not augur well for the start of our married life together. I had arranged for a new bed to be delivered at the end of this, my first day-shift, and I knew my wife would be anxiously waiting for me at the bungalow. At the end of the shift, the sergeants and all the constables were lined up on the parade ground, ready to be dismissed when the bed duly arrived on the back of the local store transport. I never knew how Sgt Maj Kaunda was aware the bed was being delivered but he must have known because he immediately took charge of the whole operation and the heavy wrapping paper was stripped off the bed. He took hold of one corner of the divan, with two sergeants and a leading constable, manning the other corners. Then suddenly, another African appeared out of nowhere, wearing leopard skin garb and carrying a ceremonial fly whisk as he proceeded to dance all around the bed singing and waving his fly-whisk in the air. Kaunda told me this was a traditional tribal dance, carried out by a local witchdoctor, as it was necessary to bless the bed and make it fruitful, so I was left in no doubt who I should blame in the future. The bed was carried on high to the bungalow with great pomp and ceremony and much singing, followed by all the other members of the shift, clapping their hands in time together and singing some traditional tribal songs with their impressive and deep melodic voices until the bed was finally deposited and positioned in our bedroom, much to my wife's profound embarrassment.

Still, I genuinely enjoyed the night shifts on duty and quite often I would collect Sgt Maj Kaunda and our other two sergeants with the landrover at about 5.30am and make our way to the local bakery to buy some bacon rolls and polystyrene cups filled to the brim with hot coffee. We would then drive out to a high escarpment overlooking the deep wooded valleys far below, where we could see the majestic orange sunrise that in turn highlighted the river mist that followed the contours of the interwoven water-courses. This gave us all the opportunity of talking to each other as equals, not only about our work ethic. It also enabled me to address their very real concerns over the burgeoning political situation and the future direction of their country.

Nevertheless, it was not all sweetness and light, because a few evenings later, Robin Mwanza was already late getting back to his home in Nchanga Township. Robin was only 17 and a member of the Ngumbo tribe from Samfya District in Northern Rhodesia. His father had died several years before this, so his schooling had been cruelly terminated. On his own initiative, he had set up a small stall in the local fish market, selling dried fish where he could make a clear £5 profit each month, which he was putting towards the cost of his further education. He had to work long hours because he still needed to send money home to his widowed mother in the village and then he had to pay his way with his guardian in Nchanga Township. His guardian frequently warned him not to be too late coming back home, as there were bands of thugs out on the streets, all looking for trouble. He knew he was late but what else could he do? He was hurrying along even as night was falling and he could hear the strident blasts of police whistles sounding out from different points in the location. He decided to take a short cut which meant leaving the main, well-lit road and taking to the smaller dark avenues, but he thought it well worth the risk.

After walking only a few yards into the darkness, he could sense there was someone just behind him and he began to run. He jumped across one of the large storm drains, used to carry away large volumes of rainwater during the monsoon season, and within a few seconds a hue and cry erupted just behind him, as several men joined in the chase and he could hear the pounding of their feet on the roadway, and then stones and rocks started to fall all around him. He was beginning to have difficulty breathing with the exertion, but he still carried on running, with fear driving him ever onwards. This time, he veered more towards the haven of light offered by the local beer-hall. First one rock hit him on the head, knocking him sideways but somehow he kept on moving although at a much slower pace, then another large stone smashed against one of his legs causing him to stumble. Even as he lay on the ground grievously hurt, he was still trying to crawl ever onwards towards the light. We had answered the urgent call from one of the police whistles and a battered and shaken police constable reported that a group of thugs, returning from a night's violence in nearby Chiwempala Township, had attacked him and then chased after a youth they had seen running away.

Sgt Maj Kaunda and I started running up the hill towards the beer-hall, weighed down by our heavy equipment and desperately gasping for breath with hearts beating rapidly, almost to bursting point. In the half-light, I could just see a person lying full length on the ground with a man standing right over the body and holding a large boulder with both hands. I shouted out a breathless 'Police – Stop!' which was all I could utter, as the man calmly looked back at me and then dropped the large boulder directly onto Robin's head, before turning and running away into the darkness. When I reached Robin he was still moving, I knelt down and held him in my arms and he spoke only one word, 'Zikomo,' meaning thank you and as I watched, I saw his eyes glaze over and the boy's spirit slowly left his broken body, leaving me angry and frustrated.

However, a week or so later, my friend Sgt Maj Kaunda went on leave and I was promoted and immediately ordered to take over the Criminal Investigation Department in the adjacent Chiwempala Township. This meant leaving our spacious three-bedroom Colonial style bungalow with flowering bougainvillea growing over the roof in exchange for a modern studio apartment in another dust laden African Township. The small enclave of Chiwempala was to all intents and purposes a typical satellite for thousands of workers employed by households and various commercial enterprises in Chingola, only a few miles distant. My wife and I arrived at our new station later one evening and the distant beating of tribal drums seemed to emphasise the fact we were now living in deepest Africa. Bright and early the next morning, I left for the police station, where I found my new Officer-in-Charge, Chief Inspector Brian

Thomas already waiting for me. Brian gave me a warm welcome and he ushered me into his office, where the first thing he said to me was, 'Look here, in this office and at home I am Brian – but out there in the station I am Sir, and by the way, I asked for you especially!' This then was the beginning of a very strong friendship that would be sustained down the decades. Brian once expressed the view to his wife, Mair, that the period we had all spent together in Chiwempala had been the happiest of all times for him in Africa.

Brian told me the CID team was in dire need of some urgent care and firm leadership, but first he took me to visit one of the location huts, where he knocked on an old battered wooden door, which was soon opened by a wizened elderly woman and after the traditional African greeting, we were ushered inside. In the gloom, I saw a thin and grey-looking young man lying on top of a narrow bed, partly covered by an old tattered blanket. Brian told how this young man had once been a healthy and well-educated local teacher, but he had been struck down by an unknown sorcerer using a Kalalozi gun. Originally, Kalalozi guns were fashioned out of bones taken from exhumed bodies, by sorcerers who would approach the intended victim and raising the gun high in the air, point it directly at the sun for a few moments before lowering it and aiming it at the intended victim. Brian told me that one of these Kalalozi guns, decorated with black and red beading, a sure sign of perverse witchcraft, was held in the Natural History Museum in London.

Later, the Kalalozi Gun would be redesigned and made out of metal, complete with a stock and barrel; quite often an aborted foetus would be used to represent the bullet, which was then fired, using a small quantity of gunpowder, into the walls of the dwelling used by the intended victim. This form of witchcraft was so virulent and powerful that it was inevitable that the victim would soon die and this teacher, too, was dead within a few weeks. Brian considered prolific witchcraft was a prime cause for anxiety, for even in a community such as ours, where schools and Christianity existed side by side, the fear of witchcraft touched everyday living.

On the way back to the station, Brian told me in confidence that I could well have been handed a poisoned chalice, because the CID squad was completely unruly and disorganised, leading them to detest authority in all its forms. In an attempt to help, he provided me with Constable Alan Phiri, a smart and well-educated police constable, who would maintain all our office records and this certainly proved to be an inspired choice. Later, that morning Phiri was waiting for me and with a dispirited sweep of his hands indicated the filthy state of our offices, where I had already noticed an empty gin bottle lying in a damaged, cane waste-paper basket. We had little time to exchange views because there was a knock on the inter-communicating door and the team of detectives trooped in. They looked scruffy, dirty and dishevelled and one of them, Detective Constable Monga, was carrying a large wicker basket containing several empty alcohol bottles. They introduced themselves one by one until finally, Monga asked me what drink I wanted to order from the local store and whether it was going to be the 'Ginnie or the Wiskie.' When I said neither, their disappointment was evident. Detective Constable Busike also wanted to know where my guitar was and would we all be going down to the riverside to play the music that afternoon as usual. Once I informed them I didn't play any musical instrument and we were all here to work and not play, there was a perceived air of open hostility. The rest of the team said nothing and as they trooped out again, I had the distinct impression I was being regarded as a massive disappointment.

I soon discovered that Monga had a paternity suit levied against him by a local Chief's daughter and he was desperately trying to defer judgment by buying a bottle of gin each week for him. Mubonda had previously had a case of assaulting another police officer put in abeyance and even Detective Sergeant Mumba was described by numerous senior officers as displaying regular instances of dumb insolence. It didn't take a genius to realise I was in serious trouble and the only positive issue I could find in all of this unpalatable mess was that between some seven detectives, they spoke a total of forty-nine different tribal dialects and languages including Swahili and Zulu. Nevertheless, dark clouds were forming and although I did not know it, much worse was yet to follow. In the meantime I bought Phiri a grey blanket from one of the local Indian stores, to cover the top of the old and battered work-table and coerced our houseboy, who was called Brush, into helping us clean through the office and apply a goodly helping of red polish to the dilapidated cement floor; as we worked, the tribal drums still beat out their resonant messages unabated. The next day, I had already been detailed to attend an open-air, political meeting in Chiwempala, organised by the local United National Independence Party or UNIP as it was called, which was a political body headed by Dr Kenneth Kaunda. The local organisers had obtained the necessary permits and my job was to appear in police uniform, spell out the legal requirements and obligations to both conveners and speakers and then position a microphone and stand, enabling the contents of the meeting to be fully recorded. The various speakers were warned not to use inflammatory language nor conduct themselves in a manner likely to cause a breach of the peace – in reality, much easier said than done.

Before the meeting started, I climbed to the top of the flattened anthill and read out the terms and conditions of the permit, amidst boos, whistles, and catcalls on the part of the 400 strong crowd, then the meeting finally got underway. The regular police recording team consisted of a smartly dressed sergeant and two constables, who knew exactly what they were doing. The sergeant told me he thought we were going to have plenty of trouble, which in turn, cheered me up no end and we agreed that if this happened, the team would close down the tape-recorder and lock themselves in the landrover. I stated my intention would be to put the vehicle into four-wheel-drive and get the hell out of there, driving over anyone who stood in our way – and they all particularly liked this idea.

Upon the anthill, the speakers began extolling the virtues of the UNIP hierarchy in general and Dr Kaunda in particular, and all seemed to be going quite well until one speaker, Jonas Ngoma, took the microphone and speaking to great applause said, 'I will speak into this thing but I will not hold it, because now it is the time for all the white people to go back home.' Without waiting for any instructions, the recording team started to pack up their gear and I think I was so shocked, I reacted by loudly shouting out the speaker's name, MR NGOMA! It came out of my mouth like a pistol shot and caught Ngoma so unexpectedly by surprise, he immediately stood rigidly to attention! The crowd erupted with absolute fury, seeing it as a sign of capitulation and soon we were battling waves of rioters coming at us from every direction. Fists were flying and we were doing our best to deflect them with our police batons, until Brian broke through their ranks with a detachment of police in full riot gear and pushed the crowd back, leaving us somewhat bruised and battered. Even while stones continued to rain down on us, I had to climb to the top of the anthill, hurriedly declare the meeting closed and quickly retrieve the microphone and stand, and for my first political meeting, I found it was all very alarming. The next day, my first urgent job was to visit the local Magistrate and swear out a warrant for the arrest of

Jonas Ngoma. Brian insisted the warrant should be executed in the early morning at about 3.am, being supported by a backup detachment from the Riot Police Platoon. After the searing heat of the day, the cold night often created spasms of heavy rain and this was no exception. My other station colleagues also considered it an excellent opportunity for me to sort out the tribal drummers who were beginning to exhaust our patience and goodwill. At 3am, we all set off in convoy and surrounded the hut used by Jonas Ngoma, but the bird had already flown the nest and could not be found.

It later transpired that he had already left for the nearby Congo, where the Russian Embassy provided him with an educational scholarship to study in Moscow; but more of him later. On the way back to the station, after a fruitless search and just as dawn was breaking, we followed the sound of the throbbing tribal drums until we came across a party of relief drummers in a wide-open space, grouped around a red-hot charcoal brazier, who explained their music was to honour the death of their revered, ancient tribal chief. I offered our condolences and then, purely as an aside, I asked them when their Chief had actually died. Their reply, uttered in a rather nonchalant manner was, 'Oh! He hasn't died yet, but we are just practising to make sure we will be ready for when he does.' The drumming was to continue at full throttle for a further ten debilitating days.

Chapter 2

The Poisoned Chalice

Chief Inspector Brian Thomas continued with his dissertation about witchcraft and one day he asked me if I remembered, months before, helping him when a passenger train had been derailed just on the edge of the location. I certainly did remember extricating a number of distraught and injured passengers and then taking them on to the local hospital for treatment before transferring some of the not so badly injured to the railway station; but then he told me something I didn't know, which was when the engineers finally came to lift the train and coaches back onto the rails, they found the body of a young man lying underneath one of the carriages, whose heart had been surgically removed in a horrendous act of witchcraft.

I soon came to realise that Brian's concern about me being handed a poisoned chalice had finally come to pass. The CID team totally ignored me, arriving at our offices early in the morning and leaving almost immediately to carry out their inquiries. Several days later, there was still no sign of the phantom squad, although criminal cases continued to pour in, leaving Phiri personally to distribute the dockets among the detectives. During some of our quieter moments, Phiri made a detailed list of all the outstanding and undetected serious crimes and I arranged coloured pins to represent the various offences. I decided to ignore the team's open rejection of me and carried on working late into the evenings until, eventually, all the outstanding criminal cases were designated on a map of the town that I had pinned on a notice board. I felt sorry for my wife being left alone in the apartment, but she, good-humouredly, soon got down to making dresses for herself on our new electric sewing machine. Sometimes though, I was aware of people coming up and peering through the officer windows, but when I looked up there would be no-one there. Although my wife was very supportive, we both knew this state of affairs could not continue for much longer and although

I hated the thought of admitting defeat, I realised there might well come a time when I would have to cut my losses by resigning. However, Guernsey folk are noted for their extreme stubbornness and after due consideration, this option seemed to me like pure cowardice.

Another afternoon and another political meeting, although this time, Special Branch warned us to expect a deliberate and violent confrontation, certainly a nerve-jangling situation. All police leave was cancelled, and everyone remained on standby. The same recording team and I went along to the meeting place, more like lambs to the slaughter, and carried out our normal routines. Brian positioned himself some 200 yards back from the throng with several landrovers and a Bedford troop carrier in full view. Lined up in front of the transport stood most of the station's police officers, making an imposing sight, dressed in full riot gear with their dark blue police helmets, metal shields, and their long-batons.

The meeting started innocuously enough with the first speaker welcoming the gathering and praising the political ambitions of their leader Dr Kenneth Kaunda, before he introduced the next guest and one of the conveners of the day's meeting, a young man called Richard Bwalya. At this stage, there must have been about 500 people gathered around the anthill and they gave Richard a real hero's welcome. Richard took the microphone and started speaking. 'I am not a police boy and I will not use this thing given to me by these white people,' and with that, he threw the microphone down into the mud, which produced enthusiastic cheers and clapping. I started to climb up the anthill towards him in order to close the meeting, when Richard took the opportunity to throw down the gauntlet by expressing in a loud voice, 'I see you, white policeman and I know you well, but do not come to my house like a thief in the night-time to arrest me with so many of your black boys. No! Come by yourself, and we will face each other man to man in combat.'

Once they heard these toxic comments, the crowd exploded into a violent, heaving mass of humanity, seemingly hell-bent on attacking us, and with some of them trying to overturn our police truck. Within seconds we were all battling for our lives in hand to hand fighting, where the Marquess of Queensberry rules simply did not apply. We faced wave after wave of faces filled with hate and as fast as we repelled them, the press was replaced by yet another wave. One man grabbed the strap of my Sam Browne belt and pulled me down to my knees, but I hit him hard in the groin with the end of my baton and he collapsed silently alongside. Still, by now we were beginning to tread over some of the inert bodies of disabled rioters, but the battle continued unabated.

In the meantime, Brian had advanced with his troops in line abreast and released them to attack the rioters from the rear. This action marginally alleviated our desperate position, but we were still being hard pressed and fighting in individual combat. The recording team and I battled our way to the top of the anthill to retrieve the microphone, when suddenly in the midst of all this carnage I heard a strident bugle call and in the distance I saw a line of our Mobile Unit riot police burst through the long grass where they had been hiding alongside the railway lines and start to assail the rioters on their left flank. Resistance soon crumbled under this heavy and sustained police onslaught and the riot was over within minutes.

Once again, I stood before the Resident Magistrate to swear out a warrant for the arrest of Richard Bwalya and as he said with a rueful smile, 'I have to say this is fast becoming a very regular feature of your police work here in Chingola.' On my return to the station, Brian told me the C.O. had been made aware of the recording, including the personal challenge issued by Bwalya. The C.O. had stated on no account was I to go and arrest Bwalya on my own and it was made clear to one and all that this was not a request but a direct order.

This left me in a very difficult position but I was staunchly supported by friends from Ted Osmond Jones to the remarkable Bill Player. Bill was assigned to the Traffic section at Chingola and we had become friends during various riots when roads were blocked and cars stoned and overturned. Bill was a member of the famous Player cigarette dynasty but we saw him more as a friend and a true gentleman. I had just reached a low point when Bill telephoned, and I can still hear his gentle voice, 'Ah! Dear boy, I suppose the Goths and the Barbarians are already at the gates of Rome? Still, I wonder if you can help me out. My dear mother has sent me another Oxfam food parcel from Fortnum and Mason in London and I wonder if you could greatly assist me by taking the pot of stem-ginger off my hands?' Decades later when he had finally retired to his farm in Zimbabwe, Bill answered a knock on his front-door late one evening and on opening it, he was immediately shot dead on the threshold by two desperate criminals.

As I saw events, the challenge from Richard Bwalya was direct and unambiguous, aimed solely at me and everyone knew, in the long run, this couldn't be ignored. In the meantime, Special Branch kept an unobtrusive watch on Bwalya's hut and reported back that he was not in residence, probably fearing arrest once he returned. The matter was left in abeyance but during this period of time, I fretted. I fretted about the challenge and I fretted about the possible accusation of cowardice if I did nothing. I fretted about the C.O.'s order but above all else, I fretted about being ignored by the whole of the squad. The one bright spot was the support my wife gave me and we talked about various alternatives, but in the end, she said whatever I decided to do she would back me up.

It is a very strange thing, but I recently found my father's diary for 1944, when we were interned in a German concentration camp and I find his misery at those times, matched my own torment exactly when he wrote, 'I am so tired today, I just fell asleep … I went to bed at 00.30am. I am so restless but I must hide my feelings somehow … I want to do what is right but this life is all wrong … A terrible day and I feel so homesick.' After waiting for two more days, I decided the time was ripe for immediate action, irrespective of the consequences. Thankfully, it had rained hard during the night, which meant most people would stay indoors. At 4 am, I dressed quietly and left for the station. The constables on night-shift completely ignored me when I took the keys for the landrover and set off for Bwalya's hut. I drove up to the hut, leaving the engine running and the headlights on full beam and I focused the vehicle search-light on the front of the hut, then I got out and banged heavily on the hut door. Eventually, a sleepy and distant voice inside demanded to know who was making such a noise at this late hour, and I answered, 'This is the police open up,' and the voice replied, 'Go away and come back some other time.' I became really angry at this response, and shouted out, 'Either you come out now or I will personally kick this bloody door down and come in and get you!'

After some time, I heard the rasping of metal on metal and for one stomach-churning moment I thought the occupants of the hut were gathering their weapons ready to attack me, but soon the rickety door opened and a sleepy looking Richard Bwalya was revealed in the entrance. I told him I held a signed arrest warrant, whereupon I handcuffed him and locked him in the landrover. When we returned to the station and entered the charge office a little later, the place was a buzzing hive of activity, and although it was now nearing 5am and still dark, all the outside floodlights were full on and police officers seemed to be milling about everywhere. I found Brian in the main station office together with a fair number of heavily armed officers, and he seemed quite nonchalant and almost jocular when he said, 'Ah there you are, I was worried about you and I was just about to come to find you. I'm glad you're back safely.' As he spoke, telephones were ringing and Brian took one call saying, 'Yes he went out on his own, and yes he's back and yes he made the arrest and yes you're down for a pound!'

I was too preoccupied to think about what was going on, although I did notice everyone was smiling. In the meantime, I had Bwalya booked and held on a charge of Causing Riot, Contrary to sections 62 and 64 of the Penal Code, and afterwards, I asked one of the orderlies to go to the police lines and bring back the CID man on call. I went off to wash my hands and when I came back, the orderly had just returned to say none of the CID men was at home. He had just finished explaining, when all the investigation team came trooping in, soaking wet even though they were wearing their waterproof capes. I suppose the adrenalin was still pumping or maybe it was just the relief of knowing it was all over, but I just blew my top and told them they were nothing but a useless bunch of idiots and not worthy of being called detectives. Brian came out into the corridor to interrupt me in full flow and asked to see me in his office.

I broke off from my tirade and on entering his office I found him standing there laughing, he looked at me and said, 'You haven't quite got it, have you? Don't you realise your lads thought you were going to go off on your own a long time ago, so they have been hiding outside that hut every damn night in the rain for several nights now, ready to help you if you got into trouble.' I have to admit I was left stunned and in total shock. I returned to our offices to speak to the team who all looked like drowned rats and I apologised to them. One of the detectives, Constable Nhliziyo, who had such an unpronounceable name, he had subsequently been named Charlie, said, 'We are sorry too, Bwana, but we have all been thrown away by the whities – and no one wants us anymore.'

'Well, I want you,' I said, 'So I suggest we all start again from the very beginning. Now, who would like a hot cup of chocolate?' Never having had hot chocolate before, the idea really intrigued them and I suggested I should go and change and return with the chocolate drink if they would take Bwalya out of the cells and charge him. I quickly went home, showered and changed, then prepared a sizeable Thermos flask of cocoa, which I carefully carried back to the station and by the time I returned all the statements had been taken. Richard Bwalya was subsequently found guilty and sentenced to a term of imprisonment with hard labour; nevertheless, we were to meet on several more occasions.

The team thoroughly enjoyed the cocoa aided by spoons of sugar but then I needed to see Brian and discuss the full implications of my actions. I duly reported and told him that I had better go and meet the C.O. and get the whole matter over and done with, but he astounded me by saying it wouldn't be necessary, as he had been running a book and taking bets on whether I would face the challenge or not, and even the C.O. had bet £1 on my going! Back in the office, I thought it time to regain control and it was then I dropped the bombshell, by telling the team that, in the last few days and working purely with Alan Phiri, we had made more arrests and cleared up more cases than the whole team had done in a month. I followed this up by explaining that by using my magic board next door I knew there was going to be a burglary either that night or early the next morning and I even knew the number of the hut which was going to be burgled. I called for two volunteers to wait inside the chosen hut and catch the burglar when he broke in. There was quite a lot of excited babble when I left to collect the dockets and information from my office next door.

Unknown to me at this time, my old friend from my previous station, in the form of a smartly uniformed Sgt Maj Kaunda, complete with swagger stick, marched briskly into the station, just as Brian was checking entries in the Daily Occurrence Book. Kaunda came to a crashing halt in front of him and at the same time in a loud voice said, 'Good morning Sah.'

'Good morning Sergeant Major and what can we do for you this very fine morning?' Kaunda then followed up by announcing, 'I have just come to kick a few smelly black backsides right into the middle of next week – Sah.'

'Ah yes' said Brian, 'I can see you must have worked with Inspector Matthews for some time, anyway, please be my guest, and you will find them all at the end of the corridor.'

The first I knew was the noise erupting from next door and a loud booming voice I thought I recognized. When I opened the door, I saw Sgt Maj Kaunda in full flow and a group of sorry-looking detectives facing the total wrath of one of their own. Charlie started to grin and spoke to Sgt Maj Kaunda, 'Excuse me, sir, we were all wrong and we have now fully apologised, and it will not happen again. Now would you like a cup of the Bwana's cocoa?'

In the end, it was all sweetness and light except for Kaunda's parting shot, which was to the effect, that if I had any more trouble, I should give him a call and he would come down personally to sort them all out, and then the whirlwind was gone. As Charlie put it so succinctly, 'My God, that is truly a real man.'

When everyone had quietened down, we agreed that Busike and Monga would spend the night in the hut waiting for the burglar, although they did not really believe a crime like this could be foretold by magic. We then took down the torn curtains in their office and threw out all the dirty rags and oddments of clothing littering the floor, and I promised to have poor Brush come in and polish the floor for them.

I was late getting to the office the next morning because I had already visited the Public Works Department to collect several newish office chairs and a bucket of magnolia emulsion paint with a few brushes. I knew something was up when I walked into the charge office where all the constables were milling around the front desk, with a few of them going 'Hah, Hah' which always indicated their amazement at some happening or other. In my office, the whole team were looking entranced in front of my coloured display board. Busike and Monga duly reported that at 6.30am just after the homeowner had gone to work and when the two of them thought nothing was going to happen, the door of the hut had been forced open and they caught a stunned and mystified burglar red-handed.

But now it was time for another hard lesson. I sent some of them off to collect the new chairs from the landrover and I soon had them all seated in a row in front of the board, showing the plan of the township. I pointed out one cluster of yellow pins that very nearly filled up a whole line of huts in the same road and we then went through the old crime dockets one by one, noting these burglaries always occurred on the same week-day and at about the same time. I told them that if we were conscientious in our investigations, we could probably solve six or seven cases, all at once. A subsequent search of our burglar's own hut revealed several items of clothing later identified by their owners as having been stolen and our man consequently pleaded guilty to having committed all of these outstanding crimes.

As a reward, I painted the offices out in magnolia emulsion and my wife had the curtains washed and mended. Brush worked his miracle on the floors with his red polish and I visited some of the Chingola travel agents and luckily found several large holiday posters of London, showing such places as Buckingham Palace, Trafalgar Square and the Houses of Parliament but more in keeping, each one had predominate photographs of uniformed London Bobbies. Charlie, who was always ready to exploit any situation, would often bring members of the public in for a guided tour, where he would point out that this was our Queenies house in London, which was guarded by some of his English police colleagues who were all very big friends of Bwana Matthews!

Even so, my education into all things African commenced, albeit slowly and gently, under the tutelage of the team. Just before we were due to set off on a night raid in the township, the team, in their inimitable fashion told me that I needed to be extremely careful when walking along any of the footpaths in the dark, because many people, suffering from serious diseases would hang their old clothes out on wooden poles, making sure they would brush against any unsuspecting passer-by and if anyone touched these contaminated materials, then the serious disease would soon pass to that person and leave the body of the sick person, so I had been warned.

My African tuition continued even when I wasn't completely ready for it, especially as the team and I had settled down into a calm and happy coexistence based on absolute loyalty and respect. We had been ordered by District HQ to mount a small expedition to investigate the alarming number of incidents of cattle rustling near the border with the Congo, just off the Chingola-Solwezi dirt roadway. We had all the necessary accoutrements, including an additional full petrol can and hessian water containers which we fixed onto the front bumpers to keep cool as we drove along; we were also fully armed and certainly everything seemed set fair. Mid-morning and we turned off the main dirt road onto a smaller village cart-track and it was only after a few minutes that Detective Constable Busike told me he thought he could smell wood smoke and within minutes we could all smell that pungent odour. Alarmingly, Mubonda who had been looking out of the rear window suddenly expostulated that he could see widespread orange flames bursting through the dense undergrowth behind us and then within seconds we were confronted by a deadly fire just in front of us and blocking off any means of escape.

Undaunted, I drove off-road, with the thought that the track we had been on would in all probability act as a firebreak, but abruptly we realised the fire had already crossed the roadway and was bearing down on us at an alarming speed. It has been said, and I for one believe it, that a raging bushfire is able to move faster than a galloping zebra. The team was becoming demonstratively anxious but I pressed on even faster through the long grass until finally I only just managed to miss a hidden boulder and at this Detective Sergeant Mumba yelled out, 'Please stop Bwana or we will be all killed.' I replied somewhat testily that if I stopped we would be burnt to death, as we could not outrun this fire and anyway the swirling smoke was becoming thicker at every passing second.

Mumba though was most insistent, 'Stop right now Bwana and we will show you how to escape this fire.' I reluctantly came to a halt and everyone jumped out of the landrover and it seemed each one had a specific job to do. Charlie took the petrol can and raced some fifty yards ahead of us, where he undid the petrol cap and started pouring a little of the petrol onto the grass and right across our line of vision, before returning to the truck. I was horrified when Sergeant Mumba hurried ahead too and bending down, set fire to the undergrowth underfoot, which went up with a mighty whoosh and then he too shot back to the landrover. In the meantime, Busike had retrieved the water containers and had also brought the petrol can inside the vehicle. In spite of the choking and eye-watering smoke, Mumba stayed outside and then told me to drive slowly over the burnt grass in front, while he walked ahead, stamping on any of the still glowing embers.

A few moments later, a sweating and coughing Mumba jumped back into the truck as Monga handed out strips of cloth to everyone, which had been soaked in water and these we used to cover our mouths and noses. All the windows were shut tight and the heat inside built up almost to boiling point. However, I was more concerned with the petrol can being lodged inside and I had the feeling the idiom frying tonight could well come to pass. After a few terrifying moments, the smoke cleared and we all stumbled out onto a blackened landscape, unharmed but gasping for breath. Before we moved off again, I had them cluster around, where I apologised for my ignorance and told them in future I would rely on them for teaching me their bush craft and in return I would teach them more about law and police regulations; funnily enough it was an ecstatic and relieved group that continued on with the rustling investigations.

Chapter 3

The First Hundred Days

After the traumas and upheaval, peace finally descended, and life took on a hectic but more routine nature. In the following days, criminal cases came and went until gradually our detection rate increased to the point Brian was delighted with our performance. Nevertheless, I could see once the people of the township realised the police were now serious about investigating crimes, our caseload would increase and our detection rate fall unless we developed a new and effective strategy to combat this. Brian felt we should be guided by the principles, which in modern-day parlance would be seen as our mission statement; sensing that we should return to the true values of police work which were the preservation of all life and the protection of property. We soon saw we were missing solid and reliable intelligence emanating from the township itself and Brian decided he would deal with the police shifts, if I would cultivate some of the outside sources and, in addition, encourage our detectives to form their own individual networks of informers, guaranteeing these sources full anonymity from prosecution, at least for the time being.

One other area for discussion was the problem of recidivists returning to our patch, more especially now as we were on one of the major coach routes from the main prison in Ndola. In clearing out the office cupboards, Phiri had come across a wodge of foolscap sheets showing details of criminals due to be released from prison, together with their photographs, lists of their previous convictions, known accomplices and the anticipated dates of their release. We decided to give Phiri the job of collating this information and then pass on any relevant details to Busike and Monga for action and it was not long before Phiri found a document concerning a criminal due for release early that morning from Ndola prison. There was a long list of previous convictions, a photograph and an address in Chiwempala location. Later that evening, Busike and Monga called for transport to pick them both up at the local market together with a person they had just arrested. They had been given the details of the newly released convict, worked out how long it would take someone to reach the township by coach and decided to wait near the bus station while making themselves look inconspicuous. They soon spotted the target and started to follow him at a discreet distance towards the busy market place and as he wandered in between the various stalls and kiosks, they watched him lift a purse from a shopping bag and then pick the pocket of a passer-by. At this point, they jumped in, arrested the man and handcuffed him after a very brief but violent struggle. This method of virtual entrapment was soon adopted by our intrepid duo, aided and abetted by Phiri, so much so that it quickly became a regular feature of their work, earning them welcome praise from the market stall holders. I had to admit to some feelings of guilt in the way we operated the system, although Brian felt the end more than justified the means.

All the same, if I had once said that the team and I had to learn some hard lessons, then I continually found myself on the edge of a massive learning curve and usually, it came upon me when I least expected it. There was the moment when the complete team was returning from an investigation in the rural areas, driving along the sweeping river bank of the spectacular Kafue river. It was a wondrous African morning, with the sun hanging high in the sky, when I decided we should stop and take in the glorious scenery and perhaps enjoy a relaxing cup of coffee. No sooner had we stopped when we witnessed a magnificent fish eagle (Nkhwazi) swooping down low over the wide expanse of the river until finally, the large bird plunged both outstretched talons into the fast flowing water and with black wings outstretched in a herculean effort, the bird emerged from the waters with a huge, writhing fish firmly held in his strong claws. I was lost in thought as the large white-headed bird with a wingspan of some 200cm ponderously carried his prize off to a dead branch of a tree on the river bank.

I was unceremoniously brought out of my daydreams by Charlie, who was chortling away in the seat alongside me. 'What's so funny?' I asked.

'Nothing much Bwana, I was just seeing the big difference between the Whites and the Bantu [African people]. The Whities, like you, see a big bird of Africa in all its glory, so you watch and praise Africa for its abundant wildlife. But the poor Bantu with a starving family to feed and no money only looks for the best way to trap and kill the bird. Even if it is the only bird left in the whole wide world, so he can feed his dying children – that is the real difference between us.' In that one instant, I came to see another of my clear cut and sacrosanct theories had suddenly taken on a rather grey and dismal aspect.

If our new strategy of developing a good intelligence network was producing results, it was sorely tested one night when a petrol bomb was thrown through the window of hut 64. The occupants were all fast asleep, but miraculously, they somehow managed to scramble out with only minor burns and a few cuts. However, all their possessions were completely destroyed, along with most of the hut and I felt cases like this were perpetrated by evil-minded cowards. I regarded arson as one of the hardest crimes to solve, because the evidence was invariably obliterated by the flames and the heat. We spent hours sifting through the ashes although our rewards were meagre, apart from a cork we found lying outside the hut, a piece of scorched cotton cloth smelling of petrol and a few shards of glass lying just inside the building. We soon came to the conclusion that we would need witnesses to come forward, although this seemed most unlikely with such abject fear stalking the township. It was evident the attack had been motivated by political considerations, because the victims were staunch members of the African National Congress Party or ANC, as it was known, headed by Harry Nkumbula.

Special Branch could not come up with any useful information, leaving each of our detectives to push their informants hard, and by offering a small cash incentive to secure a conviction. As is often the case, rumours swirled about and had to be painstakingly dissected one by one. Following several dead-ends, a name emerged which started to ring alarm bells. Solomon Safuko immediately brought to mind a sallow youth and a member of the local branch of the opposing political party, who was noticeably absent from the township. Solomon was never a leader but always a follower, and we resolved to pick him up for questioning, although it was early evening before he was finally tracked down and brought back to the station.

I knew this was going to be a long and exhausting interrogation and as such, we split the detectives into two teams, although I resolved to stay with the interrogation until the very end. It was certainly hard going because Solomon stated he knew nothing, he had done nothing, he was completely innocent so why was he here at all? Every question we asked was rebutted and, moreover, the questions and answers flowed backwards and forwards, leaving us tired and dispirited. The teams changed over and the questioning continued. We went over his movements on the day in question, time after time and his replies were then checked out one by one by the detectives, often visiting the various witnesses involved to seek corroboration, until gradually each of his statements was repudiated. While the detectives tried to verify the conflicting stories we took another break and I brought out soft drinks and a few sandwiches, some of which we gave to Solomon, and whether it was this, or whether it was when Busike drew back the curtains and sunlight flooded in, showing we had been at it all night long I don't know, but after a short pause, Solomon slowly looked at each of us in turn and then said resignedly, 'Alright I will tell you everything.'

Mubonda cautioned him, and in reply, he stated in the Bemba language, 'I understand all this and I want to say something about this case now as I have been very worried about it and I was frightened at what had been done to this house. On the date, I think it was a Wednesday, I went to a certain house in the Chiwempala location. I don't know the number of the house but the owner is a Mr Pascale Chibwe. I arrived at the house at 9.30pm, and I was the last person to arrive when I entered I found the following people present. There was Pascale Chibwe, Frederick Sichone, and African Makombo. There were just four of us.'

The statement rambled on for several pages in which he exonerated himself and blamed all the others for the arson attack, although he did identify the broken piece of glass and the cotton swab. After some time, Solomon incriminated another man called Betson, indicating he was last seen carrying the bottle of petrol. Having accused everyone else, he finished by saying, 'The next morning I heard that the house of Mr Ngosa had been burnt. I did not want to be involved with these people, so I left Chingola and went to Kitwe. I also want to say this is a voluntary statement and I have been well treated by the police. I am very happy now that it is all over.'

The teams were ecstatic because they thought the case was all but over and done with, and they looked pretty dejected when I told them although they had all done extremely well, we had only just overcome the first hurdle. Solomon was frightened of being sent to the Central Prison and appeared greatly relieved when we arranged to keep him in one of our station cells, with additional blankets and a good hot meal. I could see we were heading towards a major legal proceeding in the High Court and thought it advisable to have Solomon checked over by an independent medical practitioner to confirm he had not been ill-treated.

The team were sent off for a well-earned rest for a few hours after which we returned for a meeting with Brian, to discuss our next step.

It was evident we had a strong case for a Conspiracy to Commit Murder or Arson or both. First of all, it was decided to pick up both of the Nchanga people and regard them more as vital witnesses at this point. We agreed we would leave the others until the very last moment, knowing we would have to monitor their movements very carefully. We sent out two landrovers to pick up Frederick Sichone and Makombo individually and they were easily located at home and offered no resistance. We interviewed them separately and when they saw the exhibits we had retrieved, they both made statements acquitting themselves from any wrongdoing and blaming everyone else as well as our original interviewee, Solomon. During the night, we raided the houses of Pascale and Betson and, although Pascale appeared docile and resigned, Betson was aggressive and denied all knowledge. With all the accused blaming each other, we had a pretty cast-iron case and in the following weeks, the legal proceedings took place in the High Court, where all the accused were found guilty and sentenced to lengthy terms of imprisonment.

There was one interesting turn of events when we raided Makombo's house, because although we knew he was the local treasurer, we had not bargained on discovering such a treasure trove of information. The proper account books revealed an astonishing level of information and showed amongst other things, donations received from overseas. I was overwhelmed when one of the team found a souvenir handkerchief marked 'A Present from Guernsey' and then later, we came across an entry showing an amount of money coming in from a charitable organisation in Guernsey. Eventually, we traced part of this donation, going out in payment for the petrol used to bomb hut 64. Sometime after the case had been settled in the High Court, I wrote to the Guernsey organisation informing them of what had happened, but sad to say, I never received a reply.

Brian also had another urgent and troublesome matter to consider, because a great number of Congolese and Katangese migrants had fled the vicious fighting in the Congo and sought refuge in our area. However, their resentful rivalries often spilt over into our township through acrimonious arguments and occasionally armed encroachment into each other's sectors, where it would take only one unforeseen incident, leading to a violent conflagration affecting the whole of the location. I probably should have seen it coming when Brian asked me what weapon training experience I had besides that given at the Police Training School. There was a noticeable glint in his eye when I said I had undertaken several courses with the Royal Hampshire Regiment in the UK through Elizabeth College, Combined Cadet Force, including involvement with the Mk4 .303 rifle, the Bren-gun, (light machine-gun - LMG) and the Sten-gun.

He then carefully explained his highly original idea of inviting the leaders of both the Congolese and Katangese factions to a police open-day where we would provide a display of marching by armed police followed by a live firing demonstration of the LMG. However, my assistance would be crucial in both handling the Bren and also in helping to drill the police contingent, although as he pointed out, this work would have to be in addition to my already heavy workload. He had already selected a few officers, because of their bearing and smartness when on parade and had promoted his own driver Sekondwe to the rank of sergeant to head this platoon. Sekondwe was an enormous man well over 6ft 4in in height, with a huge smile and the most enormous hands I had ever seen, and as Brian once put it to me so succinctly, 'When the shit hits the fan, you really need Sekondwe standing right beside you!' The challenging part was in keeping Sekondwe sober and to stop him from getting into fights in the beer-hall. He had been promoted and then demoted so many times that Brian had suggested he should have his sergeant's stripes fastened by Velcro. His courage though was never in doubt, as witnessed one stormy night when the rain was lashing down outside, and we were all in the station charge office. Brian had brought along his daughter Caroline and young son Roddy when the main outside doors suddenly opened, and someone threw in a large and poisonous black-mamba snake. I think it is fair to say we were all taken aback, but with the snake wrapped around his feet, Sekondwe simply bent down and picked up the two children in a single movement, and with one child in each of his large hands, he held his arms and the children high above his head. It turned out later that the snake was already dead, although none of us knew that at the time.

My uniform was cleaned and starched, with buttons polished and my Sam-Browne belt and boots buffed up to a high gloss finish. We drilled every morning for several hours for over a week and even though we had initial difficulty in getting the constables to master the art of fixing bayonets, we eventually reached a fair state of efficiency, allowing me to move on to the Bren-gun. I had always been told that the serial numbers on the removable barrel should match the numbers on the carcase of the gun and in our case; the numbers on our two Bren-guns were totally at variance with each other. 'Never mind,' said Brian, 'I will just have to keep a safe distance away from you when you start firing that damn gun, just in case the bloody thing blows up!'

We obtained a cardboard cut-out of a typical insurgent from the riot police detachment and fixed it directly in front of an old ant-hill, some-way behind the police station, then chairs and benches were placed alongside the parade ground in two distinctly separate groups to accommodate our visitors. The display platoon was ready and formed up out of view, behind the station, and the visitors provided a rare and flamboyant sight to behold, especially those unusually tall and extremely slim African ladies who were all dressed in their bright, colourful robes. I jokingly whispered to Charlie that as a single man he might wish to consider entertaining one of these young ladies later on, but he gave me a rather baleful look and in measured tones said 'Bwana, I know you mean well, but I must tell you I am but a very poor boy in their eyes. It is as if I am looking through the large windows of a big car showroom, at some of the most desirable models, sleek and very well upholstered yet I have no money and I know they are far too expensive for me to run.'

When everyone was seated, Brian asked the two respective leaders to join him for a tour of our well-stocked armoury! After this sobering walk-through, the party returned and at a given signal from Brian, Sekondwe marched the impressive police platoon onto the parade ground. The drills were immaculate and well worth the hard training we had put in, especially the part where the platoon fixed bayonets and then marched past with the sun glinting on their bright and wicked looking metal blades. Then it was my turn. Brian invited the visitors to walk across to the firing range where we had placed the Bren-gun on a ground-sheet, with an ammunition magazine lying alongside. I stood just behind the Bren in my crisp, full-dress uniform and on the word of command from Brian, 'Take Post,' I threw myself full length behind the gun, loaded the magazine, cocked the gun and secured the safety-catch to the 'on' position shouting out 'Number one gun ready for action, sir!'

The reply came back immediately. 'At the target in front, two bursts rapid fire.'

With the safety-catch off, the gun jumped into life and the two short bursts decimated the target, cutting it in half and perhaps even more imposing were the spurts of dust thrown up around the ant-hill as the bullets slammed into the dry earth. The day had been an unqualified success and had produced a long-lasting, sobering effect on both the Katangese and the Congolese audience, to the point we never suffered any further disturbances.

During this time, I had also been fairly busy on the home front, where Monga's paternity case had been put into cold storage, once I had mentioned to the Chief that accepting regular bottles of gin each week could be construed as cases of bribery. I had been able to settle a number of claims for compensation levied against Charlie for his various infidelities amongst certain young ladies who had found an athletic Sezulu such a delightful companion. Gradually, the team appeared to be far more confident and their dress code certainly improved, although I wasn't too sure about Charlie's heavily patterned and brightly coloured linen jacket, which I called Jacob's coat of many colours. This comment really intrigued Charlie who wanted to know who this fellow Jacob was. 'Is he in the police and what's his tribe?' he asked me one day and when I told him it was all described in the Bible, he went about telling everyone his coat was specially mentioned in the Great Book in the Church and as such held extraordinary mystical powers.

Mid-morning and I was just enjoying my coffee and biscuits when my reverie was violently interrupted by a great shouting and wailing coming from outside the building. I stood up and, looking out, watched a large crowd of men and women approaching the station, with one man who appeared to be their leader dragging a poor woman along by her hair. Phiri went out to see what the commotion was all about and soon came back with that wide, all-knowing smile of his to say he thought it might be a good idea if I came outside and saw what was happening. When I entered the charge office, I immediately saw Charlie's coat of many colours lying on the office counter, while the man recounted, mainly for my benefit, how he had come back home early, only to see a big black backside disappearing through the open window. Whoever it was had left his jacket behind and he wanted the police to find the culprit and put him prison.

I gently told the complainant how sorry I was over his evident distress but this was really a civil case which should be taken before the elders of the Native Courts. However, I could see how upset he was and if he would leave me the coat I would try and find the person involved, although, at this stage, I did not hold out much hope. The aggrieved husband reluctantly agreed and left the station still clutching his errant wife. In the late afternoon, a very sheepish Charlie come into the office and although he was delighted to be reunited with his jacket, he realised it was now far too conspicuous for a CID man to wear and it would have to go. I agreed wholeheartedly with him but said, more importantly, that he had to stop his various philandering adventures before he found himself in some really very serious trouble. Charlie agreed, and gave me his usual, 'It will not happen again Bwana.'

'That's all very well, but you said that last time and the time before. And it's what you always say before you go out and do it all over again.'

'Inde, Boss, I know it is true what you say, but this time I really mean it – it will not happen again.'

'How can I believe this time will really be the last time?'

'Cabwino, boss I will tell you honestly, because the next time I shall be keeping my coat on!'

There was also a gradual but noticeable change in our relationship with the people in the township, because if they were working in their allotments when we drove by they began to wave, the children too started to wave at us and often when we slowed down to reduce the billowing dust rising in clouds from behind our vehicles, people on the roadside would stand erect, then bow their heads as a mark of respect. The market traders became increasingly relaxed and friendly in our company mainly, I suspect because everyone began to see we treated their complaints seriously and we usually managed to solve their problems. Our own intelligence network moved into top gear and we began to identify and isolate more and more of the lawbreakers. We continually harried these miscreants, breaking doors down, and raiding their known haunts until the word spread that it was far easier for criminals to move off somewhere else to avoid all this hassle. Nevertheless, it was no good criminals carrying out their crimes in our township then retreating to outlying villages, because our reach extended well outside these confines, and the words bandied about were that we would always get our man, however long it took.

But it was not all sweetness and light during this period, because political unrest in other countries in Africa caused periodic waves of refugees to swarm across our borders. Convoys of overloaded transports carrying South African families who were leaving Kenya and Uganda only added to the congestion of the fleeing tribal inhabitants of the Congo. At varying times, we had to set up border posts and everyone was involved in this action, where we confiscated rifles, shotguns, bows and arrows and a motley assortment of other weapons. These episodes acted as a wake-up call, whereby we could see we were acting like innocents abroad and what we really needed was a whole new innovative plan of action. We took time out to review every facet of our way of working, and everyone was invited and encouraged to participate. There was the question of filing a travel plan not only with our station but also notifying the District Operations Room of our movements. We were in dire need of more detailed and better maps of the area, and it was also necessary to make sure we had proper tools and other equipment housed permanently in the vehicle. It was then I came up with the percentage game routine, which seemed totally incongruous at the time but saved us from ignominy on many subsequent occasions.

The idea was to spend more time in planning our excursions, where we would work out the overall distances required to travel and by using the trip-meter on the landrover, keep a watchful eye on the mileage as we journeyed. It was the same with the passage of time; for instance, how long would the journey take? Had we reached 50 per cent of the planned route or used more than 50 per cent of the petrol? Our other major requirement was to ensure we carried sufficient fire-power with us at all times, in case of unexpected incidents in this volatile country. Gradually, our experiences turned us from purely rank amateurs into a cohesive and professional body of young men.

Sitting alone in the office one evening, I had the feeling we had missed one vital element and then it came to me in a flash. Most of the team members were highly intelligent young men who had previously been used to complete freedom of movement within their own tribes and villages. They had lived happily in a land-locked country containing a rich diversity of territory from a high plateau to a rolling savannah countryside incorporating all the attendant hills mountains and rivers and because of such a high elevated position up to 5,000 ft above sea-level, the country enjoyed a pleasant subtropical climate. They had joined the police force and, after training, moved from one dusty and dirty town to another until claustrophobic frustration reached bursting point. I resolved then to do everything I could to mitigate this situation by carefully balancing our workload, with interspersed visits to the more calm and rural regions, on a rest and recuperation basis and this is exactly what we did with some quite amazing results.

At this juncture, I was reminded of a wonderful poem about the country written by my friend David Lewis which summed up all our emotions.

I've stood witness to the sunrise,
On a distant Mountain Peak.
When the plains below,
Lay silent in the dawn.
And I've watched the lone 'Nkhwazi,'
Soaring high to ever seek,
The unwitting Bream,
Exhausted near its' spawn.

I have gazed to far horizons,
in the iridescent noon,
When phantasmic forms,
Soon vanish in the heat.
And I've heard the distant thunder,
Meting out its sombre tune,
Where November rains,
Will soon parched lands defeat.

Once, I rested in contentment,
By the camp fire's dancing flames,
With my thoughts alone,
And overwhelmed with calm.
And I stared beyond the darkness,
Where the unknown stakes its' claim,
And where those victims,
Of the night endure harm.

Now, at last, I only dream of,
Times and places long ago,
When I wandered far,
Across the torrid plains.
How I hate the English winters,
With their cold and sleet and snow,
And my thoughts again,
Turn to those 'Afric' plains.

Chapter 4

The Walking Dead

We very gradually extended our theatre of operations throughout the township, but as so often happens at times like this, nemesis soon raised its ugly head. Charlie came into the station, late one morning with a man, Joseph Kaole, who was suspected of being in possession of stolen goods. A quick check revealed Joseph had a long criminal record, although he swore that since his last lengthy prison stint, he had gone straight and was holding down a regular job, which enabled him to buy such expensive clothes. He gave an address in the Nchanga Mine location, and we decided to go and search this dwelling. Joseph told us he was staying with his brother, a member of the N'gumbo tribe, from Malunga village in Samfya District, and he would vouch for him.

We took Busike, Charlie and Sitali along with us, because Sitali, who was a junior but enthusiastic member of the team, would handcuff himself to Joseph, just to be on the safe side. As part of our recognised protocol, I notified the Operations Room of our intention to visit another police jurisdiction, being explicit they should notify Nchanga Station of our intended visit, besides keeping a record of it in their log. Some twenty minutes into our trip, we were driving up the long winding hill through Nchanga when we passed a stationary police landrover with a solitary and morose looking European officer sitting in the driver's seat. I waved, but there was no acknowledgement. Some 200 yards further on, we came across a detachment of six police constables being led by a figure I instantly recognised as being that of my old friend Sgt Maj Kaunda.

I was just about to overtake them when Charlie said, 'There is something very wrong here Bwana. I think we should stop and find out.' I pulled up and Kaunda came up to us to say he was in deep trouble since they had been called to a multiple stabbing and the kidnapping of a young girl, but his European officer had elected to stay in the vehicle and refused to budge. Kaunda was almost in tears, because his constables were only young boys and he really didn't know what to do next. When I suggested that maybe we could help, the relief on his face was immediately evident. We were virtually at the scene, where a crowd of moaning women soon indicated the hut where they alleged the assailant was holding the young girl prisoner.

Sitali remained handcuffed to our suspect and was told to keep well out of the way of any fracas. Busike was instructed to take two of the constables and make a quick search of the surrounding area. Within minutes, he called out, having come across three women lying in the long grass. All of them were suffering from the most horrendous multiple stab wounds, to the point I felt sure they could not possibly survive, especially as they were bleeding most profusely and it was obvious medical attention was urgently required. A decision needed to be taken and taken quickly and I ordered Busike to rip the door off a nearby hut where it was only secured by a small padlock and then place it across the seats in the rear of the landrover. We gently carried the three seriously wounded women and laid them out, side by side on the wooden door. I radioed the Operations Room and told them I was sending the landrover plus the injured women to the hospital, while we were going to tackle the murderous assailant inside the hut.

Busike set off and the hospital, already forewarned of his anticipated arrival had doctors and nurses were waiting outside for the arrival of the injured women. In the meantime, we posted all the police constables around the hut in a circle and it was decided that Charlie and I would rush the door and smash it in. Kaunda was to make sure, if anything untoward happened to us, that the criminal must not be allowed to escape and in response, he ordered the constables to draw their short batons and standby.

'One two three,' and we rushed the door. I was first to hit it hard with my right shoulder and the door simply gave way under the pressure. In a second, we were both stumbling over the remains of smashed furniture and broken crockery. In the half-light, I noticed massive splatters of blood, arcing high across the walls and a little girl standing against one of the walls of the corridor. The impetus of our charge carried us through and as I passed, I hastily grabbed the girl and then hit the far wall with a great clump which momentarily knocked the wind out of me. I turned around still holding the girl and rushed back to the doorway where I literally threw her into the arms of one of the startled constables.

I turned back once again, only to see Charlie struggling with a tall man who was wielding a large kitchen knife. I grabbed one of the man's arms but in one slashing moment he brought the knife down hard, cutting the third finger of my outstretched hand, right down to the bone. Charlie kicked the man hard in the groin and followed this up with a chopping motion to his nose and thankfully, the fight was over. We bundled the assailant out of the hut where he was shackled by feet and hands and then we took stock of our situation. Fortunately, the young girl had not been harmed although the seriously wounded women were identified as being her mother and her two aunts. According to witnesses, the girl's mother was demanding a divorce, which was being steadfastly refused by the husband until the point was reached that the mother announced to all and sundry that the man was not the girl's natural father.

Shortly afterwards, Busike returned, giving me access to the first aid kit although I could see I would need stitches. The wooden door we had used as a stretcher was replaced, albeit without the padlock, and a constable was detailed to stand guard over the hut until the owner returned. There was further work to be done because Sgt Maj Kaunda felt that although his officer had abandoned them, he, in turn, had let his own men down. I gathered them together and told them they were very fortunate to be working with the sergeant major and as a result, they had all done a great job. Following this, Kaunda and his men marched off with the attacker in tow to the police station and I went to the hospital for another tetanus injection and a few stitches. Sadly though, I was never to see Sgt Maj Kaunda again.

Later, back at our station, Brian told me the Officer-in-Charge of Nchanga Station wanted to charge me with malicious damage to property and he was going to swear out a court order the following day. I had endured enough for the moment and I went home, took some pain-killers and thought it through. As a result, I once again telephoned probably the best lawyer in the territory, Colin Cunningham, in Lusaka. I was surprised by the fact that after only a minute or two I was put through to him whereupon he said, 'Good to hear from you again. Now, what have you been up to this time?'

When I explained what had happened, there was silence for a few moments and then he said, 'Good God! I can't believe it – but look here, this is what I want you to do. I want you to notify your Officer-in-Charge in writing that I shall be defending you and that I shall also be contacting the Commissioner of Police.'

The next day, Brian was still seething over our treatment, and in the meantime, I had typed out the various requirements dictated by Colin Cunningham, together with the list of all the potential witnesses. At the same time, I handed in my report clearly giving times that included notifying Nchanga police through our Operations Room, and of placing a constable to guard the property where we had removed the door. I indicated the lack of response from Nchanga and questioned what the European officer was doing, only several hundred yards away from this outrage. Then, probably to add insult to injury, I made a recommendation on behalf of Charlie in regard to his courageous conduct. Brian looked at it all for some time, smiled, if a little ruefully and told me 'I think this is going to ruffle a few feathers and the old man [C.O.] will probably go berserk! Anyway, the sooner I get to see him the better.'

The next morning, a meeting was convened in Brian's office with Chief Inspector Jack Gowland from CID and me. Brian told us the C.O. was absolutely furious and had conducted an inquiry himself, personally checking all the records of conversations from the Ops Room logs. As far as Brian could ascertain, not only would there be no action taken against me or anyone else, but certain station transfers would be instigated forthwith.

Days later and I was in the shower when my wife put her head around the bathroom door and said Charlie had been on the telephone to say they had found another body. She went on to say, 'He's a really strange one that one, because he asked if you were in the shower and when I said yes, he said, OK Medami I was afraid of that!' I explained it was a current in-joke with the team because whenever we faced an extremely difficult murder investigation, I was always in the shower when it was first reported. By the time I reached the station, the team was already organised with the landrover loaded with our scene of crime box. I could see they were all on edge and so we took the time out to discuss the case. Detective Sergeant Mumba told me a body had been found near a village which was just about an hour's drive away but the disturbing news was that the body seemed to belong to a terrifying zombie, one of Africa's vicious walking dead.

After a long drive over rough bush tracks, we arrived at Kumalo village, a motley collection of circular, traditional thatched huts, where we were met by one of the frightened elders who had remained alone in the village because quite a few of the inhabitants had rushed off in some panic to hide away in the dense bush country. This tribal elder elected to take us to the body, which had been discovered only about half a mile away. On arrival, we knew immediately this was the murder scene because we could see a small crowd of villagers, gathered together and forming a sullen semi-circle. We knew too, this was a serious matter because, from our experience, whenever supernatural powers were involved villagers would stand some way off and not approach too closely out of fear of the paranormal. Still, we were not prepared for our initial view of the place which was macabre in the extreme.

The rich, red earth immediately in front of us gently sloped away, towards a small, cultivated maize field, but directly in the foreground there was a patch of ground covered with weeds. However, what really focussed our attention was the grey, withered human arm and hand, rising out of the earth, with the index finger extended, as if pointing towards a small knoll of trees, just behind us. The soil surrounding the arm had been disturbed and on closer examination, we could see parts of a white shroud peeking out. The village headman came up and welcomed us in the traditional manner by bowing low and slapping his right hand against his left arm to show he was not carrying any weapons. He was obviously very frightened and pleaded with us to remove the body quickly before this evil zombie could rise up later from the grave and attack his village.

He spoke in a low voice, saying, 'You must follow the pointing finger and look to the evil signs, calling for all zombies to come forth and meet at this place, under the new moon.'

We walked over towards the trees and for one heart-stopping moment, I saw the hand in the grave had been pointing towards a few bright red splodges covering the tree trunks. When I touched the red marks, everyone took a step backwards although I realised immediately this was not fresh blood but red paint, and not only that but, the paint was still very tacky to the touch, which meant it could only have been applied fairly recently. There were footprints and thin bicycle tyre marks seemingly going off in a direction leading away from the village. Some of the team were left to protect the site, while Charlie, Monga and I took the landrover to follow these mysterious tracks. Within 100 yards, we found another red mark on a tree, then another. The journey went on like this for well over five miles, which in itself made little sense. Then, finally in the distance, we saw a young man, riding a bicycle through the bush and as we caught up with him we could see he was riding along completely naked except for wearing a large bush hat. Slung on the crossbar, was a short wooden ladder and dangling from the handlebars hung a pot of bright red paint and a paintbrush.

We stopped the man and started to interrogate him, while Monga eventually rifled through some of his belongings packed inside the rear carrier bag and produced a document to show he was employed by the local telephone department. Apparently, it was his job to plot and mark out a proposed route for a new telephone line, and his method was to mark various trees as he went with a daub of red paint, enabling his following colleagues to position any new telephone poles and it was now plain we had wasted more than two hours on this abortive part of the investigation.

When we returned, we found the area in turmoil, with the watchers shouting and recoiling in horror at what was going on. Sergeant Mumba had begun to uncover the remains of the body and if the sight was truly awful, then the cloying stench that rose up was even worse. The badly decomposed body had been closely wrapped in a white shroud, with the right arm and hand still pointing into the far distance. Meanwhile, Mubonda had left to make inquiries around the village and had not as yet returned. We eventually succeeded in moving the sullen onlookers away, mainly by threatening to arrest them for interfering and hindering our police investigations and we quickly commenced taking our photographs, making plaster casts and recording various pieces of forensic evidence.

After an hour, Mubonda returned, bringing with him a very dour looking man and a woman who stated they were the son and daughter-in-law of the dead man and they had surreptitiously buried him in that patch of ground one night several moons ago. This was as far away from the village as they could manage, because the old man had died alone in his hut and they didn't have enough money to bury him properly. Busike indicated that there were marks in the earth surrounding the body which looked as if a wild animal, probably a hyena, had pawed and dragged at the body, eventually pulling the hand and arm free of the cumbersome shroud. We realised that the onset of rigor mortis had resulted in the hand and arm remaining in the upright position, thus causing panic and terror amongst the villagers. The smell of rotting flesh was nauseating enough and it was a most unpleasant task recovering the disintegrated body which we wrapped and securely tied in a plastic sheet and then placed in an unassailable position on top of the landrover. Days later, the post-mortem would reveal the man had indeed died from natural causes and the case of the walking dead zombie was finally closed.

In the meantime, we still had to finalise statements and only when the sun had set were we finally able to leave Kumalo's village. We drove slowly along deserted and twisting dirt paths, many gouged out by the previous monsoon rains. It was becoming increasingly dark and the bright lights from our headlamps seemed to bounce back at us from the tree-lined bush country. We ground and bumped our way over the difficult terrain until quite suddenly, the headlights picked up clouds of very fine dust, hanging heavily in the night air and within seconds we could make out a serious disturbance taking place right in front of us, with three men attacking some poor unfortunate, who was putting up a brave but faltering defence. The team were out of the landrover even before I had time to stop and they joined the fray swinging their batons with deadly efficiency, while I left the engine running and the headlights on full beam. By the time I joined the scrap, it was all over and the assailants had decided this was no place to be, as they wheeled or rather limped off into the protective darkness.

The victim had been badly beaten and although we tried to patch him up with our first aid kit, the light was insufficient for us to see properly. We decided to take him on to the clinic in Chiwempala, while he explained that he had been travelling around some of the villages in the area selling his wares and he had arranged with two men to transport him to the next village. At the appointed time and place, he was ambushed by three men, who tried to steal his belongings and he felt if we had not come along when we did, he could have been killed. We managed to squeeze the man and his cardboard boxes into the back of the landrover and an hour or so later we dropped him off at the clinic where the paramedic in charge decided he would need a few stitches, plus a tetanus injection. This paramedic often treated us all for various cuts and bruises by using mosses, herbs and even spider webs and for this, he was regarded as a good 'white' witchdoctor. Nevertheless, we still had to take the body to the mortuary. We told the victim that we would take his cardboard boxes to the police station for safekeeping and he could collect them when he was fully fit to travel.

I sauntered into the office the next morning to find the team grouped around my desk in an animated discussion because on the top lay a small parcel and an envelope. I opened the envelope and discovered it had been written in English by the man we had helped the night before. In it, he thanked us for saving his life and wrote that the small parcel contained a little gift to show his appreciation. I opened the box to find an ornamental carving set, that had originally been made in India and lying at the bottom of the box was a cloth bracelet with an attached note telling me to wear it at all times as a protection against evil spirits. So, who was the man we had rescued? We reckoned the answer probably lay with the paramedic at the clinic.

We piled into the landrover and drove off to the clinic where he greeted us with a broad smile, 'I see you Bwana and I have been waiting for you.' I showed him the bracelet but he didn't want to handle it because he said it contained very powerful protective medicines. He continued, 'The man you rescued is one of the most powerful of witchdoctors in the country – he is what is called a paramount witchdoctor.'

When I asked him what the bracelet would contain, he suggested we should go inside and look. The bracelet had been crudely made with a linen covering that had been rolled and then roughly sewn around the edges. I snipped one or two of the stitches and gently eased a small peep-hole at which point everyone took a smart step backwards. The wristband contained a motley collection of seeds, sweet-smelling herbs, very thin strands of copper wire and shards of long black hair. The paramedic looking from afar said the hairs were from the tail of a bull elephant and the whole thing was designed to provide a very powerful aura of protection for the wearer and this was certainly the most powerful medicine he had ever seen.

The medic's reference to the hairs on the tail of an elephant reminded me of a situation a year or so before when I had only recently been posted to Chingola. The following day had been scheduled to be my rest-day, but the Officer Commanding had stated he wanted me to volunteer to assist a Government game-warden in hunting down a dangerous and badly wounded bull elephant, up on the border with the Congo. I had to take one of my police sergeants and a .303 rifle and ammunition and ensure the safe passage of the game warden. Our party set off at first light the next morning and en route, the game-warden told me the elephant had a broken tusk and was obviously in great pain and had even killed two villagers. The sorely wounded animal had eventually been tracked down, near a village situated right on the border with the breakaway state of Katanga and by mid-morning, we arrived there.

The headman told us the animal had been spotted in a maize field right on the edge of the nearby river. The game-warden took out an enormous rifle, which he called his special elephant gun, and told me he would endeavour to kill the elephant with just one shot, but if this failed and the elephant charged, I should stand my ground, shoot, reload and shoot again, using my rifle. I suddenly had the feeling this was not going to be as easy a job as I had at first imagined. The day was unusually a dull one, for Africa, with the sun hidden behind dark clouds, and the effect it created was one of mystery and foreboding, perhaps a harbinger of things to come. It was with some trepidation we approached the maize field, while at the same time, a group of villagers had been instructed to form a long line on the far side and gradually walk through the maize stalks, beating sticks on metals tins, or anything else that would make a loud noise. There was the nerve tingling sensation created by the racket and gradually the sound of the trumpeting and bellowing of an angry elephant grew louder, accompanied by crashing sounds as he burst his way through the dense bush. In the dull, almost half-light, it was difficult to see anything specific, only a kaleidoscope of fast-moving shadows and then, oh, my goodness! The largest bull elephant I have ever seen suddenly emerged from the maize field and stood there, shaking his great head and trunk from side to side, in obvious pain and anger.

The animal had one tusk which had broken off almost at the base leaving only a small fractured shard sticking out. Seeing or rather sensing our party the elephant hesitated for only the briefest of moments, then with his large ears moving back and forth, he suddenly charged. The African elephant is the largest land animal in the world and I can certainly vouch for this, as this thundering menace bore down on us. The game-warden raised his rifle and waited and waited, as I became more nervous of impending doom. My thoughts were ones of utter confusion – for God's sake fire – what am I doing here, - why not cut and run for it – go on, fire for God's sake! Then suddenly there followed a massive explosion as the warden fired, with the recoil almost knocking him over. The elephant was stopped instantly in its tracks, until gradually the gigantic beast slowly toppled over onto his side, stone dead.

It seemed then in that one instant all hell broke loose, as villagers started whooping in delight and rushed towards the dead animal, although by the time we had collected our thoughts and reached the elephant, the tail had already been removed and spirited away. The game warden told me afterwards that the tail would be used as an ingredient in some of Africa's strongest black-magic potions. As I stood there pondering exactly where the elephant's tail had disappeared to, a group of some five or six pygmies emerged from the bush and started butchering the dead animal. First of all, they disembowelled the elephant in a traditional way designed to free any evil spirits from the animal's body and again I was to remember this final scene many months later in another gruesome witchcraft murder.

Meanwhile, back at the clinic, the paramedic said I should wear the wristband under my watch, as this would give me total protection from evil spirits and would also cover those I worked with, and indeed the team seemed quite happy with this idea and none of us thought any more about it. Soon afterwards, Brush decided that all this witchcraft business was too much for him to bear and he resigned; in the meantime, Charlie had already lined up a replacement called William Kabeka, who had been happily employed until recently, when his employers had unexpectedly retired to South Africa.

William appeared later, escorted by the whole unit and during our negotiations, it turned out he had been paid a far higher salary by his previous employers who worked for the Nchanga Copper Mine. William mentioned a sum I could not possibly match but Sergeant Mumba would not be put off and took over the discussions. He intimated I had to raise my offer by a small amount, provide 2lbs of stewing steak each week for William and his family and be prepared to issue a brand-new uniform at very regular intervals. Mumba, in turn, pointed out to William he would be able to live rent-free in his own private accommodation, in a very secure environment, with free electricity and free water. According to tribal tradition, William had four wives who all lived together back at his home village, and he confided to us that his favourite wife of the moment was called Serafina, who had given him his only son, Joseph, so as a further incentive, I agreed to pay for Serafina and Joseph to travel by train to join him. That was probably the best deal I ever made in my life and William, who much preferred to be called Willy, over the years became a wonderfully loyal family friend.

Willy moved in straight away and was given two days to tidy and clean his new accommodation. However, in the middle of that night, the police bugles sounded, and I rushed to put on my riot gear as I headed out towards the station. I was struggling with all my accoutrements outside on the patio, when a figure suddenly came at me from out of the darkness, holding what I took to be a long piece of wood. I raised my baton, to defend myself until I heard a voice saying, 'No Bwana, I am your boy Willy and I will stay here on guard until you come back.' And this he did, not only on this occasion but whenever the police bugles sounded.

Chapter 5

A Doberman, A Baby Lost and an African Wedding

I was entirely wrapped up in my job, so much so, I rushed home at lunchtime to read a newspaper article about one of my recent court cases. 'I happened to see Dr Naudé today,' my wife said. 'Oh! And how was he?' I replied, and then the next moment a cushion was thrown at me from across the room, tearing the newspaper right out my hands. 'What I was going to say,' she went on totally nonplussed, 'is that I am pregnant – if that is alright with you?'

'That's more than alright,' I said, 'And it really is the most wonderful news.' We were both buoyed up by the news but vowed to keep it secret from family and friends until we had safely passed the all-important three-month point.

Days later, my wife said we needed to talk seriously about our security because although we had our dog, which was a cross between a Rhodesian Ridgeback and a Bulldog, he was totally useless as a guard dog and it was this aspect which really worried her. The answer was obviously to get ourselves a new guard dog, one we could train ourselves, and I immediately started looking at newspaper advertisements. It wasn't long before I spotted an advert promoting the sale of Doberman puppies which were now ready for collection. This set me thinking, because I vividly remembered the time as a very young boy when I was incarcerated in a German concentration camp during the Second World War with my parents, and seeing a majestic Doberman sitting in the back of a Mercedes staff car belonging to a high Nazi official, and I vowed then, that one day, if we survived, I would have such a dog.

The only worry was the question of how such a large and powerful dog would react to a young baby. After lunch, I talked it over with Brian who told me I should go and speak with the newly appointed

A DOBERMAN, A BABY LOST AND AN AFRICAN WEDDING

Officer-in-Charge of Nchanga Police Station, Chief Inspector John Ellis. Brian said John was a true horse and dog man and had several Dobermans himself but more than that, he was an honourable man and would only give me a true and balanced opinion. I visited John and explained what I was contemplating, and he expressed the view that if I was careful in buying a puppy I should have no trouble. He went on to say it would be better for me to buy a dog rather than a bitch and I should sit in the run, as far away from the puppies as possible, and take the first one that came up to me. Success would be achieved as long as I remembered I did not own a Doberman, I could be his best friend, but it was his family, his home, his furniture and even his car. Afterwards, I telephoned Kitwe and spoke with Mrs Douthwaite, owner of Copperane Kennels and agreed I would drive over to Kitwe to purchase one of her puppies. The next afternoon in Kitwe, I soon realised where the kennels were because of the constant barking and after meeting Mrs Douthwaite, we sauntered over to the wired-in enclosure, filled to overflowing with excited dogs.

Nonetheless, I was soon faced with several major impediments, the first one being the colour of the Dobermans, because, instead of the expected sleek black and tan coats, I was confronted with a sea of brown-haired dogs. Mrs Douthwaite explained to me that though there were several types of the breed, she bred only champion liver and tan Dobermans, although she preferred to call their colour as being red; still, all were registered with the South African Kennel Club. At that critical point, she went on to tell me, unfortunately, all the puppies had been sold. I protested, pointing out I had telephoned her only yesterday and made this appointment but as she explained, she was in business to make money and buyers had to be handled on a first come first served basis. I was feeling quite philosophical about it and took some time to look at the puppies, who were inquisitive bundles of energy and evidently all in fine fettle; well that is, except for one rather forlorn looking puppy lying against the wire netting on the far side of the run, with a purple coloured ribbon tied around his neck.

I asked about him, but she said that he was not for sale, because he was the runt of the litter; his snout was too short, and he was not built sufficiently well to make a champion and they had regretfully decided to have him put down. It was then the external telephone bell rang and Mrs Douthwaite made off to answer it, leaving me to enter the run to have a closer look at this sorrowful, rejected puppy. I think it is fair to say we were both greatly disappointed by what we saw, I sat down on the concrete floor to observe him and the first thing I noticed was that his paws were simply enormous. He slowly raised his head and looked directly at me with large deep yellow coloured eyes and I think at this stage, he probably thought I was going to be his best chance of survival. He rose up and slowly trundled across to where I was sitting and flopped down dejectedly, with his head resting on one of my extended legs and in that one moment, I was completely lost.

Mrs Douthwaite soon returned to tell me her husband had telephoned and they had agreed I could take the dog for the same price, because they would have to cover the cost of the necessary puppy injections, but all this came with the proviso I would not be able to exhibit him at any future dog shows, I readily agreed and soon completed the necessary formalities, I received the pup's South African Kennel Club Registration Certificate No: 151171; which named him as Graf Von Schwarzwald, and I carried him to the landrover. On the long return journey, I told the puppy he was now going to be called Alex after a wonderful guard-dog, who had looked after me in that German concentration camp during the last war when I was only 5 years old; when we arrived home, our older dog decided to ignore Alex completely and made out he did not exist.

We had been cautioned that Alex should not come into contact with any other dogs until he was three months old, nevertheless, he roamed happily about the confines of the garden either with me or with Willy. Late one afternoon, I was sitting on the stoep, reading the newspaper, when I heard a high-pitched screaming coming from just behind the house. I rushed around to see a pack of six or seven African wild dogs attacking Alex and throwing him around like a rag doll. I hastily grabbed a stick and joined in the fray, wielding the club and kicking out at these fiends in all directions. One of them flew at me and latched onto my chest until I grabbed him by the throat and threw him into the bushes – he did not return. By now, Willy had appeared and he too started to kick out until the pack ran off yelping but leaving a bleeding and inert Alex lying in the dirt.

I feared Alex was dead but when I picked him up, one eye opened and he just looked at me, still, he had been badly bitten all over his body and was bleeding most profusely. We gingerly wrapped him up in a blanket and with Willy holding him in his arms; we hurriedly drove off to the veterinary surgery. The vet examined Alex and felt the kindest thing would be to have him put down there and then, but as I digested his words, Alex opened his deep yellow eyes once again and just looked at me. If this was a direct appeal on Alex's part then it worked, because I could not possibly contemplate losing him and I told the vet as much. In response, he gave Alex an injection to ease the pain and handed me several tubes of penicillin which needed to be pumped into the larger holes in Alex's body, every few hours. He also instructed me to keep him warm and he went on to explain the most difficult time would come that evening or perhaps during the night, if Alex went into shock.

Noticing I was bleeding from a wound on my chest the vet asked if I had been bitten and when I said yes, he became agitated and said I should see my doctor urgently in case the dog suffered from rabies. Up to that point, I hadn't had time to think about it, but with Alex wrapped up in Willy's arms I drove around to the surgery. The doctor, Bill Schneerburger, was quite concerned and spoke to me about the effect of rabies, and anyway I had once seen a man dying from this torturous and abominable disease. We went through the violent engagement and I tried to remember in detail the state of the dogs, especially if any of them were foaming at the mouth, which they were not. Overall, I thought I had been very lucky, but Bill gave me several injections and told me to come back each day for the next week for a check-up. Back home, I took Alex and laid him in his cardboard box, still wrapped up in the blanket, and later that night I moved him into our bedroom and put him on the floor, on my side of the bed, and in the early hours when he started to whimper, I simply reached over, half in and half out of the bed and just held him throughout the night until early morning when his whimpering finally stopped.

Looking back now, I believe the time we spent like this was how we bonded together and by the morning light, I had fallen back on the bed, leaving my arm hanging over the side with my hand resting on Alex's head. When I woke from a night of disturbed sleep and looked over the edge, I could see his dark yellow eyes looking back at me, so blessedly, he had survived the difficult night. All the same, it had not gone unnoticed that our other dog had not helped one iota during the kerfuffle and we decided there and then he had to go. Sometime later I took him off to one of the outlying farms where he would spend the remainder of his days hunting in the far bush country.

The days passed slowly, and Alex gradually built up his strength, taking a few faltering and stumbling steps as his wounds healed, until finally, he seemed to throw off all stiffness and return to some form of normality. The great day arrived when he was finally strong enough to follow Willy to the office with the morning coffee and then came the time, just as we were about to board the landrover, when Alex suddenly appeared and jumped up into the front seat, which he obviously regarded as his rightful place. As so often happens, times of peace are often followed by periods of upheaval and all too soon we were faced with total devastation in heart-chilling moments that would affect our lives for all time.

For the moment though, we all lived happily together, especially when we received an invitation to attend a celebration dance at the Police Club in Chingola. We had great fun at the dance, although my wife raised a few eyebrows amongst friends by only drinking orange juice, even though she told me it had a rather funny taste. We left the celebrations before midnight, mainly because I had to make an early morning start, leading an armed patrol into the bush country near the Katanga border. Daylight was just breaking the next morning when the team and I started loading the landrover, and with the first rays of the sun appearing over the horizon, we started off, but only a few minutes into the patrol the radio came alive with an urgent message telling me to get back to Chiwempala as a dire emergency had arisen.

Back at the station, the duty sergeant said there was a big problem at my home and I took off, running hard across the parade ground only to find an overwrought Willy, who stuttered that he had found my wife lying on the bathroom floor, covered in blood. I wrapped her up in a blanket and then telephoned Dr Naudé, who was nicknamed Luddy, for help, and it seemed only a few minutes before he arrived, evaluated the situation and discovered Wendy had lost the baby but was still haemorrhaging. Luddy said to me, 'Look, this is terribly serious, and we need to get her to the hospital in Kitwe, like yesterday.'

'OK,' I said, 'I will call up the ambulance from Chingola straight away.' But he stopped me in my tracks by blurting out that we just didn't have the time and we should put her in the back of his car and be off as quickly as we could. Luddy had a large black American style car and I carried Wendy to the car. Before we left, I telephoned through to our Operations Room and asked for a motorcycle escort to the nearby town of Kitwe and if they would let the Kitwe hospital know we were on our way.

A DOBERMAN, A BABY LOST AND AN AFRICAN WEDDING

We had just driven under the railway bridge, when Bill Player rode up alongside us on his patrol motorcycle, then he moved ahead, with the siren wailing and lights flashing, leading us at great speed down the wide open road to Kitwe. On the outskirts of Kitwe, we were joined by another police outrider, who indicated we should follow him. We were simply flying, and thanks to this police motorcyclist we soon arrived at the hospital where nurses and doctors were already waiting for us outside the main doors of the emergency department and within seconds my wife quickly disappeared on a trolley pushed by several hospital porters. Time dragged on and eventually, Dr Naudé had to return to Chingola and I was suddenly left desperately alone.

From time to time, nurses came into the waiting room to make sure I was all right but there was no immediate news. It was becoming dark outside when a doctor came in, to explain that not only had the baby been lost but the trauma had caused a serious haemorrhage and the overriding problem still facing the medical team was to try to stop the bleeding. My wife had lost a great deal of blood and was having a blood transfusion, but the prognosis was not good and I had to be prepared for the very worst case scenario. At that point, my world collapsed and where once I had everything I ever wanted, I was now looking at a very cold and empty world, completely devoid of love and warmth.

I asked if I could see her, but the doctor said it was inadvisable as she had been put into a deep sleep to help her relax and to give her body a chance to recover. He went on to say we needed to be positive but if unfortunately they could not save her, her final hours were still a long way off and the best thing I could do was to go back home and wait for him to telephone me with any news. I was left completely numb and bereft and felt altogether isolated and exhausted. I made my way through the long, lonely hospital corridors, being met at the entrance by a police officer, who told me he had been detailed to drive me back to the border between Kitwe and Chingola. He had already arranged for Chingola police to rendezvous with us and drive me home and later I transferred to the Chingola truck. Instead of driving to Chiwempala, the sergeant told me he had been given strict instructions to take me to the Police Club, and at that moment I was just too weary to argue.

Then, a wonderful thing happened for one by one and two by two my friends and colleagues began to arrive at the Police Club to show solidarity and express their sadness; never in a thousand years would

I ever forget their kindness. I have always felt great pride in having served with such an extraordinary band of men; nevertheless, I was dog-tired and soon begged a lift back to Chiwempala. Once there, I walked slowly across the parade ground towards home and as I came nearer, I witnessed a sight, forever fixed in my memory. A circle of flaming candles had been placed all along the driveway and I could see Willy and the team sitting on chairs and stools, in a rather despondent group. I joined them and then Willy switched on the outside lamps, illuminating the driveway and I was astounded to see it was full to overflowing with all sorts of produce and even several wicker baskets containing live chickens. Sergeant Mumba told me that many people from the township had been arriving at the station throughout the day, as the distressing news had spread. He said they all wanted to show their sorrow by bringing in gifts such as vegetables, eggs, fruit, cooked chickens and even live chickens. I realised then, that these were heart-given gifts from people who I didn't know and who, I felt sure, could ill afford to provide them, and I started to cry.

I passed a restless night and telephoned the hospital at first light, to find my wife's condition remained unchanged but with the alarming proviso that the next 24 hours would decide the final outcome. After talking with the team, it was agreed all the gifts would be shared out between the various medical clinics and the hospital. Although my mind was not focussed on work, I asked to look at the Occurrence Book to see what crimes had been committed over this period, but Charlie said, 'There has been no reported crime Bwana, the town is quiet and everyone including all the criminals is very worried about Medami.' This state of affairs lasted for several more days, and in the meantime Brian gave me leave of absence. By late afternoon, I was sitting at the bedside in a hospital ward, encircled by curtains, lost in thought as I watched the peaceful, sleeping features of a very beautiful young woman and conjectured about what might have been.

Later that evening, I met the doctor who told me they had finally been able to stop the haemorrhaging and my wife was now stable and out of danger although very weak. I was allowed to stay with her for a little while and the first thing she said to me was, 'I am so sorry,' in a very croaky voice, and as I said 'You have nothing to be sorry about, and I am so happy you are now on the mend.' The time eventually arrived when she was able to leave the hospital and it was a very thoughtful and sad couple who made the return trek home. Once she was back home and resting, it was if the township gave a collective sigh of relief and gradually things got back to normal, crime started to rise again and cases began flooding in once more. But this was not the final act, because one of the party organisers later confessed to spiking the orange drinks with gin and vodka, to make the party go with a swing.

As the days passed, the team and I gradually picked ourselves up and began to take more notice of events happening around us. At the station, victims of housebreaking, burglary and assault were starting to form orderly queues until just after one lunchtime we received an urgent telephone call reporting the horrific news that an 18-month-old baby had appeared to have fallen into an open sewer in the township. Brian was attending a meeting in Chingola and most of the squad were out on inquiries, which left only Charlie and me to respond. When we arrived, we found a distraught group of women wailing and sobbing, as they told us the young child must have toddled off towards the ditch and fallen into the fast-flowing open sewer, because they had looked everywhere else. Charlie and I ran down the whole length of the ditch which was approximately four feet across and at least three to four feet deep and because it was the middle of the rainy season, the race was moving at a very fast pace, with an abominable combination of water and raw sewage.

I positioned myself at a junction where the dense liquid went underground en route to the sewage farm, while Charlie was some way back on a small bridge, looking down into the stinking morass. Within seconds, he shouted that there was something floating in the ditch and without a moment's hesitation he jumped off the bridge and into the foul-smelling effluent, which came up to his waist, then in the same instant something hit him hard against his legs and knocked him completely off balance and down into the foetid mire. As he vainly struggled to regain his balance, I shouted at him to keep his mouth shut and when he neared my spot, I too jumped in and positioned myself hard against the buttress of the stone cover.

In no time at all, Charlie fetched up against me with such a heavy thump the pressure of the water quickly built up and covered us both in a torrent, until I was gradually able to push him out and then claw my own way out of this awful stinking mess. The stench was appalling and we were both soaked through, unrecognisable and inundated with raw sewage. We tried to wipe ourselves down, and just as we started to regain our composure, the tall grass on the edge of the ditch parted and a young baby crawled out, only to be picked up by his relieved and adoring parents who hurried him off to their hut, singing and dancing as they went, while totally ignoring our own desperate plight. Charlie and I walked back slowly towards the landrover together, only to be met by Brian, who pulled up alongside us and said, 'Now, just where do you think you two muck-spreaders are going?'

'Back to the truck and then we will go and get cleaned up.'

'Oh, no you won't, and certainly, not in that diabolical state. Sekondwe will drive your landrover and you two can walk back, in front of mine, but keep us up-wind if you please.'

As we walked back towards the station, we were certainly the centre of attention and followed by an ever-increasing crowd, dancing, singing and laughing, and to make matters worse, some of the young children started to mimic us by holding their noses as they shook themselves down. It wasn't any better when we reached the station, being confronted by a long line of constables and sergeants laughing to the point of mass hysteria. My wife was certainly not impressed and I was forbidden from entering the apartment until I had stripped off to my briefs and suffered the ignominy of having a laughing Willy dowse me down with stinging jets of cold water from the garden hose. Then and only then was I allowed in, on the promise I would have a further hot shower and use a perfumed soap.

The next morning, the intercommunicating-door opened and the team trooped through in relatively good humour. Detective Sergeant Mumba, acting as the senior officer, opened the discussion, by pointing out there had been numerous times when I had saved their lives, and they hesitantly suggested there had also been quite a few times when they had saved mine, which meant we were now all brothers under the skin and as such, we needed to help each other in times of great difficulty. The punchline was not long in coming, because Charlie took up the discourse to let me know he had finally found a beautiful young lady and now wished to get married, in spite of all the imposing obstacles. The main hurdle he faced was in negotiating the bride-price with the girl's father and for this, he needed a special 'brother' to plead his case and as he and I were now true brothers, he wanted me to negotiate the bride-price on his behalf, during the next afternoon.

Detective Sergeant Mumba interrupted to say this was going to be no easy task, as it had to follow strict and long-established tribal laws, more especially as the stipulated price of four cows, eight goats and numerous chickens was well above Charlie's capability to meet with any degree of certainty. The team felt with my involvement, the girl's family would possibly feel obliged to reduce this extraordinarily heavy burden, although there was no guarantee this would actually happen. I had no alternative but to agree to act as a tribal brother for Charlie and then the instructions started to flow. The meeting would be held at the Ndaba Tree (the village meeting point) the next afternoon and I was also expected to attend in my full-dress police uniform. Furthermore, I could not dictate the terms of the bride-price, because this would greatly offend the bride's family.

Detective Sergeant Mumba would also attend and act as an interpreter and I was required to give a full discourse on Charlie's wondrous abilities and chances of promotion. Besides this, I was expected to bring a small gift, such as a crate of beer for the girl's father. Willy started preparing and starching my uniform and polishing my Sam-Browne belt and boots, the beer was purchased and just after lunch the following day, the three of us set off for the Ndaba Tree, where village elders would normally sit, relax and then discuss affairs of state. When we arrived, the male members of the family were all sitting on chairs under a shady tree, with the women reclining on the ground, just behind them and I noticed directly in front, three chairs had been placed for us, whereas the very attractive young girl sat to one side with her mother, but took no part in the discussions whatsoever.

Traditional greetings were exchanged, and we were welcomed into the family. The crate of beer was gratefully accepted, especially when I agreed they could take the empty bottles back to the store and reclaim the deposit. Once the first bottle of beer had been dispatched, the joviality stopped and we settled down to some very hard negotiations. Yes, Charlie would make an upright and worthy husband, destined as he surely was for rapid promotion within the police. Yes, married accommodation would be provided free of charge, with free water and electricity. Medical facilities were also available and would be free for wives and children. Obviously, the family had not thought about these aspects and a great deal of animated discussion took place between all the male family members.

After some delay, the girl's father returned to the fray and announced the family would now reduce the bride price to only four goats, although they still required the original four cows and chickens. It was evident this was going to be the best deal we could achieve and as a tribal brother to the future groom I had to formally accept the bride-price which needed to be paid in full before the marriage could proceed. After this, the celebrations began in earnest and Detective Sergeant Mumba and I left Charlie in the bosom of his future family and returned to the station. On the way back, Mumba issued the thunderbolt, which was to the effect that as the brother of the groom, it was now my responsibility to meet the bride price, especially as Charlie had very few assets of his own to contribute towards the cost.

The goats were easy to track down because we visited our old friend, the good witchdoctor and herbalist Emmanuel Muleya and purchased four goats in reasonable condition for a bargain price. The chickens too came free following visits to numerous European owned chicken farms in the district; still, the cows remained an expensive proposition. The team let it be known, in no uncertain terms, that because I had negotiated the price, I needed to personally see the deal through to completion. Farm patrols put the word out, until finally several of the European farmers provided three cows and one young bull, all at knock down prices. With honour satisfied on all sides, the marriage was allowed to proceed and although I wished Charlie all the luck in the world, I had to admit to being slightly miffed about not receiving an invitation to the wedding.

Chapter 6

Ambush!

It was another good morning for the team at the Resident Magistrate's Court, where all of their criminal cases had been handled with the usual efficiency and professionalism by the Police Public Prosecutor and friend Inspector Duncan Pollock. Each of the accused had been sentenced to varying terms of imprisonment and the Magistrate commended the unit for their diligent work. I returned to the station feeling very happy and Phiri told me the headmaster of the local school had visited us and invited me to take tea with him at his house that same afternoon.

Later, when I arrived at the headmaster's home, he detailed his youngest son to guard the landrover, while two of his other sons went inside the house and emerged a few minutes later carrying a black leatherette settee which they put down in the shade of a tall banana tree. Soon tea appeared and we settled down to the serious business in hand. The headmaster said he wanted to make sure I fully understood how important a bicycle was to the African, in all levels of society, because it was rather like a European owning a car, where the loss could have a disastrous effect on a person's livelihood if it was ever stolen.

His comments really made me think and I promised to do something about it, although I realised the main difficulty lay in trying to recognise the various overlying and changing patterns of cycle theft throughout the township. On the way back to the station I decided to plot all the unsolved cycle thefts over the last six months on the map board, once again delineated them with coloured pins. I soon had Phiri working on a list of cycle thefts, with days, dates, places and values together with the modus operandi involved. We worked through the evening, and the rest of the team soon joined in, retrieving files and dissecting the information. At midnight, we called a time-out because although we had most of the necessary information to hand, there was still no clear emerging pattern.

The next morning, after breakfast, my wife said she was going to spend some time with friends in Chingola and I decided to take Alex with me to work. We both walked over to the office, where the team was still studying the cycle theft information and looking rather despondent. I uttered the magic words, 'I have had an idea, which will involve everyone this morning,' and they immediately perked up and soon the office was a hive of activity. Within minutes, we were in the landrover and on our way to create a road-block on the main road out of the township and this time, apart from Alex, we also took Constable Phiri along, in an attempt to vary the boring monotony of his daily office routine. We had only travelled about half a mile down the dirt road, with the dust billowing out behind us when we were flagged down by the agitated owner of a rather ramshackle and battered old brown taxi.

The driver hurriedly explained that his heavily pregnant passenger was on the verge of giving birth in the back of his taxi and she was in urgent need of some medical assistance. A quick check showed this really was the situation and Phiri was quickly dispatched on foot to the nearby medical clinic to summon the sister in charge, the redoubtable Mrs Green. In the meantime, Charlie and Sergeant Mumba helped the distraught woman leave the confines of the taxi, allowing Monga and Busike to start stripping out the bench seats and totally ignore the protestations of the agitated driver. The seats were soon laid out in the cool shade of a nearby tree and the expectant mother gently lowered into position. Things were becoming serious when the baby's head began to emerge, which frightened the life out of us, except for the experienced Sergeant Mumba a father many times over, who immediately took charge and with much urging, cajoling and pushing a healthy, baby boy was safely delivered.

None of us had any idea what to do with the umbilical cord, but providentially we were spared, by the arrival of Sister Green in the clinic van, who took matters completely out of our hands. When the excitement had eventually died down and the mother and baby had been driven away to the clinic, the taxi driver, rather belligerently wanted to know who was going to pay the fare and who was going to make amends for cleaning his seats and cushions. His strident pleas received very short shrift from the squad who pointed out he operated an illegal taxi service, which warranted a hefty fine and, following some very aggressive staring and growling from Alex, the disgruntled taxi driver backed down and within minutes we had set off once again.

AMBUSH!

We positioned the landrover sideways across the main road, partially blocking the way in and out of the township. Monga and Busike went back into the location a little way, enabling them to stop anyone from turning around and fleeing from the road-block. In the back of the landrover, Phiri had all the record books of detailed cycle thefts at his fingertips and while Mumba stopped the cyclists and Mubonda shouted out the frame number on each of the bicycles, Phiri checked these off against his records. Although a queue of cyclists quickly built up, they were all in good humour and realised we were working hard on behalf of their community. After some time, Police Constable Musongo, the head bugler and messenger from Chingola Police Station, rode up on his brand-new green bicycle, explaining that this was his day off and he was looking around the local stores for various bargains.

Alex was clearly very uneasy and when Musongo bent down to pat him, Alex moved away but I could see his raised hackles and even Charlie remarked when Musongo had left us that Alex didn't seem to like him very much. The morning passed very quickly and although we had not found any stolen cycles, I had a bad feeling that we had missed something vitally important and on the way back to the station, I tried to think through what was concerning me. The team by now seemed to recognise some of my more peculiar traits, because when they were all chattering away in the back of the truck, Mumba told them to quieten down, 'As the Bwana is at his thinking once again!' and it was only when I parked the landrover, the answer came to me and I started to chuckle to myself. In the charge office, I carefully examined the Occurrence Book and saw there had been no reports of cycle theft during the morning. Even so, I told the desk-sergeant I was expecting someone to report the theft of a very expensive green bicycle and he should make sure to keep the owner in the station until I returned.

When I returned after lunch, I overheard the desk-sergeant talking to a member of the public. 'You know, this is all about witchcraft and of course, the Bwana's big brown dog Alex knows who did it.'

The young complainant, who owned a green bicycle, had left it unattended that morning for only a few minutes, outside one of the local stores. Mubonda took a detailed statement from the young man and I took the opportunity to telephone the Detective Sub-Inspector in Chingola and made arrangements to meet him later. At 3pm, with the full team and Alex in attendance, we collected the Sub-Inspector, after which I parked the landrover just outside the Police Club where I finally told everyone what it was all about.

I asked the Sub-Inspector if he knew where the bugler Musongo lived and he acknowledged that he did. We proceeded slowly along the track, until we saw Musongo outside his quarters, carefully polishing his brand-new green bicycle, however it didn't take us long to discover this was the stolen bike and in spite of his initial protestation of innocence, we soon found a hoard of cycle parts inside his dwelling. I told them, I had eventually remembered seeing Musongo in the marketplace several weeks before when I noticed he was riding a new red cycle, again on his day off, and our records showed an identical bicycle was stolen on that day. Musongo decided to call it a day and come clean and admitted to a number of high-profile cycle thefts. So far so good!

Phiri began to devise various ways of interpreting the modus operandi on cycle thefts and soon came up with a mysterious observation, where he noticed many cycle thefts took place either at the end of a month or sometimes during the first few days of the next month and, more out of encouragement than anything else, I produced a graph of these thefts. The results were quite startling, with heavy spikes occurring during these times but crucially the stolen cycles were usually of high value, in excellent condition, and had invariably been purloined overnight.

Joseph Mulimba was a proud member of the Lamba tribe from Mulimba village near Ndola and was enjoying a new-found freedom. He was gainfully employed by a group of American Missionaries who had recently established a Mission Station, quite a few miles outside Chingola, and it was his job to drive and maintain the Mission's old Bedford lorry, in order to collect groceries and other much needed essential commodities. As far as Mulimba could ascertain, the American Missionaries were financially supported by well-wishers back home in America, who sent regular contributions to them each month. More than that though, he was inordinately proud of his most exciting money-making idea to date, which was netting him large sums of money each month in addition to his meagre salary. He had soon realised that the Missionaries, like many Americans, had an entrepreneurial streak and when he had suggested he could buy bicycles for very little money, then recondition them during his quieter periods and offer them to local tribesmen at very special low prices, the Missionaries jumped at the chance. They saw a wonderful opportunity of not only defraying their own expenses but more importantly of bringing many more people to the feet of Jesus.

Joseph had been very clever in establishing his cycle workshop a little way away from the Mission, where he was free from observation and interference. He had built a number of thatch-roofed huts where he could carry out his repair and reconditioning work and already the space was overflowing with cycle parts. As far as the Americans were concerned, he would buy suitable bicycles for between two and three pounds each, then he would be given a further two pounds for each cycle he repaired and the money made from the sale, generally reckoned to be between six and eight pounds would go directly to Mission funds, showing a healthy profit.

Towards the month-end, Joseph would leave the Mission at around mid-day arriving in Chingola later that evening, where he would buy all the necessary commodities, and load them directly onto his truck, ensuring they were covered by a large tarpaulin. During the night, and after a good meal he would start to trawl through both the townships and the Municipality looking for suitable bicycles to steal. There was always a ready supply of unlocked bicycles and Joseph would simply park in a side street some way away, walk back, and wheel the cycle quickly away. Once loaded, the tarpaulin was again secured and Joseph would drive off to the next venue. Usually, ten bicycles were enough to be loaded onto his lorry and he reasoned no-one would ever suspect an employee of such a respected religious order. He would sleep in his vehicle because he didn't want to spend any money on accommodation and he certainly didn't want people to see his precious illicit cargo! Early the following morning, he would write out a series of fake bicycle receipts, pocket the money allocated by the Mission, making sure it all balanced correctly then he would set off, usually arriving by late afternoon.

Driving back, he mused about one of his more pleasurable problems, being his large stash of money, which was beginning to swamp the big suitcase he kept under the bed. Perhaps, one day soon, he would need to take it to a bank and open an account. Back at the Mission, the bicycles would be quickly unloaded and checked over by his two employees then stripped down. Some would be painted, others would have different saddles, bells and pannier baskets fitted, to give the impression of care and perceived value to the Missionaries and buyers alike, but which Joseph regarded as being essential to disguise the thefts.

MURDER, WITCHCRAFT AND THE KILLING OF WILDLIFE

Mid-afternoon and we had finished our investigations well outside our normal geographical boundaries and in doing so we had not only arrested several wildlife poachers, but we had also retrieved a number of ivory tusks and leopard skins. The slaughter of such magnificent animals always filled me with disgust and more especially with unbridled hatred for the Indian traders or store owners who invariably paid the poachers a mere pittance for their ghastly trade.

We were heading back, when I decided to go and check out the newly established American Mission, just to let them know we could offer a measure of security and protection. They were very welcoming and I gratefully accepted their kind offer of coffee and biscuits, served on their shaded veranda. The team, meanwhile, dispersed to talk to workers and any villagers, just to make sure all was well, and later, when the Mission lorry arrived, one of the Missionaries excused himself and went off to speak to the driver. When he returned, he regaled me at some length with stories of his prowess in establishing such a profitable charitable market by providing cut-price bicycles solely for his Christian parishioners, Mubonda just looked straight at me, then rolled his eyes heavenward, in sheer disbelief. I quietly told him to take Busike and the stolen cycle log and check one or two of the cycles out, just to be on the safe side.

Joseph Mulimba enjoyed his trip back because it had been completely uneventful as usual. As soon as he had parked up near the stores building, one of the Missionaries came along to inspect his selection of bicycles. Joseph dutifully handed over the completed receipts, then he unloaded the essential supplies and put them in the storerooms, before driving off to his own compound. His two associates offloaded the bicycles, while he went off to his hut to wash and change his clothes. He took the opportunity to put his ill-gotten gains into the burgeoning suitcase under his bed and then he just relaxed for a few minutes.

In the meantime, Mubonda and Busike approached the two unsuspecting associates under the pretence of looking for a bicycle for Mubonda's young son. They examined several models and checked the wheels, brakes, and frames before asking the price and then they told the two men they would need to think it over but would return very soon. I had just finished my coffee, when the two returned and told me what they had discovered, and this must have been the same time the two assistants were telling Joseph the good news, because they thought they had a reasonably dandy chance of making another quick sale. Meanwhile, Mubonda told me they had secretly checked three bikes and all of them had been stolen a month or so earlier.

It was a lovely cool evening and Joseph was very relaxed when he saw a European and two African men walking towards him, and from the way they walked and the upright manner in which they held themselves he knew straight away his new-found way of life was about to end. It took several weeks for us to sort the mess out because many of the bicycles had been stripped down and parts exchanged one with another but eventually, we traced over 575 stolen bicycles, which we were later informed was a new world record! Joseph was very helpful and was finally charged with forty cases of theft which he admitted and then he asked the Magistrate for 535 further cases to be taken into consideration, and after that our detection rate rocketed and was never beaten again. When the case was finalised, we extended a warm welcome to the headmaster, to take afternoon tea with us all in the station.

After a short period of probation, I had been accepted into the permanent CID establishment and in recognition, I had also been given a brand-new, grey coloured, long wheel-based landrover; with no police insignia displayed. This was deemed to be much more appropriate for our vital plain-clothes police work. However, our euphoria did not last long, because several days later, during one of our regular riots, our new truck had been stoned and seriously damaged. The end result was that it had to go in for repair and we reverted to an old and battered replacement vehicle.

In times of serious public disorder, all police transport was required to have security wire-mesh grilles fixed to the more vulnerable parts of the vehicles such as windows, windscreens and radiator housings. My boss, Chief Inspector Jack Gowland, had called a special meeting to discuss some new force standing orders and it was during one of these meetings we all went outside to inspect my replacement landrover. For some reason, I had taken Alex along with me and he was quite content to sit in the front seat looking out at what was happening all around him. Jack noticed that, although most of the protection screens had been fitted, the windscreen still lacked the proper protective covers and he urged me to get it completed before the next meeting. By late afternoon, we adjourned to the Police Club for a sundowner, which usually meant several ice cold beers for us and a bowl of cool water for Alex. The only other occupants were Chingola's executive officer, Don Maclean, and Peter, the bar-steward, who was a gentleman, always smiling and well turned out in his crisp white uniform. However, this time, he was assisted by a newly appointed part-time bar worker, a tall man I had not seen before.

On these occasions, discussions with colleagues were invariably animated and covered a wide range of subjects although nearly always geared to police work. Jack reminded me of a Force instruction to vary our transport routes to avoid repetition which could lead to any of us being bushwhacked by troublemakers, and as such, I had always varied my routes anyway, as part of normal patrolling techniques. I told Jack I had driven down the main road, passing the Church, and I intended going back via the market and the beer-hall. That statement very nearly proved to be my undoing – a little later, we all left the bar and Alex and I set off for home.

The short period of twilight had given way to nightfall and the lampposts leading out were all lit, with groups of men and women standing underneath with their tin baths filled with water, ready to catch a harvest of flying insects attracted by the brilliant lamplight, by scooping them up ready for frying. The market was almost deserted when we passed, but the beer-hall was doing a roaring trade. On a gloomy stretch of the road, the headlights pierced through the dusk and soon picked out a group of youths blocking the way and when I slowed down, others came suddenly at us from both sides. They started beating fists and sticks against the sides of the landrover, causing Alex to go berserk, horrified that these people were trying to damage his vehicle and shortly afterwards the crowd began to rock the vehicle from side to side in an attempt to turn it over on its side.

I managed to send off a desperate radio message to police control, giving brief details of our attackers and my position, and although I had locked the doors automatically, I quickly came to the conclusion our situation was precarious and untenable, to say the least. A voice rang out over the tumult calling for someone to bring petrol to burn the white policeman, and I decided there and then, we had to get out by any means possible and in damn short order. I grabbed a long-baton and slid back part of the windscreen to let a snarling, slashing Doberman, quivering with anger, to scramble out onto the bonnet. I followed suit but being heavier and more cumbersome I received several heavy blows on my head and shoulders but at least we were out and by now the adrenalin was really flowing. Alex threw himself about, moving at lightning speed from the bonnet to the roof of the vehicle and then back again and I laid about me with the long-baton, hearing yelps of pain and feeling the crunch of broken bones as I made direct contact with the fingers and wrists of my antagonists. In this maelstrom, I soon came to realise we could not continue like this for very much longer. I called out to Alex and he came to my side immediately and I was just about to jump off the bonnet into the heaving morass when I heard a voice shouting, 'No – Stop!' In the half-light I could just make out the figure of a tall and older man wielding a long and heavy piece of wood, charging full tilt into the mob.

The rabble recoiled with shock, giving me the opportunity to throw myself forward, fiercely wielding the baton in short stabbing motions and closely followed by Alex, whose large, white, crocodile teeth were quickly slashing and scything through the serried ranks of our opponents. Eventually, the crowd realising this ambush was not turning out to be the easy conquest they had been promised, decided discretion was now the better part of valour and took to their heels, violently pursued by an enraged and vociferous Alex.

Within minutes the police rescue patrols arrived and an exuberant Alex returned to my side, still spitting out torn pieces of cloth. A few minutes later, Brian drove up with a scratch rescue team, sitting me down on the front seat of my truck and giving me the once over, checking my various cuts and bruises. He told me his wife, Mair, had invited Wendy over for a cup of tea, on the pretext that I had been delayed by work and we both agreed we should just leave it like that and not say anything more about the incident, although I knew I would not be able to hide the bruises, cuts and another black eye for long.

Back at the station, the team made a great fuss of Alex, and from all appearances, he seemed none the worse for his adventure. I was finally able to properly thank my saviour, John Shinde, for his valiant intervention and as it turned out, he was the respected leader of a community of Jehovah's Witnesses, who had regularly suffered at the hands of roaming bands of violent insurgents demanding money. This brief respite gave me the opportunity of calmly reviewing what had happened during the evening and I came to the firm conclusion, that if I had fitted the necessary security grilles on the windscreen, then I would have been unable to escape and Alex and I would not have survived the attack, a very sobering thought indeed. As I went over the events of the night in my mind I came to focus on the activity of the assistant bar-steward at the Police Club. The team was in high dudgeon over the incident and left straight away to question the man, but the bird had flown and was never traced. When we finally arrived back home, Alex flopped down on the floor and my wife remarked a little wryly, 'I don't know what you've done to this poor old dog today, but he is completely tuckered out.' And as far as I was concerned, he certainly wasn't the only one!

The next day, I visited John Shinde at his home to thank him properly and I offered to take his photograph and have it framed for him, but he refused out of fear the camera would steal his soul, a commonly held belief. However, he welcomed my suggestion we should place a police constable on guard duty during night-time, and it was a darned good job we did, because, at 1am, the bugles summoned us to repel an attack on John Shinde's community huts and buildings, where the attackers were dispersed with some alacrity, suffering a few sore heads and broken bones in the process. The next evening found me with an armed patrol investigating some other serious breach of the peace in the township, when the operations room notified us of another attack being mounted against the Jehovah's Witnesses' compound. This time, the constable on guard had been lured away by a ruse, leaving the main force of subversive elements free to attack the compound. When we arrived on the scene, some of the buildings were already well alight but it was obvious that the main thrust of the attack had been directed against John Shinde's own hut.

Smoke and flames billowed out from broken windows and the main door had been ripped off its hinges. I leapt across the storm drain in front of the house and raced into the building, quickly followed by Charlie and Monga. In the half-light, I could just make out John's bloody face as he sprawled on the floor with an evil looking man standing just behind him. This man held John up by his torn coat collar with one hand, while he gripped a wicked looking metal cargo-hook in the other. I shouted at him to stop but he continued to raise his arm high in the air and took no notice of me whatsoever. By now my .38 revolver was in my hand and as his hand started to sweep downwards towards John's bloodied and unprotected face, I fired.

In the confined space the explosion was deafening and at the same time the man clutched at his chest and literally flew backwards against the backdoor, dropping the cargo-hook in the process. This violent movement was so traumatic that the door gave way and both man and door disappeared from view, tumbling down a short flight of steps. Brian was already outside organising the police in checking debris and making the properties safe with strategically placed armed guards and having recounted my recent involvement, we went looking for the body. There was a great deal of blood on the steps but no body, and in the following days, no further information came to light, although in my own mind I felt sure the attacker could not have survived my bullet.

A few days later, John Shinde asked to see me and when I visited him, I found the Jehovah's Witnesses smartly turned out with their brilliant white bandannas picked out with vermilion coloured hieroglyphics, all packed up and ready to leave. John said they had decided to return to the bush country, so they would no longer be intimidated. I offered him transport to the railway station, but he declined, preferring to march instead at the head of his own people. Before he left, he gave me a pewter image of an African head which he said was of him and in memory of our special relationship and the fact that the image bore no resemblance to him whatsoever did not seem to worry anyone. The community set off singing their hymns and we followed a little way behind until we reached the railway station where finally Alex and I could say goodbye to a very brave and Christian gentleman.

Chapter 7

Lepers and Presidents

It was the beginning of yet another hot and humid day and I was closeted in the shower when the telephone rang. My wife answered and shouted out, 'It's for you. They've just found another body.' Within a scant few minutes, the team and I were at the scene, not that it had been difficult to find, with the early morning workers taking the time out to gaze at the corpse gently swinging backwards and forwards in the damp morning air. The body of a relatively young man was hanging from an almost horizontal branch of a tall tree. The body was stiff and cold to the touch and had obviously been suspended there for most of the night. However, there were several intriguing features to this case, such as the use of thin but high tensile wire to form the noose, deep scratch marks around the frontal area of the throat, and the fact the body was suspended only a few feet off the ground. The wire too had cut deep into the flesh and it looked for all the world as if the victim had been garrotted.

Detailed examination of the body showed patches of green lichen smeared on the soles of the shoes and these matched the marks on the tree trunk, making it clear where the man had scrambled upwards, towards the main branch. There were firm indications that he had stretched out full length, before tying the wire around the branch, then fixing the noose about his neck, before finally rolling off into the next world. As we were taking care of the forensics inevitably involved in such cases, the agile Monga scaled the tree and tried to lower the body gently to the ground but the metal wire proved far too strong to sever, until with the aid of a pair of wire-cutters, he was able to snap the restraining wire and the body fell earthwards. I just managed to catch the rigid torso as the dead man's feet hit the ground, but rigor mortis had already set in, creating chemical changes, and as such, the trapped air inside the body was expelled with a massive, 'Aah!' With that explosive sound, we suddenly found ourselves completely alone with the body, because the watching crowd had taken

62

to their heels in some disarray, running for their lives in every direction, which later gave credence to the myth that they had heard the spirit of the dead man speaking directly to the white policeman.

In the meantime, a search of the area by the side of the nearby railway-line undertaken by Busike revealed a small hideaway covered with interlaced banana fronds and he could see that the large leaves had been securely bound to a slight wooden framework with the same type of wire as used in the hanging. Once the body had been wrapped up and transported to the local mortuary, we began our careful examination of the pitiful hide. There was insufficient room to stand upright, but we could see a rumpled blanket, lying on a long, wet strip of cardboard and a small, rickety orange box that had been used as a table. There were a few assorted items of dishevelled and dirty clothing, together with a pencil note, scrawled on a tattered and torn piece of paper lying on the table and written in the Bemba language, which stated, 'I am Moses Chungu and my chief is Chitimbwa from the Abercorn region. I have lost my job and my house and my wife and my family. Today I only had enough money left to buy a small chicken but when I came back, someone had stolen it. So I have lost everything and now I will lose my life.' Later the post-mortem revealed the skin under Moses's fingernails was his own as he frantically tried to claw at the wire in a vain attempt to save himself.

This was not the end of the saga, because a final twist in the story still needed to be played out. Later, at the station, Brian dropped a new docket on my desk, which no-one at Chingola Central wanted anything to do with, as it concerned the theft of 120 black and white chickens from a local farm. Before I could do anything about it, the DSI from Chingola, arrived on his bicycle and asked to see me; it was only recently he had helped us in solving a case of cycle theft. He could hardly write his own name but, my goodness, he had an excellent brain and a superlative, retentive memory. Previously, when I was in charge of a police shift at Central Station, we would sometime sit together in the charge office in the late evening and talk about life in Northern Rhodesia in the good old days and I knew he dearly loved a cup of hot English tea. Our team liked him enormously and soon he was relaxing in our office with his tea and a biscuit, as he told us this story.

He said some three years or so ago, when he had only just been posted to Chingola, there had been a theft of more than a hundred chickens, all black and white, from a remote farm deep in the bush. The complainant's name on the docket matched his description and our stolen chickens were also black and white and came from the same farm. He spoke about how he had finally traced the culprit to an area near the railway lines, where, in amongst the trees he had found the chickens, all with their throats cut, hanging from the branches of trees and bushes. The man had been arrested and sentenced to a long term in prison but perhaps by now, he had been released. Anyway, for what it was worth, he said once he had finished his tea, he would be pleased to show us the place where he had originally found the chickens, in case the modus operandi had remained the same.

We set off, and he directed us to exactly the same place where we had been investigating that morning's suicide. Leaving a constable to guard the transport, we marched off in crocodile formation through the dense bush with the DSI leading. We were in the middle of the rainy season and the overgrown vegetation had started to turn green and was dotted with beautiful white and yellow wildflowers. We meandered along for perhaps three or four hundred yards until our man flattened out some of the tall elephant grass and we stepped through the thick undergrowth. It suddenly gave way to reveal a green and dark oasis of shrubs, with a clearing in the middle. The impact was so immediate it resembled a scene straight out of a Breughel painting, except that none of the people there were animated in any way.

It was difficult to take it in all at once, because every bush, every tree, and every branch held a chicken dangling by its legs, but with its throat cut. There must have also been fifteen to twenty men and women on this greensward, some standing alongside large cooking pots with wood smoke spiralling upwards and some sitting on wooden stools, plucking chicken feathers for all they were worth. Long strips of coloured plastic hung from the branches of several trees to provide a limited protection from the invasive rains and shabbily dressed men and women passed us, as if in slow motion, carrying bundles of wood which they had just gleaned from the forest floor, their shuffling only serving to reveal and emphasise the enormity of their suffering.

The DSI indicated one man amongst the group who approached us with his arms held out as if in supplication. Coming up to us he said, 'So I see you once more Mr Policeman, I think you have come to take me away again to see the white magistrate.' I could see from his deformed hands and swollen fingers he was in the advanced stages of leprosy and then I noticed that all the other people grouped around us were also showing distressing signs of this terrible disease. I had Mubonda caution the man who identified himself as Isaac Nyanguni, a member of the Nsenga tribe from Lundazi and in reply, Isaac said 'I admit it, that I did steal these chickens, not for myself you see, but to feed these poor people who have nothing. Loneliness and hunger for them comes like a thief in the night and steals their minds.' Then he turned to me and said in English, 'Please, sir, I beg you to let these people eat these chickens first and I will come with you and agree to everything with the Magistrate.'

After some deliberation I soon realised the chickens were no good for anything else and decided to take only two of the birds as police exhibits and we returned to the station, taking the leper with us. Later, in the office, Isaac the leper sat on the floor, as the charge was read out to him. He promptly agreed and signed the form, albeit with the greatest of difficulty because of his deformed fingers. Once he had done this, he looked up at me and asked if I was afraid of lepers. In reply, I adopted a soothing approach, which in retrospect probably sounded condescending because when I turned to leave, I received a powerful punch in my lower back followed by an excruciating pain on the left side of my body. Isaac had moved like lightning, covering the distance between us at incredible speed, hitting me in the back then bending down and biting a sizeable chunk out of my hip and drawing a little blood in the process.

Some of the team grabbed him and hauled him off, but he merely laughed, saying, 'OK, Mr white-policeman, now tell me once again you are not afraid of lepers.' Although my mind was in turmoil, I tried to pull myself together and calmly told him he would now be charged with assaulting a police officer in the execution of his duty, and with that, I left the office. I may well have appeared nonchalant, although inside, my stomach was gripped with fear. I walked out of the station and then ran hell-for-leather to our apartment, stripped off and jumped into the shower, turning on the hot water full blast. The wound was not deep but clearly showed teeth marks and bruising. I used a scrubbing brush liberally smeared with antiseptic soap to vigorously cleanse the injury, and then followed up with copious doses of stinging iodine.

After some time, I dressed and then found the telephone number of the prison near Ndola, where I eventually spoke to the medical officer who had handled Isaac's treatment. I recounted my story and after a judicial pause, he said, 'So Isaac has been up to his old trick again has he? I suppose he didn't tell you there are two types of leprosy, one is certainly virulent and contagious and the other isn't. Anyway, let me assure you Isaac's condition is not contagious, although it might well be a good idea if you could make sure he receives a long prison sentence so I can continue with his medical treatment back here in the prison.'

After lunch, I read the statement Isaac had made in answer to the charge of assault on a police officer in which he had said, 'I admit it all, why should I deny it.' Isaac was brought back from the cells, and Sergeant Mumba told him the police were now making inquiries about the theft of a chicken belonging to Moses Chungu. In reply, he expressed his views in quite a forthright way. 'That man Moses was a complete fool to leave the cooked chicken in a place like that, even if it was only such a small one. I have been from prison only for a short time and it took me a long time to walk to the farm and take all those chickens to feed my people. By the time I passed along I was very hungry and I saw this bush-hut by the railway line. The place was very badly made with only banana leaves and it was tied up all wrong with only wire or string. Through the opening, I saw the chicken on a box so I took it.' Charlie told him Moses Chungu had killed himself because someone had stolen his chicken, the last of his food, and at this, Isaac just crumpled and remained totally oblivious to all of us for a few minutes until finally he roused himself and looking straight at me said, 'I have never made a profit by stealing myself. I only took food for my people, my poor lepers who have nothing in this world and no-one to help them. This is the first time I took food to feed me and now I have killed a man.'

Before passing sentence in court, Keith Pollock, the magistrate, called for a short adjournment and asked to see me in his chambers. His approach was more quizzical than anything else as he felt there was a deep undercurrent in the case, he didn't fully understand. I confirmed that what I was really after was a very long prison sentence for Isaac, not only to enable him to be fed properly but also to continue with his lengthy medical treatment for leprosy. Once the Court had reconvened, Isaac was sentenced to the maximum term in prison, as he was a re-convicted felon.

I was still left feeling guilty over the large number of lepers I had seen in the bush and I finally tracked down a representative of the International Red Cross, who readily agreed to come with me into the bush one morning and see for himself the plight of these unfortunate people. When we came to the clearing, we found it completely devoid of lepers, who seemed to have melted away into thin air and would continue to remain invisible in the lonely and painful darkness of their underworld.

The new day started out well and breakfast was ready, at which my wife suggested that as she was going shopping in Chingola, it might be a good idea if I took Alex with me. Alex always relished these special days we spent together, especially if it meant trips in the landrover with the squad. It was a wonderful bright and sunny Rhodesian morning as we walked over to the station; well, I walked and Alex bounded along full of a real zest for life. If ever a dog had a positive attitude it was Alex, he just seemed to think life was for living and learning, and learning was something very special to him. I went to report to Brian and found him engrossed in discussions with Charles Skinner, head of Special Branch. I had known Charles for some time, so he immediately cut to the chase and told me Dr Kenneth Kaunda, leader of the United National Independence Party and likely to be the newly elected President of the country at independence, was going to visit a particular household in our township that afternoon. It had been arranged that I would keep watch on his activities from a camouflaged hideout and report all the comings and goings, paying particular attention to the times and the people who were visiting the house. It seemed ludicrous to me, as I was one of only three Europeans living amongst more than 40,000 plus Africans and my presence would hardly go unnoticed. As Brian put it so succinctly, by quoting Alfred Lord Tennyson, "Ours not to reason why, ours but to do or die." 'So off you go sunshine!'

In the late afternoon, the rain started to fall, just as Charlie and I were dropped off by a vehicle some way away from our pre-selected vantage point. We wore dark green water-proof capes and I had my old bush-hat with the wide brim pulled well down in a futile effort to disguise my European features and to provide some protection from the all-pervading drizzle, which, still managed to run down the back of my neck. Promptly at 5 o'clock, a black saloon drove up to the target house and a man got out and entered. At four minutes past the hour, a smartly dressed youth ran over to where we were hiding and announced in a very loud voice for all to hear, 'Mr Kaunda sends you his compliments and gives you his word he will stay here until 6pm after which he will leave for Kitwe. You may now go back to the police station or join him for a cup of tea and a biscuit!'

Knowing full-well our position had been completely compromised, I elected for the cup of tea and a biscuit and followed the young man down to the house, allowing Charlie to stroll back to the station. I was warmly welcomed by the owner of the dwelling house who was a genial man of mixed race. He introduced himself as Aaron Milner and he could have only been a few years older than me. He said he had only recently joined Kenneth Kaunda's political party and was peacefully striving to help move the country towards Independence. I believe that immediately after this meeting he was appointed to the party's central committee and later he would become a Member of Parliament and a valued Government Minister appointed by the Prime Minister Dr Kenneth Kaunda. During my time in Africa, I always found people of mixed race to be kind, charming, hard-working, intelligent and energetic in spite of being shunned by most Europeans and rejected by nearly all the African tribes. The dwelling itself was very comfortable and built of concrete block, but well furnished. We sat around the table with Dr Kaunda, soon to be the first African President in the country's history and talked of many things.

Very soon, out came our host's family photograph album of yesteryear, showing a stately English home and various family gatherings, then African scenes with European men and African men and women grouped together in front of tribal villages. I felt we had spent a very happy time talking about everything under-the-sun – except politics – and in rising to leave, I said jokingly that when I returned to the station I would need to amend my records accordingly; we all laughed, and then my host reached for a blue box-file, opened it up and took out a card with my name on it, saying, 'Yes and while I'm at it I will amend yours too!' I was to meet with Dr Kaunda only once more in Lusaka but in a drastically different set of circumstances when I detained an armed suspected assassin at a political rally, just before Dr Kaunda was inaugurated as President of Zambia.

Kenneth David Kaunda was certainly a charismatic figure, also known as KK, one of eight children born to an ordained Church of Scotland missionary and teacher. Later KK would also become a teacher himself, although the call of politics became too strong for him to ignore. He formed the Zambian African National Congress Party, which was later renamed the United National Independent Party and on being elected

President in 1964, KK turned the country into a one-party state, which he effectively ruled until 1991.

Time passed and we were in the midst of yet another government economy drive aimed at reducing the ever-increasing cost burden, where police vehicles had to be used sparingly and long distant jaunts were actively discouraged. I was disconsolate having just purchased a new fishing rod and I felt the team also needed some rest and recuperation, after continuous days and nights combating criminal activity in the town. The team knew exactly how I felt and suggested this might be a good opportunity to visit our friendly market store and do another deal for blankets and other household items on a sale-or-return basis as we had done previously. They pointed out that we had been looking for one criminal called Felix Kalombe for many months, who was wanted for a whole string of burglaries. Monga had been checking the files and it was clear that whenever life became too hot for him, Felix would return to his home village for some time until the hue and cry died down.

In spite of any misgivings, Brian gave permission for the exercise to get underway, with Busike and Monga posing as salesmen. They visited our friendly Jewish storekeeper and replenished their household stocks, ready for resale; although this time they were also given two smart new suitcases to carry their goods. Bus tickets were purchased, and later in the evening our two intrepid travellers, disguised as local traders, set off from the bus station with their cycles strapped to the roof of the coach. Nothing much happened for several days until finally, we received a telephone call from one of the Native Court officials to come and collect two jubilant detectives and their handcuffed prisoner.

We were all in exultant mood, because the landrover had been expressly released for the journey and we were soon on our way, and I was pleased to see the first item Charlie had packed away was my new fishing rod together with one of those comfortable fold-up chairs, together with the cool-box, closely followed by my camp-bed. We stopped off en route to buy some beer, eggs and bacon and Charlie made sure I had not forgotten my hip-flask filled to the brim with precious brandy. It only took about two and a half hours driving until we pitched up at the Native Courts to be welcomed by a relieved official and an exuberant Monga and Busike, with not just one prisoner but two! Monga explained they had soon located Felix Kalombe who was seen in the company of another man they came to know as Sylvester Mutadi.

MURDER, WITCHCRAFT AND THE KILLING OF WILDLIFE

By clever use of the indefatigable African bush telegraph, they had soon found out that Sylvester, too, was an escaped prisoner from Ndola and in the early morning, assisted by two court orderlies they raided the hut, bursting in and arresting both criminals. Not wishing to lose out on our fishing time, we bundled both the handcuffed felons into the landrover and even though it was somewhat crowded, we were an ecstatic group camping by the side of the mighty Kafue River. We found an excellent spot to bivouac and firewood was collected immediately and a fire started. The two prisoners were shackled to the wheels of the landrover but all in all, they seemed relieved that their days of running were well and truly over. We took turns in mounting guard and early the next morning, following our ritual breakfast and a hot cup of coffee, liberally dosed with a goodly measure of brandy, we were all set for a spot of fishing.

With great aplomb, my chair was carefully placed by the water's edge with my rod and box of fishing tackle alongside and, wearing a floppy linen hat to offset the burning sun, I was soon busily engaged in casting the line out into the depths of the river. Although the fish were not biting I was not too discouraged, because we were happy and relaxed being in each other's company. Nevertheless, I changed my routine and with Monga's excited exhortations, I added a brilliant red float to the line, and then just sat back and watched it bobbing up and down in the clear blue waters, although once again, not with the expected results. Busike presently appeared having settled our two prisoners down, and he quickly showed me how poor my fishing skills really were, because only using a short length of heavy twine, weighed down with a few rusty old washers and a bent hook, he was soon pulling in fish upon fish; leaving me so mortified I gave up in despair. Monga, in the meantime, had already started to expertly gut and fillet the fish and soon the cool-box was full to the brim with succulent river bream.

Lunchtime, and with the barbecue well and truly glowing, we were ready to enjoy the remainder of our fish, cooked to perfection, and it was at this point, Sylvester informed us he had once worked for many years as the talented head chef in a large hotel in Ndola and he would be more than willing to do the cooking for us. This seemed like a brilliant idea and it would certainly leave us more time to enjoy some of our cold beers, sitting in the shade of the overhanging riverside trees. I nonchalantly asked Sylvester what crime he had committed to be sent to prison for such a long time and he answered in quite an innocent manner, that he had been convicted for poisoning some of his regular restaurant clients, who had dealt him a very serious blow by inconsiderately dying on him!

From time to time we would visit some of the outlying villages not only to show our faces but in most cases to alleviate the boredom if events were on a downward spiral in our township. Our main preoccupation was twofold; we would raid various known hideouts looking for illegal game trophies such as elephant tusks and then pursue the location of illicit stills where a lethal concoction called Kachasu, was distilled from locally produced maize beer. We decided to pay a visit to a distant village that had been carefully built on a high plateau with a sweeping view down into the plain below. This provided the villagers with an unrivalled vista and by using some of their young village children to tend their goats along the ridge, they were invariably made well aware when anyone approached unannounced along the rutted trackway to the village.

We were all in good humour driving towards the village and it wasn't too difficult to spot several of the young children running off hurriedly towards the village. By the time we arrived, a hastily formed delegation was already in place to greet us, led by their headman, who assured us they would never brew illicit spirits as they knew only full well it was illegal. Now, I have always been accused of having a big nose, and certainly, on this sunny morning, I detected the overpowering odour of freshly manufactured beer with just a hint of additional richness. We had brought Alex along with us and while we proceeded to meander through the village, checking the huts, Alex padded happily beside us, completely absorbed in this, our fun day out.

The walk took on more of a celebratory event with the women singing and clapping, and the men smiling and welcoming us, giving me the distinct feeling we were a long way from any potential brewery. After a half an hour, we sauntered back to the centre of the village, where a group of older men were sitting on low wooden stools, placed in a semi-circle around a glowing fire. Large metal cooking pots were suspended from various spiked racks and a woman was busy stirring the contents, as she sang a traditional tribal song. I noticed, however, that the smiles had somehow disappeared and did I detect a nervous murmuring amongst our jovial followers? It was then Alex started circling around the group; sniffing the air and then smelling the sandy soil until a point was reached when he began pawing at the ground.

A deathly silence followed and my response was to take a gourd filled with water from the elderly cook and begin spraying it gently on the place where Alex had been digging. Almost immediately the water was absorbed by the sandy soil and a small hole suddenly appeared. Without a moment's hesitation, Charlie fetched a shovel from the landrover and started enlarging the hole and after only a few seconds, he hit an iron plate. We moved the occupants sitting around the fire to a safe distance and then we started clearing the sand, which revealed four metal rings, placed at each corner of the metal plate. It didn't take long for us to attach a chain to two of the metal rings and gently pull the metal plate, still complete with the blazing fire on top. As the metal plate slid back, a huge chasm was revealed, comprising pipes, pots and containers housing some very obnoxious smelling liquids – confirming that we had found their cleverly disguised illicit still.

Chapter 8

A Touching Murder and a George Medal

Our debriefing session had started promptly at 8am when everyone was ready to go through their individual cases. Our detection rate had been rising steadily and had already attracted some excellent comments from senior commanders. We dutifully went through a litany of housebreakings, cycle thefts and, assaults until we came to some of the cases being personally handled by No.2193 Detective Constable Busike. Busike was a young man, not overly tall but wiry and energetic. He was inclined to be serious and had gradually become what I called the conscience of the team, indefatigably fighting his corner to right any perceived injustices. He was a member of the Lozi tribe which inhabited the flood-plains of the mysterious Kingdom of Barotseland in the western portion of Northern Rhodesia. The Lozi extended their influence over a wide range of territory, incorporating a number of ethnic groups including the Batonga tribes and their influence even spread through parts of Angola, right up to the border with the Congo, and it was Busike's sacred tribal knowledge that would one day save all our lives.

Busike was handling several important burglary cases, which shared the same modus operandi, involving the much larger commercial establishments, such as markets, beer-halls and the local cinema. Only cash was being stolen and Busike reported a sole case where he had clear evidence of fingerprints. However, he was embarrassed to report that somehow, he had made an embarrassing mistake in lifting these prints because it seemed the burglar now had two thumbs on one hand! When the laughter had died down, I told everyone, Busike had not made a mistake because a year or so before I had arrested a man called Simon Chibwe, for a similar offence and I knew Simon had two small thumbs on his right hand. The fingerprints were sent off to the Criminal Records Office, who duly confirmed that Simon Chibwe was indeed the perpetrator.

I resolved to take a more proactive approach and suggested that, because I knew Simon Chibwe used only cash to fuel his obsession for consuming beer and spirits, it was more likely we would find him in the local beer-hall during night time. I was the only one of the team who knew Simon well enough and I proposed to disguise myself as an African labourer and visit the beer-hall, accompanied by everyone in the team, the next evening. This statement caused great consternation, which continued unabated well after the meeting ended. Several hours later, the whole team trudged back, and it was apparent Charlie had been appointed as their spokesman. He broke into his well-rehearsed speech. 'Bwana, this plan of yours is going to be very dangerous for us all.'

'Yes, I can see that.'

'OK, so we do not want to cause offence to you and make you really cross, but did you know that all the white people smell?'

'No, I did not know about this.'

'Bwana, if we all go, you must not wash, shave or use the white people's smelly soap, and you must not put that other really smelly stuff under your armpits.'

'OK.'

Charlie then continued in the same vein by adding, 'We will now have to find you some very old tribal clothes.'

'OK.'

Sergeant Mumba cut in with a question 'What are you going to do about your white skin and hair Bwana?'

I had already thought about this and told him I intended to wear a big bush type hat, dark glasses and cover any exposed parts of my skin in Soya sauce. After that, it was agreed, albeit somewhat reluctantly, we would go out later the next night.

During the ensuing day, the team raided the station's lost property store and contacted some of their more discreet sources, until they eventually arrived at a very passable disguise for me to wear. The stale, sweaty smell rising up from the assortment of clothes made me gag, but I was determined to proceed. Lost Property turned up a large, moth-eaten and battered old bush hat and the contribution from the team's contacts was a long, worn out and filthy khaki greatcoat that fitted well and the whole ensemble was finished off with a pair of heavily repaired trainers. However, the team had not yet finished with me, because I had to go through an hour or so of training until I could imitate the loping walk of the lithe, average African youth.

It all went incredibly well and night had already fallen when we eventually sloped into the beer-hall, with the lampposts giving off a dismal, shadowy light, greatly helping to subdue our impact. We sat together at some trestle tables in the open air, near the main entrance and sure enough, forty minutes later, I spotted a well-dressed Simon Chibwe entering the beer-hall. We moved quickly towards him and Monga and Charlie stood by his side blocking off any escape route. We identified ourselves and hurried him outside, where Busike handcuffed him, but as he did so a passing man, saw what was happening and shouted out, 'The police boys are here and are taking one of our brothers away to prison.' Within seconds, there was total pandemonium, forcing us to take to our heels, dragging our prisoner with us. We ran into a large brick building nearby, barricading ourselves in, and I hurriedly sent Charlie out of the backdoor to fetch urgent help from our station.

An angry crowd gathered outside and started throwing stones at the windows, showering us with shards of glass. Mubonda reported having heard someone shouting to the mob to bring bottles of petrol to burn out the police. This was soon followed up by another outcry, 'There is a mzungu [white] policeman there, and we should kill him too.' At that moment, I realised we had run into the local bakery where flour and other inflammable materials could combine to form a wicked explosion. Taking full advantage of a temporary lull in the attack being mounted outside, we ran out from the rear of the building and onto wasteland, finding whatever shelter was offered by large mounds of earth and builder's rubble that had been dumped there. Still, the stones flew, and although we retaliated by throwing some back, we were gradually being forced to retreat step by step.

The situation looked extremely serious, and matters were not helped when we noticed a line of some twenty or so men blocking off our escape route and this was immediately followed by the crisp slapping noise of bowstrings being released. There was the disconcerting whirring sound of arrows in flight until it dawned on us that these arrows were not being aimed at us but were being directed towards our antagonists. The line of men hurriedly ran through our ranks to confront the rabble, where they formed up on a clear piece of land and started chanting, raising their feet high in the air, in a Sezulu chant, then bringing them crashing down hard onto the earth until the very ground began to shake. At a signal from their leader, they launched themselves forward in a ferocious attack wielding their cudgels and it was all over in a matter of seconds and the mob, realising their perilous predicament, hastily evaporated into the darkness.

The leader of our rescuers was William Tambadzai, a Sezulu from Murewa in Southern Rhodesia. As soon as Charlie had left us, he realised that there was insufficient time to reach the station, so instead, he called on his own nearby tribal brothers for help, which was unstintingly given. Back at the police station, Simon Chibwe was so relieved to have survived the night's catastrophic events unscathed, he willingly pleaded guilty to all our outstanding store and shop break-ins. However, I came to the conclusion this had been another close-run thing and we were all very fortunate to have escaped unharmed.

This period signified a growing culmination of arrests for a wide range of criminal activities and these all needed to be painstakingly processed through the courts. At such times, we could count on assistance from Assistant Inspector John Maxwell from the Farm Patrol section, and the team liked John enormously because he always waded in to help. He recounted that he had recently come across a new dambo (reservoir) on a farm out in the bundu, (bush) and as he had just bought a second hand Panhard car, he intended to go swimming there early on Sunday morning and invited me to go along. I readily agreed, but as usual, the plans of mice and men went awry and with yet another murder reported early on the following Sunday morning, I had to regretfully cancel.

This murder had taken place very near the same location as our previous disturbance when we had been rescued through the intervention of the Sezulus and on arrival, we found a dead man lying face down in the dirt roadway. The body had been discovered and guarded by several municipal policemen, ensuring everything had remained completely untouched. We roped off the area and took our photographs and made a detailed examination of the body which revealed serious cuts and bruises to the face and body. The body was identified as being Daniel Fumbelo, an unemployed labourer who lived just alongside the Sezulu enclave. The municipal policemen told us there had been a serious altercation some hours before between Daniel Fumbelo and one of the Sezulus and Sergeant Mumba and Charlie were dispatched to make inquiries, allowing the rest of us to record various witness statements, after which, we had the body bagged and carted off to the mortuary.

When we ultimately returned to the station, I found Mumba and Charlie in my office with William Tambadzai, our latter-day rescuer. Charlie explained that William was the person who had killed Daniel Fumbelo the previous evening, but the dead individual was in truth a bad man and no-one in the team wanted to charge William with murder. It was obvious that everyone was seriously distressed by these events, but nonetheless, I told them justice had to be done but more importantly it had to be seen to be done and we really had no viable alternative, even though William was our valued friend. This news was badly received, and I then had to carefully explain that we could only help William in the way we went about things and it would be important how we prepared the case for trial and especially William's statement. William's statement should be taken down by Charlie and written in the Sezulu language, because the High Court had recently issued a directive that wherever possible, serious criminal charges should be conducted in the defendant's home language, ensuring complete understanding as to what was being said by both the police and the defendant. As for the statement itself, I suggested we should be scrupulous in steering it towards a case of manslaughter, thereby attracting a much lighter sentence. We should only pursue the truth and highlight the fact there was no premeditation. Furthermore, we should emphasise the point that Fumbelo was the person who instigated the affray, and William had then been forced to defend himself.

I also undertook to speak on William's behalf at the trial and explain to the court how he had previously helped us in such very difficult times and to confirm to the judge that he had voluntarily given himself up to the police and in the meantime, I would provide every assistance to his lawyer who would be appointed, free of charge. Everyone seemed much relieved and William Tambadzai was finally charged with murder and his statement read, 'I admit the charge that I did kill this person. There were two people and one of them made a big mistake and touched my wife, Ness on the buttocks. This was at the gates of the beer-hall. I asked him, you touched my wife do you know her? He answered yes, I was staying with her next door. Then the man wanted to start fighting with me. There were three Policemen who stopped us. I then left with my wife and my two younger brothers called Dominico and James. We left them there but on the way, I saw the two men coming again. One of them came up behind me and beat me with his fist I did hit him then with my fist and he fell down.' This statement was signed by William and acknowledged by Charlie.

William was kept in our cells overnight and when I went in later to check if there was anything he needed, I found William and Charlie crying their eyes out. Eventually, at the High Court, I was able to speak on William's behalf giving a brief account of how he was the respected leader of the Sezulu enclave in Chiwempala, and he had once saved us from an angry mob. This was followed by an oration from his lawyer in mitigation and the judge in his wisdom reduced the case to one of manslaughter and followed this with an extremely light prison sentence.

Unfortunately, that was not quite the end of the story because later that evening I received the grave news that John Maxwell had indeed gone to the farm to swim and had been joined by several local children. They were all happily splashing about in the water when John became alarmed to see a large crocodile sliding down the grassy banks into the water. Within seconds, the beast was bearing down on them and John knew only too well the crocodile is one of the greatest killing machines in Africa. In spite of this, John placed himself between the fast-approaching crocodile and the children. He urgently lifted one of the children onto the bank, out of harm's way, when the crocodile attacked him, virtually severing one of his legs, and notwithstanding this terrifying assault John lifted the other child clear before the crocodile returned and savaged his other leg. Once again, he fought the beast off and at this moment, an incredible, courageous African woman came to his aid by jumping into the water and dragging him out, where they both applied tourniquets to John's bleeding wounds.

Somehow, and with a superhuman effort, John managed to drive the long distance along the dirt roads to the hospital, with the woman working the clutch pedal and John manipulating the gear lever on the steering-wheel column. John eventually survived, but only just, and in recognition of what I regard as one of the bravest of actions, John and the woman were each awarded the coveted George Medal. I only found out recently that my friend Ted Osmond-Jones who had sold the car to John, took it back, cleaned it thoroughly and then returned John's cheque in full. Over the years I kept in touch with John and I know he was in constant pain throughout the remainder of his life. I am gently reminded of words by F. Scott Fitzgerald – 'Show me a hero and I will show you a tragedy.'

There was, however, one case in particular that springs to mind, not only because I failed to solve it but also because it was one where I found myself being remanded under court-martial conditions. On an early weekday morning, when the menfolk were all off working in the nearby township and the women of the village were all away tilling the maize fields or tending to their vegetable gardens down by the river, a group of young dissolute and unemployed youths descended on the small cluster of huts, where they started to harass and abuse a number of young boys who had been left behind to look after their goats. This gang soon became increasingly belligerent and hugely frustrated at not finding any adults in the village that they could inveigle into making cash donations. They took four small boys, herded them into one of the hovels, which they locked and barricaded before setting fire to the thatched roof. The dried reeds soon started to burn furiously and spread quickly across the whole roof space, adding a devastating dimension to the appalling cries of agony from within, until tragically the roof collapsed and the cries dwindled away.

We faced a daunting and soul-destroying task in sifting through the burnt debris and removing the charred and disfigured bodies of these very young boys, and we knew all the forensic evidence we so sorely needed had been totally destroyed in the fire. This meant we had no specific eye witness accounts of the murders and the only item we found was a burnt segment of a heavy embroidered piece of sculptured linen, looking as if it had originally belonged to part of an antimacassar set. Inquiries were immediately instigated throughout the length and breadth of the countryside, but despite our very best endeavours, results proved elusive. Finally, when the enormity of the crime reverberated through various communities, gradually, incomplete pieces of information began to emerge.

The full blame was levied against members of a group affiliated to one of the political parties and, although no names were mentioned, ultimately, this heinous crime was laid firmly at the doors of a nearby illegally constructed village. A meeting was hurriedly convened by Jack Gowland and although the Officer Commanding was away from the district, a senior inspector from the uniform section attended in his place. I gave a summation of events and added the fact we were waiting for an analysis of forensic evidence from Force HQ, which was likely to arrive within the next three days. It was agreed that on the fourth day, we would mount an early morning raid on the village, surrounding it with a full contingent of riot police, thereby giving us the opportunity of conducting a house by house search, looking for corroborative evidence and with it, perhaps the missing section of the antimacassar.

Only two days later I was surprised to receive a telephone call from the Senior Inspector to the effect that I should take my team early the next morning to a part of the Chingola police camp, where I was expected to cut down some of the tall elephant grass and await the arrival of several detachments from the mobile unit when all would be revealed. We duly appeared at 7am the next morning and started strimming our way through the tall grasses until, only several metres in, we suddenly revealed an extensive barbed-wire enclosure comprising a number of buildings, looking for all the world like a German concentration camp, from the Second World War and one, in fact, in which my family and I had been illegally incarcerated by Nazis invading forces in 1942. In reality, this was an internment camp, built many years before by the British, who were mightily concerned that the horrors of Mau Mau insurgency could possibly spread southwards from Kenya.

We didn't have long to wait before several troop carriers arrived, escorted by a number of police landrovers, whereupon they began to disgorge their cargoes of despondent tribesmen, wailing women and crying children. It turned out they had all been rounded up in an early morning operation mounted against their illegal village and then forcibly shipped out, a course of action which was in direct contravention of our previous meeting. The Senior Inspector purposely unlocked the chains of the main gates and started urging the reluctant people to pass through, but I soon scuppered that. Decades before, in 1945 when we had finally been liberated by Free French forces in Germany, I had made a sacred promise to my father, to the effect I would do everything possible in the future to stop vulnerable people from being imprisoned in concentration camps, in such a barbaric fashion as had happened to us.

The Senior Inspector threatened to have me arrested pending court-martial for wilfully disobeying the lawful order of a superior officer, which was bad enough in itself but my team to a man were horrified and angry at this treatment and soon made their feelings felt. Matters were not improved when Charlie stabbed his fingers against the Senior

Inspector's chest, then looking across at me asked if it would be alright if he slit his throat! Then, as I was being marched off to appear before the C.O., the team had a brief discussion amongst themselves and hastily took up strategic positions and effectively blocked off the main gates.

I was ushered in to stand in front of the C.O. who appeared completely relaxed because he indicated I should sit down and explain my actions. When I had finished, he said of all the senior officers that I should appear before, it was my lucky day, because he had been in the Royal Air Force during the war and many of his colleagues and friends had been shot down and imprisoned in various camps throughout Germany and for that reason he did not intend to pursue the matter any further. I replied that I was grateful for that, but I felt I may have saved several police jobs because I was sure once the media had been made aware of people being illegally interned, there would have been a widespread outcry.

The C.O. seemed disconcerted to learn that the illegal village had been burnt to the ground and with it an opportunity to find further evidence had been lost. Although the matter had been laid to rest, the damage was irrevocable and the case was lost for all time. Sadly, no conviction for these reprehensible murders was ever achieved and I took it as a personal defeat, and I have to say this abject failure is one that still rankles with me to this day.

After lunch, the team trooped in, somewhat confused by the morning's events and asked me for a detailed explanation. When I had finished they all still appeared mystified, and it was Sergeant Mumba who put everything firmly into perspective when he said, 'If that defective European officer thought he would punish those people, he needs his head examined because they would have been housed, fed and watered, provided with bedding and given the benefit of electric light, all free of charge; some punishment.'

One afternoon, when driving past the old ant-hill, so beloved as a meeting point by political parties, I could see it was occupied by a large congregation consisting entirely of women, dressed in a variety of brightly coloured dresses and robes, who were dancing, swaying and clapping their hands in time to the music. I drove a little nearer and then stopped and switched off the engine, enabling me to hear them sing some of the hymns I had learnt at my Sunday School, back at Les Camps Methodist Church in Guernsey. It all seemed too good an opportunity to miss so, I jumped out and walked over towards the anthill.

I had no wish to disrupt the singing but within a few minutes one of the indisputable leaders descended from the anthill and came towards me with the traditional greeting. She identified herself as Alice Lenshina, head of a Christian group who had formed her own religious body called the Lumpa Church. She must have been in her mid-forties, and she had great nervous energy about her. As we talked together the singing continued with marvellous voices raised in harmony, and in answer to my question as to whether she had a permit to hold a meeting like this she told me, if a little sharply, that God did not need a permit for his people to sing his hymns and she and her followers completely rejected all earthly governments.

She went on to say that she preached a total Christian doctrine backed by hymns and she had set her face solidly against witchcraft and sorcery. However, she and her adherents had become sick and tired of being harried by various political gangs to make regular monetary contributions and had decided that in future they would refuse to pay all government taxes. She added they intended to return to Chinsali District in the Northern Province and create a completely new way of life there, but in the meantime, what was I going to do about the required police permit? I thought carefully for a moment and then told her, perhaps it would be much better if I hadn't seen her at all, and at this, she burst out laughing and walked back to the anthill, I was not to see her again.

Alice Lenshina was a self-styled prophetess who would start an armed uprising in Chinsali a little later, resulting in more than 700 deaths, including some of my friends and police colleagues. She was to be kept in prison for many years and would see her Church disbanded, although never quite eradicated.

Guardians of the Herd.

The African Leopard.

The Majestic Elephant

From paintings by renowned international artist and wildlife conservationist, friend and fellow Guernseyman, Peter Le Vasseur, who has graciously given permission for his work to be reproduced in this book.

Steve in working uniform. Injured in a confrontation with extremists, and displaying another broken hand.

Police Training School in Lusaka. New police intake in 1960, at a passing-out parade. Steve is in the 2nd row and 3rd from the right. He would never meet any of his colleagues again after this photograph was taken.

The Fish Eagle. The bird is named Nkhwazi, and is the national bird of Zambia and the emblem of the Police Force.

Victoria Falls. Standing on the edge of the Falls, known as 'The Smoke that Thunders'; first seen by the intrepid explorer David Livingstone in 1855, alongside the mighty Zambezi River.

Police recording team. Attending every political meeting and rally and recording all the speeches aimed at countering hate-crimes and any acts of treason.

Anti-Poaching Patrols. The continual fight to stop the monstrous slaughter of vulnerable wildlife.

Arson murder scene. Official police photo, identified by Steve's bush hat. It was here that four young children were burnt to death in a terrifying and senseless act of violence.

A police flight. About to embark on an urgent Search and Rescue Mission to find a lost hunter.

Devil dancers. Displaying and perpetuating a strong belief in magic and witchcraft, in all strata of African society.

Village talking drums. Used to spread the word from village to village, sending news over long distances. In times of great danger, they could call on their tribe to come to their aid if they were under attack.

Poachers' hideout. An illegally constructed village being used by an array of poachers to decimate wildlife that included elephants, rhinoceros and zebras.

Alex the Doberman. Regarded as a witchdoctor by local tribes. A fearsome crime fighter with 'crocodile teeth,' who saved Steve's life on several occasions and also protected his family, keeping them safe from harm, from intruders and snakes.

An identity parade. An official police photo showing an alleged murderer being identified by a masked witness placed under police protection.

A good witchdoctor. Unmasking a violent criminal by divination. He was also a herbalist and helped the police on many occasions to solve crimes that had been motivated by black-magic.

The border with Katanga. Village children hoping for a monetary reward from visitors crossing over from Katanga.

My boy Alex. The Doberman on guard against depredations by man or beast and keeping a watchful eye over the wide bush country.

The ever-present crocodile. One of Africa's awesome killing machines, overshadowed only by the Hippopotamus. They are prolific along most Zambian rivers, lakes and dams; and it needs to be remembered that once they focus on a target they very rarely fail.

Investigations by dugout. Certain areas of the country were inaccessible except by river and dugout canoe.

A witchdoctor from Solwezi. A member of the Kaonde tribe, who tragically killed one of his patients with his potions.

Police launch on Kafue River. Investigations into the atrocious slaughter of crocodiles, on the borders with the Kafue National Park. The park is designated as a safe haven for a great diversity of wildlife but this, in turn, acts as a magnet for poachers.

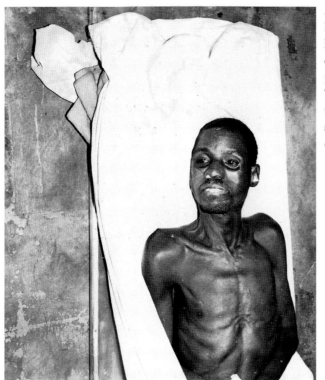

A murdering witchdoctor. He had committed one of the most horrendous and evil murders ever dealt with. He died during a police chase to have him arrested. This official photograph was taken just before his postmortem, after he had been dead for two days.

Zambezi sunrise. The team camped here, right on the borders between Southern Rhodesia and Mozambique, and on the edge of the placid flowing Zambezi River.

Lonely Giraffes. Wildlife in the Luangwa Valley is under serious threat from poachers.

A prowling leopard. A proud animal with a price on its head, prey to trophy hunters and poachers alike.

President Dr K. Kaunda. First President of Zambia inspecting a police contingent at the Training School.

The CID team on duty. This photograph was taken shortly before the potential assassination attempt on the life of President Dr Kenneth Kaunda, in the capital Lusaka.

Police First XI Cricket Team. Steve is in the back row, far right.

Early colonial-style police station. Eventually converted into a police museum.

A traditional witchdoctor. A member of the Shona Tribe that occupies areas of Zambia, Mozambique and Zimbabwe.

Cannibal's knife and arrow. The knife from a cannibalistic murder on the border with Katanga; the arrow that wounded Steve; and the sample carving used for the creation of the Speaker's Chair of the Ghana Government, which Steve helped to design before joining the police force.

United Nations air crash. The tragic crash of an aircraft with the United Nation's Secretary General Dag Hammarskjöld on board at Ndola, resulting in the loss of all passengers and crew. Steve organised one of the outlying search parties attempting to find the plane.

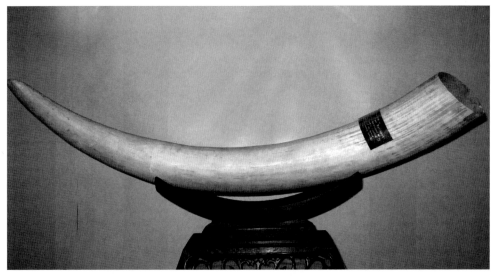

Game department award. Presentation made to Steve for his unstinting work in investigating poaching and endeavouring to stop the slaughter of wildlife in the country.

Antelope in the game park. Seen in its natural habitat within the Kafue National Park.

Painting of a lion by Peter Le Vasseur.

The Glorious Hippo. The greatest killer of people throughout Africa. By Peter Le Vasseur.

Chapter 9

The Birth of Twins and No Dogs Allowed

Perhaps after all, things were going too well for us and the gods decided we needed to be brought back down to earth, but the clouds of wrath were building up when Brian interrupted one of our morning sessions to make us aware of the recent Order of the Day issued by the Commissioner of Police. This was to the effect that dogs owned by the European members of the inspectorate would no longer be permitted to occupy the front seats of force transport, as this spot should be rightfully occupied by the next senior police officer. It was obvious the order had been issued on the grounds of ensuring racial harmony, but the team to a man were totally aghast. As Charlie put it so concisely, 'This is not a good thing for when the good people see Alex in the front seat, they know all is well, and when the bad people see him they think now would be a good time to leave and go elsewhere.' The team inwardly seethed and even Sergeant Mumba said he would be happy to give up his seat for Alex, but an order was an order.

A week or so later, when returning alone from a routine investigation, I was stopped by the charge office Sergeant who told me in hushed tones, that the Assistant Commissioner CID, from Lusaka, had telephoned and wanted to speak to me urgently. I was being instructed, nay ordered to return his call, punctually at 2pm. The Sergeant went on to add 'The Bwana Assistant Commissioner is not a very happy man!' Promptly at 2pm, I telephoned Assistant Commissioner Denis Brockwell, only to be greeted by a very gruff voice. Mr Brockwell forwent the usual pleasantries and cut straight to the chase. 'So what the hell do you mean by sending such a damn stupid letter to the Commissioner?'

This approach took me completely by surprise and I could only stammer out 'What letter, sir?'

'Now don't start getting smart with me, you know damn well what letter. I have it here right in front of me'

'Excuse me, sir, but I haven't a clue what you are talking about.'

'Well then just let me refresh what appears to be your serious failing memory.'

I was caught in the middle of a nightmare, but Mr Brockwell pressed on unabated, 'As you well know, the letter is addressed to His Most Gracious and Glorious Excellency, Mr Commissioner of Police, and goes on Dear Sir or Madam.' He broke off in a more conciliatory tone to tell me he knew I had a good sense of humour and from time to time his staff had shown him some of my more humorous reports but the timing of this letter was ill-judged, as the Commissioner was under immense pressure to maintain racial harmony within police ranks.

When I stated that I still did not know anything about the letter, he simply sighed and continued reading.

'We are all your CID boys here in Chiwempala and we work hard for the excellent Bwana Matthews. The Bwana's big dog Alex is our true friend and colleague and he helps us arrest many bad people. Sometimes we have too much month left at the end of our money and in these very hard times the Bwana takes us all into the bush to hunt for rabbits, and our dog colleague Alex catches the meat for us by jumping out of the landrover on top of them from the front seat.

'We therefore urgently request permission to ignore the police orders about dogs, having to sit in the back of police vehicles. We respectfully remain your most devoted servants' – and here followed a signed and printed list of names, ranks and serial number numbers.

'Postscript: We wish to say to your Excellency, that our Bwana is also very careful with your precious landrover and always takes the doors off first before we go hunting.'

When Mr Brockwell finished reading, there followed a stunned silence until he said, 'I gather you remember the letter now?'

'No, sir! I know nothing about the letter, but I do have a very good idea who wrote it.'

'Oh my God, are you saying these detectives actually wrote the letter to the Commissioner themselves?

'Yes, sir, I think so.'

At this point the Asst/Commissioner started to chuckle and told me, 'Just you wait till I tell the Commissioner about this, it is really going to make his day, but what he will make about the story with the doors of the landrover I dread to think.'

Although we remained on tenterhooks for some days, nothing further was heard and later, it transpired that the team had visited a scholar in the township, whose job it was to write such letters for a hefty fee and it was this scholar who had formulated the letter on their behalf.

As is the way of the world, time passed and memories dimmed until we were told to expect an imminent visit from the Commissioner, who was on his final inspection before his well-earned retirement. Our detection rate was still sky high and some of our detractors continued to assert we were not fully recording all the reported cases. I judged the Commissioner's inspection would also be aimed at either confirming or refuting these unworthy thoughts, and it would be a good idea to ensure we were smartly dressed, the offices spick and span and our records and dockets well up-to-date. In the days preceding the visit, the place was a hive of activity until we could do no more but wait, although I thought Brian's humorous remark about no dogs in the office was quite uncalled for.

The Commissioner arrived early one morning in a cloud of dust and after a brief sojourn with Brian; he strode into our offices with the comment, 'Just keep on working as normal,' as if we could. He started with our occurrence book, making detailed notes, before asking to see our case files and cross-referenced them all. At 10.30 and right on cue, a smartly dressed Willy arrived with the Mary Rose, porcelain coffee pot and matching cups, milk jug and a side-plate of tempting biscuits, which he placed alongside the Commissioner and then hastily retreated. I had to admit to feeling things were certainly going our way until I glimpsed a large, slow-moving, shadow to my left and on turning I saw Alex sidle in and before I could stop him, he moved quietly to stand alongside the Commissioner and there he rested his head on the table top. Silence reigned and none of us dared to breathe, let alone say anything until almost as an automatic reaction, the Commissioner raised his hand and softly scratched Alex's ear. Pleased with this recognition, Alex silently turned and padded out of the office, after which the Commissioner turned around, and said, 'I suppose that was your colleague the valued rabbit hunter, and the terror of criminals?' None of us uttered a word in reply. The inspection continued with our occurrence book being taken out into the main charge office to be reconciled against our reports and entries. After an hour or so, the Commissioner returned to say our records were in really good order and were some of the very best he had ever seen and we had obviously worked very hard, then he was gone, driving away fast, in a billowing cloud of dust.

Several days later I sat in the Magistrate's Court, watching a long line of criminals taking their turn in the dock, where justice was swiftly dealt out by the magistrate and the malefactors, with bowed heads, continued their slow walk to the waiting transport and prison. When I returned home, my wife told me she was becoming extremely weary with Alex following her around so closely and to make her point, she rose, as did Alex, and I suddenly realised what this mystique was all about. 'I think you had better make an appointment with Dr Naudé because Alex has the firm idea you may be pregnant again.'

Immediately after lunch, Wendy drove off hurriedly to see Luddy Naudé and several hours later returned with the wonderful news she was certainly expecting. Bearing in mind our last débâcle and miscarriage we decided to do everything by the medical book, starting with a whole series of tests and examinations. Knowing our previous medical history, the newly built Llewellyn Hospital in Kitwe immediately appointed a woman gynaecologist from South Africa to maintain a watching brief. It was certainly exciting times as the weeks passed until eventually, the moment arrived for an X-ray to be taken.

On arrival at the hospital, my wife was whisked off by our newly appointed gynaecologist and I was escorted to the frugally appointed waiting room. I waited and I waited and it was noticeable that the afternoon sun was fading fast, only to be followed by the faint onset of dusk. Eventually, a nurse came in and announced that there had been a certain development and I was now wanted by the doctor. I was ushered into the packed room and offered a seat alongside my wife and after a brief nod of welcome, the doctor, announced in a very strong voice to all and sundry that we were expecting a healthy baby, which would probably be due about the second week in January but there was an added medical complication. I thought to myself, 'Oh my goodness, here we go again,' when she added that the complication was not just one baby but two. She went on to say, 'There is something else we need to discuss, which is the equipment here in Kitwe is not too sensitive, but you should be aware there is another shadow in the background, although we have no idea at the moment what it is exactly, it could be three!'

Shell-shocked, and with no recollection of the journey back home, the following days passed in a blur of confusion and as the weeks went flying by it soon became apparent to everyone that my wife was becoming larger, until the point was reached when we had to announce the news of our eagerly awaited twins. Certainly, time passed happily enough for both of us, intermingled with regular visits to see Doctor Naudé. The babies were flourishing, and my wife seemed to be in very good health, and as she grew in size, she managed to compensate by making her own maternity dresses. Once a month we toddled over to the hospital to see our gynaecologist, who always reassured us and seemed genuinely pleased with the babies' development.

Alex continued his shadowing routine, although by now we had little concern he would not take to the babies whenever they made an appearance. As our friend John Ellis had said, 'Just remember it is his family and he will be prepared to willingly give his life for their safety.' We had talked together about me being in at the birth and my wife had said she would welcome me being there for moral support. The dramatic day finally arrived and once in the labour room, I was given the onerous job of making the tea for everyone and in giving my wife a gentle back massage. The consultant took me to one side and frightened the living daylights out of me by saying they had just come across a major problem because although one of the twins was in a superb position for the birth the other baby was upside down and facing backwards. If the hospital staff were not extra careful there would be a great danger the umbilical cord could be caught around the second baby's neck.

Because the medical equipment in those days was not as efficient as nowadays, we had no idea if we were expecting twin boys, girls or even one of each, when at about 1am, the first baby born was a daughter with wonderful delicate fingernails and even a light brushing of blonde hair. Now, we were set for the much-anticipated difficult time but at this critical point a miracle occurred, when the second baby turned over and around on its own and was born only some ten or fifteen minutes later. So, our firstborn now had an identical twin sister to contend with. My wife lay back exhausted and with everyone congratulating her on a really fine and spectacular birth all the poor girl could say was, 'Are there any more to come, doctor?' The consultant personally checked our twin daughters out and pronounced them both to be in fine fettle and tip-top condition.

We eventually decided on the names Annette Jane and Karen Leigh, then came the magical day my family came home. I collected them from the hospital and on arrival back at the apartment, we were momentarily concerned about Alex, who was over excited to see my wife, but calmed down immediately he saw the babies. A very gentle sniff there, followed by a caring nudge and at that moment I believe he decided this was to be his new job in life, which was to act as guardian and protector of his twins. It was wonderful to see him quietly lying alongside the carry-cots but at times he could be extremely difficult and I remember poor Willy trying to sweep the floor, when, at every stroke, Alex would gently put his mouth around the long-handled broom and take it out of his hands. Alex didn't like people peering over the cots and would softly barge through and use his great size to move them away, but his one big hate was when the telephone rang. He would pounce, pick the handset up in his mouth and then spit it out onto the floor. However, for Alex, duty meant duty and often when I asked him out for a turn in the landrover he would often rise up, think it through, and then slowly lie down again.

After such a traumatic inspection by the Commissioner, we soon rallied, and put such matters far behind us and went back to our normal routine police work. On this one particular day, however, when I thought everything was progressing so well, we were rudely interrupted by an angry commotion coming from the charge office. Phiri went out to see what was going on and soon returned with our old friend the paramedic from the clinic, who was so angry, he had the greatest difficulty in speaking. He eventually spluttered that his clinic had been broken into during the night and many items had been wantonly destroyed. In all the time I had been working in the township, it seemed that medical compounds were sacrosanct from such criminal events. The clinic cared for many Africans and their families and this offence was a grave development.

We found windows smashed, papers were strewn all over the floors, storerooms ripped apart and valuable medicines left lying about on chairs and benches. The place had been completely ransacked and vandalised. The squad went into action and quickly and methodically took photographs and dusted various surfaces for fingerprints. They finished an hour or so later and out of respect, they pitched in to help with the cleaning-up process. Once that had been done and a measure of normality re-established, I asked for a quick inventory of his medicines and drugs to see what, if anything had been stolen and after another hour or so, we were mystified to learn that the only missing items were the entire stock of insulin, syringes and swabs.

We sat discussing the case while trying to unravel the meagre evidence that we had, to see if we could make any sense of the confusing images. It was extremely difficult to understand the whys and wherefores of the break-in; for instance, had the insulin been stolen to support a family member who was suffering from diabetes but lacked sufficient funds to purchase the medicine? We felt we lacked enough information to make a valid assessment, yet something told me time was of the essence. Each member of the squad was allotted a specific job; for example, Monga requested a list of all the diabetic patients held on file and then he had to visit each family, to ascertain how their treatment was progressing. Busike left for the Municipal Police Offices to let them know about these events and to see if they might be able to offer any useful information. Sergeant. Mumba and Charlie took the landrover, driven by Sekondwe, to visit the market place, the bus and train stations to check on anyone who might be carrying large bags, packages or suitcases.

Brian took it upon himself to brief all the shift constables and later in the evening, this approach produced our first important lead. One of our patrolling constables had heard a rumour which was spreading like wildfire, to the effect that a sorcerer held the elixir to everlasting life and, for a few miserable pounds, he would guarantee recovery from all illnesses and diseases, by giving patients a special injection. I was becoming extremely apprehensive that some unsuspecting person would be given a lethal dose of insulin and we immediately upgraded the search as an urgent priority.

Just as dusk was falling, Mumba, Charlie and Sekondwe were returning after a frustrating and fruitless search, when the landrover headlights picked out the figure of a well-dressed man, clutching what appeared to be a black leather medical bag. The man was talking to a woman by the side of the road but the moment he was caught in the glare of the headlights, he reacted rather like a startled rabbit and ran off down one of the side streets. Sekondwe stopped the landrover in its tracks and set off on foot at a fair old lick after the man and in the meantime, Mumba and Charlie approached the woman who confirmed the man had indeed offered her the opportunity to attain everlasting life.

Within a few minutes, Sekondwe returned with a restrained and protesting man, who was straight away bundled into the back of the landrover. At the station, he was identified as Amos Sitoyi, who was then brought to my office for questioning. He was cautioned but elected to say nothing at first; making the point this was his legal right. Well, that was until I started to remove a whole assortment of packages and syringes from his medical bag, whereupon Amos remonstrated with me in English that I had no right to disturb any of his precious, magical products. The one real and unsettling aspect was the fact that one of the insulin ampoules had already been used together with a syringe. All Amos would say was, 'If the people here want eternal life then who am I to disagree?' In answer to my next question about what would happen if some unfortunate person was to die having taken one of his injections, he cynically answered by saying, 'Well that is their problem and certainly not mine.'

I was so distressed by his complete lack of remorse that without thinking I simply picked him up by his coat lapels and slammed him hard against the office wall, allowing him to slowly slump to the floor. Alongside me, Busike gently coughed and whispered, 'I thought you told us Bwana, we should not be beating these terrible criminals at all.' At that moment I felt most contrite and started to apologise, but Charlie cut in to say, 'OK Bwana, we saw nothing, so if you want to kill this load of shit, we will only be next door.' The team made as if they to leave the office, whereupon Amos looked up and said he would tell us everything, as long as we promised not to kill him. He said he had only given one shot of insulin but in order to save both his stock and his money he had adulterated it with just a little water. Amos elected to take us to where the woman lived and within minutes we had parked outside a hut in the location. Amos indicated an old and battered, wooden door which was partially open, and Mumba went over to the doorway and called out.

Mrs Musewa, the homeowner, was lying on her bed and although she should have been feeling on top of the world – well, that was what the sorcerer had told her – in fact, she was feeling very ill. She thought back to earlier in the day when she had been approached by this man offering her everlasting life and the offer seemed too good to miss. She had paid out more money than she should have from the pot of savings she kept under the bed and now she began to regret her spur of the moment actions. The injection had been quite painful and now she felt sick and she had become so dizzy she had to sit down on the edge of her bed. After some time, Mrs Musewa thought she heard a voice calling out, followed by a knock on the door. She slowly rose up and staggered to the partially opened door and saw a well-dressed man standing there who introduced himself as Detective Sergeant Mumba from the local police station. The sergeant was very kind and asked her to come to the police truck to see if she knew one of the men. It was now becoming difficult for her to move but the sergeant took her by the arm and carefully led her across to the landrover, where she soon recognised Amos and when the European officer saw her, he became very worried.

When I saw Mrs Musewa's condition, I became extremely concerned and realised we needed to get her to the hospital as quickly as possible. We urgently called for another police vehicle to take everyone back to the station, and lock Amos up until we had a chance to sort the mess out. Then Mumba and I took Mrs Musewa to the hospital, and by some good fortune, we came across Dr Caiger, who had the woman admitted to the wards straight away. She told him she was beginning to suffer from blurred vision and Dr Caiger told me quietly that we had probably got the woman to the hospital just in time, because more and more sugar from her bloodstream was being absorbed. Several days later, we were relieved to learn the patient was making a sound recovery and in the station under interrogation, Amos admitted his guilt on a wide range of multiple charges. The next day he pleaded guilty before the magistrate, where he received the maximum prison sentence. However, some good had come out of all this; one was life had been saved and there were excellent responses we had received from our informant network.

Around this time, a con-man called Jim Chisambe had finally decided that now would be a good time to leave the independent state of Katanga, especially as it was becoming far too dangerous, with armed gangs roaming the streets and attacking anyone on sight. The night before boarding a coach taking him on to new vistas in Northern Rhodesia, he had broken into a number of shops in Elizabethville and stolen a wide range of clothing, including expensive suits, shirts, ties and shoes together with a large leather suitcase. He was quite a jack-the-lad and would eventually be known as Gentleman Jim Chisambe. Jim's first port of call was the copper mining town of Mufulira, where he did reasonably well, fleecing many of the local traders and store owners by using a number of ruses to get them to part with their money.

When he felt he had finally exhausted all of his nefarious schemes, he moved on to Chingola, where he was soon embroiled in discussing how he could bring untold riches from Katanga to the very doors of gullible merchants. His engaging personality and display of obvious wealth, as witnessed by the cut of his clothes, soon saw him enjoying a new found prosperity, until eventually the penny dropped and the merchants realised they had been duped. As usual and before justice could catch up with him, Gentleman Jim was off again to another thriving community. This time though, he was caught and convicted, but then he managed to escape from prison just before we could get our hands on him. After a little while, we were informed he had been caught once again in Ndola and sentenced to several years in prison with hard labour. We arranged with the prison authorities to extradite him so further charges could be brought, although the authorities stipulated the movement of Gentleman Jim had to be undertaken by armed police as he was by now regarded as a high-profile escape artist.

The first part of the operation went well enough, once Ndola police delivered him safely to the Kitwe station, but then we heard disturbing reports that a loaded revolver had been found stuffed down the back of one of the vehicle seats. We decided to drive over to Kitwe, to collect Gentleman Jim, who I found to be a smart and highly intelligent young man with a good command of English, besides speaking French and several other African languages. We took no chances with Jim, who was handcuffed and then installed in the landrover, sitting between two detectives. I told him we knew a revolver had been hidden in the Ndola Police vehicle and I showed him that I was armed too and he would not escape under any circumstances.

His reply astonished me. 'My dear sir, you have misunderstood me completely. I do not want to escape from here because you are doing me a very big favour in getting me to Chingola, where I shall certainly be able to make my escape. I really want to be as near to the border with Katanga as possible. I will agree to all your charges because I know I will never go before the magistrate. I will now do everything possible to help you reach Chiwempala safely.'

An hour or so later we were sitting in our office, while Jim was cautioned and charged with a wide range of offences and as each charge was read out, he nodded his head sagely in agreement. We took his fingerprints and at the end of all the procedures, we handcuffed a smiling Gentleman Jim and delivered him safely to the prison authorities.

I thought that had been the end of a really productive day, but early the next morning I changed my mind completely when one of the constables from the charge office brought me in an envelope with my name written on the outside. When I opened it up, I found a plain postcard inside with the words:

'Dear Mr Matthews,
'Thanks for giving me such a splendid ride -wish you were here!
'Jim Chisambe,'

A call to the prison elicited the embarrassing reply that during the previous late evening, an African nun from the nearby convent had requested a private prayer meeting with a staunch Catholic, called Jim. This prayer meeting in the cell lasted only 20 minutes when the nun called the guard to unlock the door and she left. Later, during the night, one of the guards checked the cell, only to find the woman had changed clothes with Jim for a substantial payment, allowing him to escape dressed as the nun. Gentleman Jim was never apprehended, and I still have visions of him living a very happy life of luxury in the Congo.

Chapter 10

Arrows of Misfortune

The Zambezi River is well over 2,000 miles long and rises high up in the wetlands of North-West Zambia before flowing down through six other countries until it reaches the Indian Ocean. The memories of an exciting life in this part of Africa often flood the mind without invitation and I am ever grateful for their appearance but tinged with great sadness at their parting. Such was the case when conducting an anti-poaching patrol near the border with the Congo, a country mired in chaos and upheaval, having gained independence from Belgium in 1960. Our investigations had finished a day earlier than expected, where poached leopard skins had brought the hunters only several pounds for each skin, while the unscrupulous Indian storekeeper had received twenty-five pounds in a murky deal, where eventually the unprincipled agent in Paris netted the princely equivalent of £250.

We had started back to our base and after several hours of driving, we decided to pitch camp for the night. Willy went out into the fast fading light to collect dry wood for the fire, because our campsite had been chosen on high ground well away from the cold and damp river mist, the ubiquitous mosquitoes and the depredations of rapacious crocodiles and the raiding hippos that have killed more people throughout Africa than any other wild animal. It was always a priority to secure the high ground with all-round visibility over the vast and glorious bush country.

I loved these times, sitting around a blazing campfire and looking out over the bush and seeing the occasional brilliant flashes of forked-lightning in the far distance. Leaving Willy to prepare the evening meal, I was expected to provide the team with copious quantities of beer and then after the meal and before the storytelling began, it had been customary for me to furnish an unusual treat to test the team's palette. Sometimes it would be one of their favourites, tins of pilchards in a rich tomato sauce, however, this time it was baked potatoes, carefully wrapped in foil and laid out amongst the red-hot ashes of the campfire.

On this foray, I had brought only three of our unit, Detectives Busike, Monga and Charlie, having left the others back at our police station under the command of Detective Sergeant Mumba. These three were chosen because their field-craft was exceptional, whereas the others were real townies; even so, one of the most important members of the team was Alex, who had grown to be simply enormous with what Charlie called a mouth full of crocodile teeth. The squad always asked for Alex to come along with us, realising that with him about, there was no real need for them to stand guard throughout the long and cold African nights. Alex held a special place in tribal lore, because with our investigation into so many witchcraft cases it was said by local tribesmen that the government had paid a paramount witchdoctor a vast sum of money to turn himself into a dog, to hunt and smell out evil and I don't think we did anything to dispel this rumour. Despite having Alex along, we always took some elementary precautions. Busike and Monga would string out fishing line away from our camp to form a semi-circle and then fix it at various points with short twigs positioned several inches above the ground. The line into the camp would then be secured with several empty baked-bean tins, filled with a few smooth river pebbles, that would rattle out a warning if disturbed by either man or beast.

Once the fire had been built up, the tribal storytelling commenced. Busike came from Barotseland, whose king the Litunga, had once been given an admiral's uniform by Queen Victoria, and he invariably regaled us with time honoured stories of how his king would leave the palace, travelling in a large and ornamental dugout canoe, paddled by a host of his warriors. Monga, on the other hand, was a member of the Batonga tribe, who were all noted cattlemen, and he told breath-taking stories of a hard life, living off the land, in tending the cattle and the exceptional courage needed by their young men in facing the terror of attacks by lions. Charlie, on the other hand, was a stranger in a strange land, being a member of the Sezulu tribe from Southern Rhodesia. In the 1800s, there had been an alliance between a leader, called Mzilikazi, known as 'The Great Road', and another brilliant general, the great military genius Chaka Zulu. Mzilikazi had eventually fought his way northwards to create the great Matabele nation. I learnt many things through their storytelling, for instance, that stars were not really heavenly bodies at all, but were mere holes cut through the fabric of the sky by valiant warriors who had fallen in battle and the greater the starlight shining through, the more courageous the warrior's departure had been, as he sliced his way through to the bright light beyond. These were heady times for all of us young men and had we known it then, these were certainly some of the happiest days of our lives.

Early dawn in the bush, and already there was the sound of movement around our encampment. Willy rekindled the fire and the gentle sounds of rattling pots and pans being prepared for breakfast seemed strangely reassuring. Within minutes, the flames cast flickering light and shadows against the backdrop of our bivouac. Alex rose and gently stretched out, before resting his large head on my chest, which was his way of saying good morning, because he very rarely barked. Shortly afterwards, Willy appeared with the magical cup of coffee and having been designated as the blanket man for the team, he gently started to peel off the blankets, in case any warmth-seeking poisonous snakes had sidled in during the night.

The African sunrise is something wonderful to behold, with the brilliant reds and oranges melding together as daybreak spread across the sky. Hot water was brought for me to shave, leaving me to endure a team audience, fascinated to see the European face covered in foaming lather. In the meantime, Alex checked out all the various nooks and crannies around the camp and when he was fully satisfied, he climbed up onto the roof of the cab, to cautiously scent the air and finally when he was at peace, he would settle down and maintain a keen watch over the surrounding countryside. After breakfast, the fire was carefully extinguished and our equipment stowed away in the landrover and with the sun rising higher in the sky, the day seemed to hold enormous promise.

Trundling along the twisting bush tracks, Charlie mentioned something we had all been thinking about because we were only a few hours drive away from a small fishing village we knew extremely well. It was here that the village headman would lend us several of his young sons who would take us out in two dugout canoes, punting the craft way out into the fish-rich reaches of the river. As Charlie pointed out, the cool-box was empty but it could soon be filled with succulent river fish and if he could use some of the Bwana's vinegar, he would douse the fish and remove the taste of river mud. It had not gone unnoticed that we had a day in hand and after only a few seconds deliberations, the die was cast and we turned off towards the village.

We made good time and driving into the clearing in front of the small and dilapidated Indian trading store, we could see it was a hive of activity. Dried fish had been laid out in the sunshine along the sides of thatched roofs and quite a few stalls displayed a wealth of fish varieties besides vegetables and dried meat. A group of villagers stood in front of the store and as we approached, this gathering suddenly parted and one man rushed forward and without hesitation threw a long-handled spear straight at us. The spear oscillated in flight before fixing itself firmly in the radiator grille of the landrover. I shouted out the order to 'de-bus' and we all scrambled out of the vehicle as quickly as we could, my .38 revolver already out of the holster and pointed directly at our assailant. Almost immediately, Charlie was at my left side with his loaded Greener shotgun and Alex stood to my right with teeth bared, hackles raised and growling violently.

In the midst of this confrontation, the village headman arrived and apologised most profusely by explaining some of the crowd were new and did not know who we were. This was not an acceptable explanation, but the atmosphere gradually became subdued. The spear was removed from the security grating and luckily enough, no real damage had been done, although it had only just missed the main radiator housing by an inch or so. In this more receptive mood, it was agreed we could go fishing and the headman would certainly be pleased to provide the dugouts and the rowers, and yes, we could surely buy a chicken for our lunch. The headman clicked his fingers and a haggard old crone with only one tooth in her head, stepped forward. She told us the price of a chicken was now £1, in spite of the fact the last time it had been only 2/- and although the team were angry at the price hike, I agreed to pay this exorbitant amount, more in an attempt to placate the villagers. Once I had handed over the money, the old hag cheerfully informed me for that pitiful amount, I had to catch the chicken myself!

Amidst a great deal of laughing and jeering, I tried desperately to catch my chicken, but lithe, village chickens are well versed in the art of evading capture and my forays were proving fruitless. In sheer desperation, I launched myself full length, only to see the bird neatly sidestep my grasping arms and scamper off between the huts. Just as I was getting up, there was a massive explosion, making my ears ring, which was simultaneously followed by a great whooshing sound as bits of bird, and feathers were flung against nearby hut walls. Charlie had been so distressed to see me grovelling in such an embarrassing manner, he had used the shotgun to blast several of the village chickens to eternity. Instantaneously, the mood turned once more to anger and with our loaded weapons in full view, we backed away and left somewhat hurriedly, stopping off about a mile down the dirt road to give us time to calmly evaluate this disastrous situation.

We decided to make camp nearby and Charlie considered it would be a good idea if he went back to keep a discreet watch on what was happening in the fishing village. I agreed, because, on our way into the village, I had noticed several wooden planks on the small bridge leading to the community were in urgent need of repair. We carried the necessary tools to do the job and I cogitated that perhaps this could possibly lead to some form of reconciliation. Later in the afternoon, a breathless Charlie returned, to say things appeared to be normal and that the people were calmly going about their work. That night, we set the fire much higher and maintained an armed guard on a two hours on and two hours off shift basis. I ensured all the weapons were cleaned and loaded and although the night passed quietly enough, I don't think anyone managed to sleep very much, including Alex, who just padded up and down the whole time.

By early morning, we had enjoyed another good hearty breakfast and were back at the bridge where it was apparent several of the heavy metal bolts securing the thick wooden planks, had come apart and fallen into the river. It was obvious someone would have to jump into the stream and work from there, and I thought as leader of the team, it should be my job. I selected Busike to standby with the .303 rifle in case of an attack by crocodiles, although I was not too sure whether I preferred to face crocodiles or Busike armed with a wavering rifle. Notwithstanding this, I stripped down to my briefs and climbed over the wooden railings into the cold water. After an hour or so of hard work, the job was nearly finished when we were interrupted by Alex's unusual angry barking and growling.

I climbed back onto the bridge to see what was going on, but not a word was spoken, Monga put a steel helmet on my head and Busike passed me the fully loaded rifle. I doubt very much if I cut an imposing figure with a helmet on my head, a rifle in my hand and wearing only my underpants. Willy decided discretion was the best option and immediately tucked himself safely inside the back of the landrover. In front of us, some 100 yards away, stood a mob of angry, gesticulating villagers edging forward ever so slowly. Charlie appeared from the rear of the vehicle carrying his Greener shotgun and my Remington hunting rifle, which he passed to Monga. I handed my .38 revolver to Busike, so we were all armed and ready. Stones started to fly and in that same moment, I flipped the safety catch and raised the rifle to my shoulder, firing one shot well above the heads of the crowd. The bullet slammed into the trunk of a nearby tree sending splinters of wood flying into the air and the crowd stopped dead in their tracks. I turned around just in time to see Monga had been hit by a stone and knocked off the bridge into the water. I bent down to grab his arm and haul him safely back onto the bridge and suddenly; I felt a stinging pain in my right leg. It turned out, no sooner had I been distracted in helping Monga, when a villager carrying a bow and arrow, quickly moved forward and fired a barbed missile high into the air towards us and it was his arrow that had hit me in the leg. An enraged Alex took off after the man, rapidly overhauled him in a matter of seconds and set about savaging him in a most ferocious manner.

Charlie fired the shotgun over the head of the crowd and shredded leaves began to fall like confetti and in that one instant, the crowd turned and ran off hell-for-leather, leaving us standing there. I was heartened by the response of the team who rallied around and Charlie came and confessed to me that it was all his fault because on his last incursion to watch the village, he had met and then deflowered the headman's daughter, although he did qualify this by saying he thought she had been deflowered many times before. Busike snapped the arrow in two and gently pulled the clean shaft through the bleeding mess, and Monga arrived with the first-aid kit and started to clean the wound. Meanwhile, Busike washed the arrowhead and looking closely at the barb, whispered he thought it might have had poison smeared on it some time ago, but we should get to the nearest clinic as quickly as possible. Alex returned quietly satisfied, and with my leg bandaged, we set off for the nearest clinic at a cracking pace. The journey took about an hour before we arrived at the clinic, enabling me to obtain the required medical treatment.

Many miles away, Silas Mwamba sat alone in the dark, on a rickety and broken cane chair, just outside the entrance to his wattle and daub hut. It was early the same morning, and cold streaks of pale light were slowly beginning to steal across the sky. He thought the cold of the morning was but a precursor of the heat of the day yet to come. His village was gradually coming to life, dogs barked, cooking pots rattled and cattle snorted in anticipation of the approaching daylight. Silas was a respected figure in the village or rather he had been until recently. He was the village headman of some 150 souls, living in 35 closely built huts. He was a staunch member of the Bemba tribe, owing allegiance to a paramount chief called Chitimukulu.

He said to himself this day was going to be a great and wonderful day, the day he planned to kill his third wife and sadly he realised he should never have married a much younger woman who had proved to be nothing but a troublesome burden. Although diminutive in stature, her lack of height was counterbalanced by a virulent and shrill voice and she took great delight in criticising him in front of all the village elders. Yesterday though, his wife had declared that she intended visiting the native court at the nearby Boma (administration centre) and put her case in an effort to annul what she called a disastrous marriage. This was almost unheard of, because the Bemba people had a long tradition of honouring marriage, where divorce was almost impossible to achieve.

It was not a question of cost, because the tribe had a long-standing custom where the groom usually made only a small gift to the bride's parents, with no bride-price in cows or goats required. They had not been blessed with children, in spite of visiting the local witchdoctor and making offerings to the all-powerful Bemba god called Leza, who lived in the sky and specialised in problems of fertility. No, it was not the cost of the marriage, but it was, more importantly, the anticipated ridicule and loss of face that worried him, but not anymore because this was all before he had thought about creating the ingenious accident, which was soon to befall his third wife.

After a solid breakfast of porridge made from ground maize corn, called mealie-meal, which was washed down with a small cup of mowa, an opaque beer also made from maize, he waited patiently for the third wife to emerge from the hut, and even as she came out, she was still moaning. They took their battered old bicycles and set off for the native courts some five miles distant. Silas smiled to himself. 'Carry on moaning you mangy old bitch,' he thought, 'Because this is going to be your last day on earth.' He congratulated himself on his meticulous planning, knowing the accident would take place far away from prying eyes. He had previously found a large, thin stone with a bulbous end, which he wrapped carefully in an old linen cloth and hid it in the pannier basket on his old bicycle. He intended using this to kill the virago, sorrowfully describing afterwards how she had tragically fallen from her bicycle and hit her head on the stone. This was all going to be absolutely fool-proof.

Silas rode on ahead and, at the appointed place, he dismounted and waited patiently for his third wife to catch up. When she finally arrived, she too dismounted and began walking slowly through the dried-up riverbed. Smiling, Silas approached her with the stone hammer hidden behind his back in one hand and with the other hand he pointed to something far away, on the edge of the nearby forest. As she turned away to see what he was pointing at, he raised the hammer and brought it crashing down on her unprotected head with all the force he could muster. She just turned a little and stood there, looking at him with blood coursing down her face and in a moment of blind panic he hit her again. This time she simply folded up and slipped to the ground. He left her where she had fallen, alongside her bicycle and he carefully placed the bloodstained stone hammer beside her head. Afterwards, he set off for the District Officer's office to report this very sad accident and on the way, he felt so light headed he started to sing some of the old Bemba traditional folk songs. As he cycled along, he mused that in reality, it had all been so ridiculously easy.

At the Native Court, he reported to the uniformed district messenger and feigned a terrible sadness. The district messenger, in turn, listened to his story with patience and understanding and then went off to report the matter to the newly appointed African District Officer and it was at this point matters began to go disastrously awry for Silas. The messenger soon returned and let it be known that the police were visiting there on another matter and would, therefore, take charge of any inquiry. Silas was shown into a large room holding four young men, who were standing around a young European man, who was sitting in a chair with his bloody, outstretched leg being gently bandaged by an orderly from the local clinic. The messenger approached the group and Silas watched him bend down and talk quietly to the European. One of the men came over to Silas and introduced himself as Detective Constable Nhliziyo and from his heavy accent, it was obvious he was from one of the Southern African tribes.

The detective told him his Bwana had been injured in a fight with some very bad people and that a hunter's poisoned arrow had pierced his leg. He said that the Bwana was a great 'mfiti' (wizard) and had a special dog to protect him. The dog could recognise evil in all its forms and he advised Silas to only speak the truth when talking to his chief. When Silas Mwamba looked up, he saw the European leaning forward and looking at him with steadily focused eyes and his heart sank. Then there was a sudden movement and an enormous brown dog with blazing orange eyes came forward into the light. The dog looked directly at him and Silas began to know the real meaning of fear and sweat started to break out on his forehead. The great dog began to snarl and show his massive white teeth and at that point, Silas knew full well he was lost.

This was where I came in because I was sitting in this outer office while a clinic orderly rebound my wounded leg. He had examined the arrow and he too thought poison had been spread on the arrowhead He suggested that, although I needed stitches, he would recommend leaving this for the doctors at the hospital to complete, in case they needed to clean the wound again. Once more, my leg was thoroughly cleaned, the damaged skin trimmed and the wound tightly bound together with surgical tape, but at least I could walk unaided.

A smartly dressed district messenger came into the room with an older, rather nervous villager in tow and leaving this man in the doorway, the messenger walked over to me and gave me a breakdown of recent events. He added that the man, Silas Mwamba, had been due to appear in the native court that morning, having been summoned by his wife, to have an unhappy marriage dissolved, an almost unheard of occurrence within the Bemba tribe.

Alex came around to my side and looked closely at Silas, and commenced smelling the air. The short brown hair on the nape of Alex's neck began to rise slowly and he started to growl with disapproval; in retrospect, I believe Alex could already smell the putrid fear of a guilty man. I had a brief discussion with both the district officer and the messenger and it was agreed we would visit the scene of the incident, evaluate the situation and retrieve the body. Charlie was given the task of looking after Silas and with that, we set off. It was only a very short distance to the riverbed and on arrival, we could see the inert body of a woman stretched out in the sand with a battered old bicycle lying alongside. While everyone stayed back, I followed my normal procedure of standing a little way off and examined the track in minute detail. I always did this because after numerous murder cases, I believed a murder setting invariably told the full story of a violent death, but what I failed to realise was that many of those watching thought I was communicating with the spirit of the dead victim and so the myth persisted that I had the unrivalled ability to converse with the spirits of the dead.

Even from where I was standing, it was obvious the poor woman was dead. We took photographs from a number of vantage points, making notes as we went. There were various wheel tracks in the sand of the dried-up riverbed and a large number of smudged footprints. When we came to the body, it was immediately apparent a brutal and bloody murder had been committed and Alex seemed to know the drill well enough, because he stood looking at the body, sniffed the air, then he barked twice. Meanwhile, back at the landrover, Charlie was telling Silas that Alex was explaining to his Bwana the truth of the case and at this, Silas collapsed. It was obvious that with the bloody protuberance of the stone lying face-down in the sand, the woman's head could not have come in contact with it as she fell and besides, there were two distinct wounds to the head. The wounds were massive and would have required much more force to produce than a simple fall. The area around the head was clean and without the expected traces of sand or soil. The exhibits were identified and tagged and placed carefully in plastic bags and then I returned to interview Silas.

First of all, I talked to him about his paramount chief, Chitimukulu, and I told him I had met with his chief several times and knew him quite well. I told him I knew, for instance, the chieftain-ship is always named after the great Chiti Makula (Chiti the Great) who in the eighteenth century, lead the Bemba people out from their traditional homelands in the Lunda Empire in the Democratic Republic of Congo, to eventually settle around Kasama in our Northern Province. It was immediately evident that the news that I knew his chief had greatly unsettled Silas and I followed this up by saying that perhaps it would be a good idea if I went off to speak with his Chief again.

As far as I was concerned from the evidence we had collected, we could place Silas at the scene of the murder with motive, means and opportunity and I instructed Charlie to take out his notebook and caution Silas about the suspected murder of his wife. Silas shuddered and after a dramatic pause said, 'I admit this. I did kill my third wife by hitting her on the head with the stone. She was taking me to the court and she never stopped criticising me. That is all I have to say except if the police had not been here, I would be safe by now.'

We wrapped the body in the tarpaulin we had brought and placed it on the roof rack. The victim's bicycle was hung on one side of the landrover and we handcuffed Silas to Charlie. I noticed several blood stains on Silas's shirts, and we took this too as an exhibit.

The district officer was certainly grateful for our intervention but was mightily concerned about conditions in the fishing village, He explained it was an illegal and troublesome community, sometimes preying on unsuspecting travellers, often beating them and robbing them of money and other valuables. The village operated a smuggling ring up and down the length of the river with its headquarters in a village shebeen (vice den) and they controlled a criminal gang, slaughtering local wildlife. I promised the D.O. I would soon return to the village and rectify that totally unacceptable situation.

Nearing Chingola, I made contact with the Operations Room and asked them to contact the mortuary to receive the body and book a time for the pathologist to perform a post-mortem the next day. On the way in, I dropped off the camera film at the mine newspaper offices, who promised to send enlarged prints around to the pathologist early the next morning. In spite of the late hour, we deposited the woman's body at the mortuary, with the head attendant personally helping us slide her into one of the chiller-drawers. Silas was ensconced in the prison for the night and it was a very tired party that arrived back at our station with every sinew crying out for a good night's rest.

In a successful attempt to maintain our high detection rate, we had moved away from the usual pyramid system where every case was funnelled through the CID Officer-in-Charge and we instigated a revolutionary method whereby each team member had his own cases. The next day, and with everyone's blessing, Charlie had assumed the role of investigation officer in this murder and dramatically declared that, as such, he was determined to attend the post-mortem examination with me in spite of his overriding fear of retribution from the spirit of the dead wife. Dr Caiger was the pathologist, who liked to work carefully and methodically and was always particularly interested in our witchcraft murders.

At the mortuary, the body had already been carefully laid out on the white ceramic slab. Dr Caiger examined the enlarged photographs of the body taken at the murder scene and as a first step, shaved the victim's hair, which revealed the two massive trauma wounds. It was obvious both had been administered with great force, shattering the skull. Dr Caiger said straight away, as far as he was concerned the husband was guilty because one of the wounds had been caused by a severe downward thrust and the other created by a sideways blow, neither of which were consistent with falling down, He further added that he regarded the stone itself as the murder weapon by reason of the fact it had, in his opinion, been thrown bloody side down, leaving the exposed clean area unaffected. Although on its own this had sounded the death knell for Silas, the post-mortem still had to continue along a strictly prescribed legal path.

The first cut of the scalpel went in and a stifling gas eruption was emitted from the incision. Standing alongside me, Charlie very nearly fainted and the sweat began to pour from his forehead. I told him to go outside and get some fresh air and he gratefully retreated, as we carried on. The finale lay in the blood match of the victim to the splatters on Silas's shirt and after another hour, the post-mortem had been completed and I emerged from the cold mortuary into the warmth of the sunshine.

Charlie was waiting for me, and far from looking sheepish, he seemed quite ebullient, saying, 'Bwana, I have not been idle while you have been messing about with dead bodies. I saw a woman called Lucky Mulenga crying and when I asked what the trouble was, she said her husband had died and was taken to the big building of the dead [mortuary]. She then met the head mortuary man, who told her he could make the husband better if she had sex with him. She agreed and they went inside the building. However, the husband did not get better.'

Charlie continued, 'While all this was going on another woman came up, called Magret and she said exactly the same thing. Now I know a crime has been committed by this bad mortuary man, but I do not know exactly what crime to call it!'

I spoke with the two women and following this, told Charlie the cases were very serious ones of rape. Rape involved the three Fs – Fear, Force or Favour. In this instance there was no force and no fear involved but there was a case of favour and I told Charlie that, although he had done well, he had more than enough on his plate with this murder and we should now call on Sergeant Mumba and Constable Mubonda to come down straight away and start taking statements. These two stalwarts soon arrived and their investigations revealed yet another unfortunate dupe.

The head mortuary attendant was arrested and forthrightly admitted his crimes and I had the dubious duty of telling Dr Caiger he had just lost his headman. He seemed to think it incredible that his employee, who he had trusted implicitly, had enjoyed sexual romps on this very damp and ice-cold ceramic slab in his mortuary.

Silas Mwamba was charged with murder and subsequently tried in the High Court, where he was found guilty of the murder of his third wife. He was duly sentenced to hang and before he was taken away, he asked to see me in the cells where he invited me to attend his execution and stand alongside the gallows, to see him leave this earth on his journey to the stars. Regretfully, I had to decline his very generous offer. However, we were not finished with this part of the country because we still had some unfinished work to attend to. Days later, I returned in the company of an armed detachment of riot police to the village by the river, where all the trouble had started, but these subversive villagers had already fled. There was one sequel to this story which was brought about by rumour instigated by my own team and spread assiduously throughout our patch, to the effect that even though I had been hit in the leg with a poison arrow which would have killed any ordinary man, my magic was so much greater, enabling me to overcome this evil while suffering no ill effects.

Chapter 11

Death of a Spy and Promotion

It was one of those curious situations, which was built up through hunches and a series of thought-provoking coincidences, and yet, oddly enough, it was a case where I was totally involved, although never fully cognisant about what was happening. A brand-new school had just been built in our township, providing much-needed education facilities for young Africans, where the European headmaster was assisted by several African and European teachers. Brian had already met the headmaster and as the time arrived for the official school opening, the headmaster decided to stage a braaivleis (barbecue) for all those people who had provided their much-appreciated services and as a gesture of goodwill, we too had been invited to attend.

A few days before the anticipated celebrations, the team and I had been up on the border with the breakaway state of Katanga, to investigate the most recent cases of cattle rustling and the slaughter of wildlife by marauding Congo militias. This slaughter not only helped to feed the guerrillas but the heinous poaching of ivory and animal skins also provided them with desperately needed funds. In any case, we were on our way back and had just parked near the Border Customs post for a welcome rest, under the leafy canopy of a large tree. Enjoying this brief respite, we watched the long queue of vehicles crossing over from Katanga, with each driver handing identification papers to the border guards for clearance. However, there was one driver, a European with fair, curly hair, who must have been about forty years old, who instantly caught my attention. Remarkably, the man left his car and walked back with the guard towards the Customs post and as they walked, he handed the official an envelope, which was promptly secreted within the official's uniform. The body language of the guard seemed to be completely subservient; meanwhile, the driver immediately returned to his car. The barrier was raised, allowing him to continue his onward journey, accompanied by an enthusiastic salute from the guard. The fair-haired man drove by our group, with Katangese registration plates on his vehicle and more out of habit than anything else, I jotted the car registration number in my notebook.

Saturday evening and with the gloom of twilight quickly merging into the night, our party assembled in the grounds of the new school, ready to be introduced to the headmaster, his wife, two or three African teachers and a young European woman teacher who had only recently arrived from England. I already knew many of the guests, from the African general manager of the post office to a number of senior managers from the municipal offices and we were all soon engaged in some light and well-meaning banter. The BBQ was well prepared and included steak and some of my favourite beef and pork boerewors sausages, made to a special Afrikaans recipe, washed down with cold beers. The teachers mingled with the guests and we were quite a convivial crowd, then sometime later, I saw a fairly tall European man arrive and join the young woman teacher and when he turned around, I instantly recognised him as the man I had seen at the border post. From time to time, I watched him and I thought I noticed a certain reluctance on his part to have his photograph taken, because whenever a camera was raised, he would turn briefly to speak to someone else nearby. I was talking with the recently promoted African postmaster when the young teacher and the man came over to speak to us and although I noticed he did not give us his name, the woman explained that he was a teacher from Katanga and held a British university degree. They seemed a very happy couple and after they left us to mingle with some of the other guests, we returned to our banter, sausages and beers.

For several weeks afterwards, life continued much along the same lines until Brian handed me another BBQ invitation from the school, on the basis the last occasion had been such a tremendous success that the school had decided to hold another one. Once again, we all assembled together and were enjoying ourselves, especially as the party now contained many more faces I knew pretty well, including the local chief reporter from the Nchanga Mine newspaper called Kevin O' Flynn, who had become a good friend. The same visitor from Katanga made a late appearance and I still don't know why I did it, but I asked Kevin if he could try and take a surreptitious photograph of the man. Kevin told me later that he had taken several photos and would have them printed out and sent around to my office early on Monday morning, free of charge, providing I would give him a story if there ever was one.

When the party finished, I went back to my office just to check for any messages and there was one, from my boss Chief Inspector Jack Gowland, instructing me to telephone him whenever I returned, irrespective of the time. It was not too late when I made the call and Jack told me there was a God Almighty flap on and I had to be at District HQ at 1400 hrs., the following Monday afternoon, as a senior officer was coming from Division to speak with CID and Special Branch personnel. Monday morning and I eventually cleared my desk of all the routine notes and messages, examined the weekend cases and discussed with the team how their various cases were progressing. Willy had prepared a light cold meat lunch with an avocado salad and my wife and I sat down on the stoep to relax and talk.

Once I said I had to go into Chingola for a special meeting, she asked me to post several letters for the family back home in Guernsey and, just to make sure, I left a little earlier than originally planned and called in at the post office on the way to the meeting. I posted the letters and I was just leaving when the postmaster came running out of his office and called out for me to stop. We were always teasing each other about how difficult it was for an African to climb the ladder of success whereas it was always so much easier for the Whites to gain promotion. The Postmaster started by telling me he had just received a telegram destined for the woman teacher at the new school, and as he said, 'I want to make the point that there is a man from the university in England who cannot spell properly but who is teaching English to poor uneducated African children, it is a real disgrace.' He then showed me a copy of the telegram, written in English, which gave a date for the man's next visit in two weeks' time, together with information about his flat car battery and other nondescript issues. I noticed quite a few of the words had been incorrectly spelt and told the Postmaster that it was obvious, it must have been the telegraphic assistant in Katanga who had made the errors. The Postmaster just laughed out loud and said, 'You know, I thought you would say that, so I contacted the Katangese office to make sure, and they told me the man had already written the telegram out, and all they had to do was copy the words down exactly as written.'

Again, I don't know what made me do it, but I asked for a copy of the telegram; instead, he handed me the actual document. Sometime later, the meeting was convened in the C.O.'s office, with Jack Gowland and some officers from Special Branch, including a few of my colleagues from other stations. The meeting was chaired by an imposing Senior Superintendent from Divisional HQ, who opened the meeting by telling us this was the last in a series of meetings he had held in the mining towns of Ndola, Mufulira, Kitwe and Luanshya. The reason for this meeting was because the Force had received a top-secret file from MI6 in London, about a dangerous communist spy who was operating throughout the Congo regions and who had access to valuable and secret contacts in Northern Rhodesia. He said the spy had once been a British soldier and a deserter who had been last heard of in communist-held Albania in late 1944. He added, somewhat pointedly I thought, that the meetings so far had yielded no information whatsoever, but he would still pass around a poor-quality photograph of the deserter, showing him in a British army uniform, and taken only days before he had run away. He said the matter was of such great national importance and sensitivity, absolute secrecy must be observed at all times.

The photograph was passed around with the added proviso if we did recognise the person, we should say nothing at this stage, but once we left the meeting any officer with pertinent information should return for further discussions. This was really quite exciting cloak and dagger stuff and when my turn came, I looked closely at the photograph and although the reproduction was grainy and faded, I could still see a young man with fairish hair and dressed in a khaki uniform. If I focussed really hard on the photo and tried to imagine what the subject would have looked like some eighteen years later, I felt sure this was as near as I could visualise as being our man from Katanga. After that, the meeting closed, and I went first of all to our postbox to collect the photographs Kevin O' Flynn had taken and with the copy telegram in hand, I cautiously returned to the C.O.'s office and knocked on the door.

I entered on command, but my initial reception was not exactly welcoming. 'So you think you know more about this man than anyone else do you?'

'Yes, sir.'

'Well, I suppose you had better tell us about it then.'

I told them briefly of my first sighting at the border post, giving the Katangese registration number of the vehicle. Then a short discourse on the school BBQ and the suspect's relationship with the European teacher and finally I gave them the recent photos Kevin had taken, together with the telegram I had acquired from the postmaster, with all the spelling mistakes ringed in red ink. The Senior Superintendent took a long time studying the documents and then cross-referenced them with his MI6 file before saying, 'Well I am not altogether sure, and although I agree it does look very similar, I suggest you go back to your station and do not, I say again, do not talk about this to anyone until we come back to you. OK?'

'Right, sir.'

Life became a marked anticlimax for several days until one mid-morning, Charles Skinner from Special Branch came to see me. Phiri was sent off on some minor administration task and Charles told me that anything we talked about would be classified as being top secret and could not be discussed with anyone else, including Brian. I was not happy about this situation and although Charles was insistent, I still refused. Charles was very understanding, although he said he could not proceed any further unless I agreed. Later that morning I received an immediate summons to meet with the C.O., where it was forcefully put to me that my present attitude could easily jeopardise an operation of national importance. I told the C.O. that my main concern was being told to keep the matter secret from Brian, who was not only my superior officer but also my friend. The C.O. immediately interjected by saying, 'Look here, Brian Thomas is my friend too, and that is why I don't want him involved at this stage, so you will just do as you are damn well told – got it? Dismiss.'

A smiling Charles was waiting for me outside in the corridor and took me into his office where he explained once again that the information he was about to give me was presently classified, going on to say there was a very good reason to believe I had correctly identified the army deserter from Katanga, especially as the spelling mistakes in the telegram had revealed a precise and simple code. As a result, an RAF aircraft had already arrived at Ndola airport with two operatives on board, who had travelled with vast quantities of electronic equipment. They were now being transferred to Chingola in the guise of radio engineers and their cover story would be that they were working on the installation of new long-range radio equipment for the Federal Government in Salisbury. They would be given private accommodation in the police camp, but I should not make contact with them directly at any time, because if they needed anything, they would contact me through Charles. Charles produced a site plan of the school with the bungalow assigned to the European teacher clearly indicated. At the same time, he handed me a set of keys for the bungalow and he finished by advising me to go back to my station and continue working as normal and await further instructions.

Nothing happened for several more days until I received a telephone call to attend a clandestine meeting with Charles at the Hippo Pool, a national beauty spot just six miles outside the Chingola Municipality. The Hippo Pool was a wide stream of water flowing down to lower levels in a series of small pools that were prolific with wildlife, including hippos and crocodiles. We sat under a large tree, out of the sun's glare, on the edge of the swiftly moving water, while he updated me on certain aspects of the current operation. The female European teacher was being sent to Southern Rhodesia on a training scheme for four or five days and as a result, I would be required to be fully armed and in a position to collect the two operatives from their bungalow the next night at 2.30am, taking them to the teacher's bungalow, where they would enter with the aid of the keys I had in my possession.

The fine details of the operation were left to me and I decided I would need some specialist expertise from within my own team. I chose Charlie, Busike and Monga and I apprised them of certain aspects but only on a need to know basis. Busike and Monga, with their superior field craft, went off to secretly scout the area and find a suitable place where we could hide the landrover well away from prying eyes. Besides this, I also wanted to know if there were any tracks running through the bush to the school which would make our progress both rapid and invisible. I told Charlie I would need to rely on his excellent night-vision and exceptional hearing to provide a prior warning in case of any interference from any external sources. Busike and Monga soon returned to say they had found a good place to hide the landrover which was only a short walk from the school, and they would camouflage and guard the vehicle while I was away.

It was 1.30am when I booked out the landrover, under the heading of a routine criminal investigation and then picked up the other three just outside the main gates of the police station. We had previously agreed that we would wear dark clothes, although Charlie quite rightly pointed out that the grey colour of the landrover would stand-out under the light of the full moon. I dropped them off at the chosen spot before continuing on to Chingola with Charlie, leaving them to quietly cut and collect the branches with long grass necessary to camouflage the truck.

2.30am and we arrived at the bungalow, when almost at once, two dark figures wearing balaclava headgear emerged from alongside the tall hibiscus hedge, carrying several heavy-looking holdalls, which they hefted into the back of the landrover alongside Charlie. They totally ignored both of us and we proceeded in complete silence and I have to say even now, after many decades, I still find this aspect to be one of extreme melodrama. We stopped near the school, parking the vehicle in the chosen thicket and Busike and Monga immediately began camouflaging the truck, while we unloaded the holdalls and set off in crocodile file.

Crouching down, we waited in the darkness, listening for any tell-tale signs of activity then, at a given signal from Charlie, we quietly moved towards the bungalow. I unlocked the back door and the two operatives slid inside, with the heavy bags. All along, there were two main issues to consider, one was a possible full moon revealing our positions and the other, the likely intrusion of the old night watchman doing his nightly rounds. We had discounted the chance of dogs barking because in attending the barbecues, I had not come across any dogs at the school. Anyway, at this precise moment, our luck changed with the emergence of a bright full moon and it was just like daylight. Our immediate reaction was to draw back into the shadows because we knew that the night-watchman liked to snooze beside his charcoal brazier on cold nights like this, but perhaps it was the sudden onset of moonlight that galvanised him into some form of lethargic action.

During our lonely vigil, Charlie had peeked out from time to time in the direction of the night-watchman's resting place and alarmingly, he suddenly sighted this shadowy figure moving in between the school buildings, checking both doors and windows. He was coming directly towards us when I hurriedly locked the back door and tapped out an S.O.S in Morse code on the window. Then we high-tailed it out of there, as quickly and as quietly as we could into the dense bushes. There was one heart-stopping moment when he came around to the back door and tried the handle but being satisfied it was securely locked, he soon moved away and returned to the warmth and safety of his brazier.

We moved back stealthily to the back door and once again I unlocked it and as I did so, the door opened and the two operatives emerged with their empty bags and, locking the door again, our party moved off rather like thieves in the night until we reached the hidden landrover. It was a tantalising situation because one week went by and then another and yet I knew from judicious inquiries, the teacher had now returned and our man from Katanga had visited her on several occasions. I knew too that the operatives were still here, because they had been seen wearing their white engineering outfits and having a quiet drink together in the police club. The next Saturday evening, my wife and I, aided and abetted by Alex the Doberman, decided to have our own BBQ at home. This was Alex's favourite meal of all time, where he would lie by the side of the charcoal grill, waiting patiently for his first cooked sausage to cool. Halfway through the evening the telephone rang, and it was Charles Skinner, to say the balloon was about to go up at any minute and I should do nothing but wait by the telephone for further instructions, then he rang off. It was all very mysterious and melodramatic, especially as nothing at all happened during that night.

I was up early the next morning and just munching through my breakfast cereal while listening to the Federal Rhodesian news on the radio. Suddenly, there was a news flash announcing that a serious traffic accident had occurred the previous evening, when a European driver, visiting from Katanga, had been killed in a massive car accident, when a tyre had apparently blown out as he travelled at high speed, along the road by the Hippo Pool near Chingola. No one else and no other vehicle had been involved in this tragic accident. I thought this was an unlikely tale and I waited all through that day and the next without anyone making contact with me but at last, on Wednesday, Charles contacted me to say I would be wanted again at 3am, enabling various objets d'art, as he so quaintly put it, to be retrieved from the teacher's bungalow.

This meant we would need to go through the same operation once more, but this time in reverse order. There was not a murmur from the team who duly assembled early in the early hours, where we had previously agreed we would use the same hidden parking place and once again, we collected the operatives at 3am. Charles Skinner had already confirmed the grieving teacher had subsequently been repatriated to the UK, leaving the property empty. This time we all went in and Charlie held the holdalls, which were gradually filled with a wide range of electronic equipment and it was not lost on us that the greatest number of these electronic bugs came out of the main bedroom.

We had just finished with the bedrooms and lounge and were grouped in the darkness of the kitchen when we heard low voices coming from just outside the bungalow, followed by the sound of keys rattling in the front door lock. We crouched down as the door was opened and several people entered and crossed over the hallway in the darkness and entered the first bedroom. It was here the people, whoever they were, softly closed the door behind them. All too soon we could hear the sound of what seemed like a man and woman's low pitched voices. For the first time, one of the operatives whispered to me 'You deal with this and we will wait for you back at the landrover. Are you armed?' I whispered that I was armed and at the same time I drew my .38 Smith & Wesson revolver from its holster. The operatives slid out of the bungalow very quietly, allowing Charlie and me to move towards the spare bedroom. Taking a deep breath, we barged in, with my revolver drawn. I switched on the lights, only to be confronted by the imposing vision of the headmaster and two African teachers stretched out naked on the double bed.

In the aftermath, the headmaster had no alternative but to disclose his recent extra-mural activities and his subsequent resignation was regretfully accepted. The school was closed for the duration and all the teaching staff were relocated. I never knew the real name of the man from Katanga and I was never told what happened to the European teacher. The RAF aircraft returned to collect the operatives and I was later informed I had been given a commendation, but this was never confirmed in writing and no-one ever said well done! It was as if nothing had ever happened.

Perhaps I did have a commendation, of sorts because sometime later, when returning from inquiries, I was called into closed-door discussions with Brian Thomas and Jack Gowland. Unbeknown to me, the newly appointed Commissioner of Police had agreed to appoint quite a few African officers to the rank of Assistant Inspector, a move I considered long overdue and most welcome. However, he had also stipulated in fairness, some seven European Assistant Inspectors should, by the same token be moved up to the full rank of Inspector. According to Brian, the competition had been rife within all Divisions and our own Commander had elected me to represent his Division. Jack Gowland took up the story to say, unfortunately, Special Branch had also identified a suitable candidate within our Division, and it had been agreed we would both go head-to-head to clarify the selection of the eventual winner.

This sudden and unexpected turn of events left me a little breathless until the arrival of the C.O. who proceeded to take over the discussions. He said that before moving forward, he wanted to talk to the whole of the CID team and they were quickly summoned, filling Brian's rather small office. The C.O. explained what was being proposed and then asked them what their thoughts were. Total silence reigned, which didn't exactly fill me with any confidence until Sergeant Mumba stepped forward, cleared his throat and said, 'Sirs, I think the Bwana will make an excellent Inspector.'

'But will you support him in the proposed exercise?'

'Oh, yes, sir.'

'Why.'

At this juncture there was a definite pause as Mumba carefully considered the C.O.'s question, then clearing his throat once again he answered, quite innocently I thought, 'Bwana, it is a very wise father who will always look after his children.'

The C.O. turned his attention to me next and asked what our latest case was. This concerned some disturbing information only recently received from Emmanuel Muleya, our friendly, neighbourhood witchdoctor, to the effect that an evil sorcerer, hiding out in the bush, was dispensing spells from a book of magic and using a magic wand. The C.O. thought this was really an excellent situation and instructed me to prepare a schedule of the investigation right away; meanwhile, he would appoint two independent adjudicators to ensure fair play on all sides.

Later, Emmanuel was brought in to make a detailed statement in which he unfolded a story of terror and mayhem brought about by an evil sorcerer bringing down monstrous spirits to torment illiterate and gullible Africans. The suspect lived far away in the bush in a secret hideout, as most sorcerers did, but he was gradually building up a close-knit band of novices ready to spread their heinous activities into darker regions of the territory. Emmanuel categorically stated that the sorcerer dressed in leopard skins, used a book of spells and a magic wand to dispense his spells and call forth the demonic spirits and at that moment we began to realise the full significance of what we were hearing.

Knowing there was a book of spells being used would surely create pandemonium in government circles, more especially as the last book of spells ever discovered dated back to the late 1800s and now resided in the British Natural History Museum in London. To make matters worse,

Emmanuel confirmed that the wizard was forging weapons in his den and had already killed a number of unknown men, thereby using their rendered down bodies to imbue the pangas and spears he was making with the powerful spirits of the dead. At the same time, he was engaged in wildlife poaching, selling on skins and tusks to fund his evil way of life. Emmanuel had a reasonably good idea where the hideout was, and we spent quite some time studying maps and in making notes.

After a while, Brian confirmed that the adjudicators would be Woman Assistant Inspector Betti Jones and Assistant Inspector John Maxwell. This was really good news, because they were both good friends of mine, although the disheartening news was that because of the highly secret nature of Special Branch affairs, no adjudicators could be ascribed to their exercise. The extremely sensitive nature of our forthcoming operation made it necessary to talk it through with the team and once the full story was told with an explanation of the possible scenarios, a few eyes rolled upwards in their sockets in consternation. Sensing their unease, they were invited to return to their own offices and discuss the implications and their feelings together, without any fear of pressure. They trooped off with hunched shoulders and I could hear voices echoing from next door as they raised their concerns. They were still at it after lunch, until finally, they meandered back in and grouped around my desk.

Sergeant Mumba kicked off the discussion by saying this was going to be a very dangerous case and they had all been thinking about it very carefully. Charlie wanted to know if we would be taking the guns and seemed a little relieved when I said I would be armed and he could take his favourite shotgun. Busike felt the adjudicators would be moving through the bush like a herd of elephants and would no doubt warn the evil people of our approach. This was a salient point and I made a note that the adjudicators would need to stay well back. Monga thought if we were going to do it, it should only involve our team because he didn't trust anyone else – another good point. Charlie then summed it all up by saying, 'This is a very difficult spot for us poor boys because we are always frightened by bad spirits. But if the Bwana is with us, we will be safe because his magic is more powerful than the black shit we have to chase all the time.'

Saturday night, and we planned to raid the sorcerer's den just on midnight. We were all wearing dark clothes apart from John Maxwell, who had been ordered to appear in uniform, although this was much against his will. Phiri came with us on the understanding that he was to operate the muted radio and stand guard over the hidden landrover until our return. By now, Charles, accompanied by his candidate, had arrived at the station and they, with Jack and Brian, elected to remain there on standby in case we got into difficulties and with this rather cheerful thought, we left for what was fast turning into a circus act. We stopped a long way away from where we thought the hideaway was, leaving Phiri to camouflage the vehicle while we took to shank's pony, even though the going would prove a little difficult for John Maxwell, who was jolting along manfully on his artificial leg.

Making matters worse, the moon suddenly emerged from behind dark clouds and illuminated our procession in a pale light. We were on the edge of a large maize field and to our right, an unusual stone building with a slate roof stood out starkly against the skyline. By now, John's artificial leg was beginning to squeak, necessitating a brief pit-stop, where the leg was unstrapped and at this point, out came a tube of lubricating graphite to ease the various seized up joints. It was probably one of the most surreal episodes ever seen, with a beautifully formed artificial leg, complete with a polished boot, and a grey police sock, lying on the ground in all its glory. Just at that moment, the door of the building opened and a shadowy figure stepped out clutching a storm lamp. It was then we heard a thin wavering voice say, 'If you are good and kind spirits please bless my house, but if you are bad spirits, rest awhile and then please leave us alone.'

Busike and Monga went off to scout the ground and to locate the target area. It was not very long before they returned to say the place would be visible for miles around because the sorcerer had built an enormous fire in front of his forge and they could see him with his congregation. We left John and Betti in the middle of the maize field and pressed on towards our objective and as we drew near, we developed a much better sense of our surroundings. Busike and Monga clutching their long wooden batons circled the hut from the rear and were ready to cut off the retreat of any recalcitrant believers, while the rest of us prepared for the frontal assault.

We moved forward carefully and slowly towards the entranced worshippers. The sorcerer was standing directly in front of the congregation, wearing leopard skins and adorned with beads. He gripped the open book of spells in one hand and clenched a red wand in the other, which he waved about with some enthusiasm. A few minutes later, with the strident signal on my police whistle echoing eerily on the night air, we rushed into the circle and caught them all completely by surprise, to the point where they gave up without a fight. Once the wizard had been handcuffed, I had a close look at his book of spells which turned out to be a 1936 Methodist Hymn Book that he had been reading upside down. His wand too was a red number 9 knitting needle, so in short order, everything turned quickly into a massive anti-climax, even though we discovered several blood-stained elephant tusks inside the forge.

We took our man back to the maize field to collect John and Betti and it was John who just could not stop laughing at our predicament and the laughter continued unabated back at the station when we made our report. However, Brian said we had caught an evil, practising witchdoctor and wildlife poacher and put a potential threat to rest. It was close to 2am when John and Betti returned to Chingola and I invited Brian, Jack, Charles and my erstwhile competitor to join me for cold beers on the patio of our apartment, which they happily accepted. The cold beers came out and the ham and cheese sandwiches so thoughtfully provided by my wife were quickly devoured and all in all, I felt the evening had been reasonably successful and I certainly looked forward to the next round.

The following day, I was told to make myself available that evening for round two of the promotion stakes. It was pointedly remarked that Special Branch was a much more civilised police unit and we should all come together at about 5pm and not the usual midnight jaunts so beloved by CID. Jack Gowland and I turned up to find not only were there no adjudicators, but we were not going to be allowed to attend any of the Special Branch discussions. When Jack said this didn't seem very fair or right, we were told that Division had already agreed to this proviso, so we could just go and do the other thing! My friendly contender invited us all for dinner at his house afterwards, at 7pm, and straight away, I could see my hopes of promotion were fading fast.

7pm came with no-one making an appearance, then 8 and just before 9 o'clock, the party returned in high spirits and we finally adjourned for our long-awaited dinner. The moment I entered the bungalow, I knew I had finally lost the race because the young and very attractive South African lady of the house was there to warmly greet us in a figure-hugging, full-length gown. The table had been beautifully set, with scented candles and a bottle of white South African wine stood ready in the ice-bucket. There was little time to cogitate because we were immediately ushered to our places, where the wine was dispensed by our host and the first plates of sumptuous fillet steak and vegetables arrived. First to be served was Charles and then Jack, followed by me and there was just a brief moment to consider our host had perhaps been neglected when his plate arrived. Our host was on the point of raising his glass of wine in a toast of welcome, when his wife sashayed over to him with a full plate of food and dumped the whole lot right into his lap, with the immortal words, 'Man! When I say dinner is at seven, it is at seven,' and with that she left the room, leaving us totally confused and embarrassed. Jack decided on the right course of action, by thanking our host and getting up from the table and leaving and then we all shortly followed suit. Several weeks later, I was confirmed in my appointment as a Detective Inspector and held the first all-night party for the whole team, with Brian and John Maxwell as our honoured guests.

Chapter 12

Contraceptives, Cricket and Cannibals

The first thing I knew anything about such great and exciting news, was when Brian came in to tell me how pleased the C.O. was with the information the CID team had asked Mrs Green, sister at the local medical clinic, to give them a lecture on the all-important subject of contraception. Brian seemed a little put out that I had not thought it necessary to let him know about this momentous request, but as I explained, even I didn't know anything about it. Within hours, the whole subject escalated out of all proportion, because the C.O. notified Division, then Division notified the Assistant Commissioner CID in Lusaka, who in turn consulted with the Commissioner. Suddenly the proposed lecture took on a life of its own when it became recognised this was the first time any African organisation had made serious inquiries about this vital topic.

The day of the lecture arrived and Charlie seemed to be the main instigator and knowing him as well as we did, Brian and I viewed the whole process with jaundiced eyes. However, we were pleasantly surprised to see a table and chair had been put out for the guest speaker in the quadrangle. A semi-circle of chairs had also been laid up for each member of the team, although I was moderately disconcerted to see a chair had also been provided for me. Mrs Green bustled in, glowing with pride and anticipation and she soon had the team nodding appreciatively at the sagacity of her remarks and when, rather like a magician, she suddenly produced a large and highly polished mahogany phallic carving, they just gasped in admiration at her dexterity in applying the condom. At the end of the lecture, Mrs Green handed each detective several free-sample packets of contraceptives and with a few words of encouragement and a final wave of the hand, she was gone.

At work, we were all enjoying a few quiet moments when someone in authority dictated that the British character must forcefully come to the fore. It was further decreed that the police cricket team should once again take to the field and I was given special permission to take the landrover, complete with my riot gear together with a police constable, who was detailed to keep in contact with the Operations Room in case I was needed elsewhere. It was certainly not the first time I went to a full-scale riot clad only in my cricket whites.

Charlie often volunteered for this onerous duty and almost straight away showed a marked willingness to learn more about the mystifying aspects of English cricket. His positive approach resonated with my colleagues and in an attempt to answer his inquiries, they proceeded to teach him the rudiments of bat and ball and to be fair, Charlie showed exceptional prowess under their tuition. The cricket team presented him with an old cricket bat and Charlie was ecstatic, keeping it in our offices where he regaled everyone with tales of his vast athletic experiences on the cricket field, 'With all those amazing Whities.'

Then, suddenly, it was a return to riots once again and on one of these occasions I noticed Charlie walking nonchalantly amongst the rioters and I wasn't the only one who saw his vulnerability which made him such an enticing target, because a small group of rioters rushed towards him and I held my breath, but I needn't have worried. Charlie had hidden his awesome Zulu knobkerrie up the sleeve of his jacket and stood there perfectly poised, but at a well-judged moment, the knobkerrie slipped down, he grasped the shaft and within a blur of seconds, four rioters were laid out unconscious in the dust. Later, during the debriefing session, Brian let it be known that unfortunately the knobkerrie, although a veritable weapon of war, could not be used in any future riots. Charlie for his part took the news in good heart and I had the distinct impression his eyes were firmly fixed on other horizons and perhaps alternative methods of protection.

We had realised early on that in arresting rioters we were only picking up the easily sacrificed foot soldiers and we never reached the main organisers. After some deliberation, I was given the task of creating a snatch squad and with Busike and Monga being the youngest and fleetest of foot, they were designated as the snatchers. The concept was for me to identify and target the ringleaders and then our two would dive into the mob, grabbing one or more of the offenders. The rest of us would follow, chuntering along in their wake, securing the area and the prisoners until such time as the riot-police would arrive in force to extricate us. The point was made time and time again; in order to achieve success, we all had to operate as one cohesive and well-coordinated group, rather a forlorn hope.

Another night and the bugles sounded, shrill and loud. When I arrived hot-foot at the station, the team was already in the landrover and fully prepared. In the market square, Brian and his uniformed police were steadfastly arrayed in front of an angry mob and he used the loudspeaker to announce, 'I call upon those rioters herewith illegally assembled to peacefully disperse.' The answer was immediately forthcoming, as stones and verbal abuse were hurled at the police lines. Straight away, we were released into this maelstrom and for the first time, I noticed that, although he was wearing his steel helmet, Charlie did not have his riot shield nor his regulation long-baton, because these items had been sneakily replaced by his precious cricket bat.

Unperturbed, Charlie meandered along, giving me a running commentary as he went. 'You see Bwana – dis am de square cut.' Whack! and a surprised rioter pitched over, then, 'Here is de full toss.' Wallop! as the bat caught another miscreant under the chin and he too, quickly succumbed. The final stroke in Charlie's repertoire came with a powerful 'Drive-to-the-boundary Bwana', catching the poor unfortunate in the groin and leaving him writhing in agony in the dirt. Over to our right, we saw two criminals barge their way inside a hut and we both followed, but when we entered, we could see they had already made a quick exit by breaking one of the hut windows. I became momentarily distracted, seeing Busike running past on his own which was tantamount to inviting the mob to ambush him and in my haste to race outside, I forgot two cardinal rules; try not to leave the same way you entered, and before emerging into bright sunlight, pause for a moment in case someone is out there waiting for you!

I rushed outside and in that single second, everything became a blurred kaleidoscope. In a flash, I saw the raised iron bar and then felt the sharp, excruciating pain as it connected with the right side of my face. There was the mystifying way the ground rose up and the final thought was this was how life would end; in the dirt, then total darkness. Charlie had been right behind me and using the edge of his cricket bat, he dealt my assailant a cutting blow, consigning him to relative obscurity. As the stones began to rain down, an amazing thing happened (according to statements made by Brian Thomas), because the rest of the squad raced up to my prone body and holding their metal riot shields over their heads, they formed the ancient Roman 'testudo'' (or tortoise formation) designed to protect all of us from the missiles raining down. Charlie though stayed out in front, swatting as many of the projectiles away as he could with his bat, although he did take a few hits to his body. However, it was only a few minutes before a detachment of riot police arrived and I was finally retrieved, minus a tooth or two.

Early the next morning I was in the office, sporting yet another black eye and somewhat the worse for wear. I had been checked out by the hospital and patched up where necessary after one of my broken molars had been carefully removed. In this particularly vulnerable state, I was ripe for some of the team's well-meant homilies. Mumba suggested that, although the day had not proved to be one of our best, we should not be downhearted. He quoted an old tribal saying which went, 'If you aim for the tree, you will fall to the ground but if you aim for the moon you will fall in the tree.' I wasn't at all sure about this but Mubonda brought a sense of reality to the occasion by suggesting in future, instead of gallivanting off to the Mine Hospital at a moment's notice and leaving them all behind, I could be treated just as well at the local clinic. Finally, Charlie appeared, covered in bumps and sticking plaster and still clutching the remnants of a splintered cricket bat. Placing the remainder of the bat firmly down on my desk, Charlie drew himself up to his full height and standing to attention said, 'Bwana, I think the white man's game of cricket is far too dangerous for a simple Sezulu warrior like me and in future I would much prefer to face dangerous lions in my home Kraal.' Having learnt these lessons the hard way, the snatch team went on to trap and arrest many of the ringleaders including six firebrands in one week alone.

We had appreciated a brief, lull, although upheaval and chaos continued to reign supreme in the Congo and Katanga. Katanga had sequestered a large part of the mineral-rich mines, left behind by the Belgians at independence, and this led to the large-scale rustling of cattle in Northern Rhodesia. Various militias and tribes from both areas conducted regular incursions into our country and then herded the animals back across the border. Not only cattle were targeted, but also wildlife and Police Farm Patrols had asked for our assistance. We were deputised to carry out an armed but limited exploratory patrol and rifles were issued with a reasonable supply of ammunition. Starting off well before daybreak, this exercise also gave us the opportunity of reaching those farms and settlements situated well off the beaten track, ensuring they were all safe and secure.

It was my birthday and I was anxious to return by early evening, to enjoy a birthday bash in the Police Club with my wife and a few friends. En route and as a matter of normal routine, we stopped off at one of the border farms to ascertain the occupants were untroubled. The young owner had a slight foreign accent and inside the farmhouse, I noticed a few birthday cards. It turned out this was also the farmer's birthday and I observed a framed print of a German family coat of arms. During our discussions, he asked me what I had been doing on this day in 1944 and I told him I had been incarcerated in a German concentration camp, in Biberach with my parents. He told me his father had been a general in the German Wehrmacht and was home on leave having been wounded in fighting on the Russian front. The family had a lovely hotel in the Black Forest and this birthday had been a wonderful family occasion. Still, some seven weeks later, a large convoy of cars manned by elements of the Gestapo and feared SS troops arrived at the hotel and after brief introductions, they took his father down into the hotel basement and there hanged him from one of the ceiling beams with piano wire, as retribution for the attempt that had been made on Adolf Hitler's life.

We were soon on our way again and at the next settlement, the village headman told us that since they started bringing all their cattle in at night, they had experienced no further cases of rustling, although, he had heard that Ngulube village, which was only five 'clicks' away from the border, had suffered a large number of cows being stolen. I loved these visits to African villages, always a hive of activity that showed off their ancient crafts and skills in such primitive conditions. Here women with young babies strapped to their backs would be pounding maize into a fine powder with long wooden poles and where river fish were carefully laid out in the sun to dry. Where blacksmiths hammered metal into spears or axe heads and sometimes we would come across men smelting copper in small clay furnaces, while young children operated the home-made, skin bellows.

An hour or so later we drove into Ngulube village, finding it uproar. A village elder explained that numerous refugees, fleeing from the Congo, had recently crossed over the border, with harrowing tales of being chased by a company of rampaging Congolese soldiers, who were likely to arrive in his village at any moment. Even so, he continued in a more sinister vein by saying several parishioners from the Catholic Mission situated just the other side of the border were spreading rumours that their beloved Italian priest had been brutally murdered by enraged and drug-fuelled Congolese militiamen.

Rather reluctantly, I agreed to venture further up onto the border to investigate, although our primary function would be to establish the possible truth of having foreign troops on our soil. When everyone was back in the landrover, and with Sergeant Mumba sitting alongside, I turned around in the driving seat to speak with the squad, only to find them sitting quite upright, almost at attention, with rifles firmly grasped between their knees, but with a contraceptive sheath dangling from each rifle muzzle. Charlie was grinning away like a Cheshire cat and said this was their special way of saving the trouble of having to clean the dust or rain from the barrels of each rifle at the end of the patrol. Finally, we set off to confront a possible armed enemy, with rubber condoms lolloping from side to side with each swaying motion of the truck; so much for family planning! I wondered then, how many commanders in the past, had gone forward to confront a potential enemy in battle, with condoms dangling languidly from the rifle barrels of their troops.

Large parts of the border between Northern Rhodesia and the Congo were unmarked but had many well-worn tracks leading off into the bush. We soon came across a bent old woman who told us a few Congolese soldiers had crossed the border but immediately realised their mistake and had beaten a hasty retreat. When asked about the priest at the Mission Station, she started to cry and told us she felt he had been killed but added somewhat meaningfully that someone should go and make sure. With the border leaking like a colander, I knew if we did cross over, we could always say we were lost, that is if we were ever given the opportunity to explain. I talked it over with the team and we reached the unanimous decision we should go and have a look. Not for the first time they came up with the statement that they would go because they knew my magic would protect them, but if anything untoward did happen to them I had to promise not to leave their bodies behind – a very sobering thought.

We had a rough idea of direction and distance and after only five minutes of careful driving, when breasting a small hill, we saw the Mission laid out in a deep hollow just below. I stopped the truck and cautiously examined each facet of the Mission through my binoculars and it was evident most of the buildings had been destroyed, with large swathes of wreckage blackened by fire. Even more worrying, I could see no sign of life. We drove down very slowly when suddenly two armed and uniformed Belgian mercenaries emerged from the side of the road. They explained partly in French and broken English that their transport had broken down and their C.O. had told them to make their way to the Mission, where they would be picked up a little later. They clambered on board and we gently edged our way into the driveway, where a tall and lanky youth abruptly appeared, wearing a long black ecclesiastical coat and white trainers.

He explained that when the Congolese soldiers had first appeared, the old Priest had run off into the forest, but he was the trainee priest and knew it was his duty to return and he had been back here at the Mission for only a few days. He followed this up by offering us some hospitality in the form of rather warm local Simba (Lion) beer. We all trooped into the dilapidated building and sat down on a motley collection of wooden boxes, planks and broken chairs in the partly destroyed and ransacked dining-room. He bustled off, but soon returned with opened bottles of beer and we noticed he seemed a little unsteady on his feet. After a few minutes he tottered off again for more refills and on his return, he really was quite unsteady on his feet and given to occasional bouts of giggling which was all rather unnerving.

When it came to the third round, Charlie elected to do the honours and spare the partially inebriated trainee priest the trouble, and he disappeared into what we reckoned was the kitchen area. He reappeared almost immediately and practically dragged me into a kitchen, occupied by a damaged cooking range, a large, heavy wooden table and two refrigerators, although there was no electricity. Charlie gently swung open the door of the larger refrigerator and there, resting on a white enamel oval plate was a cooked, human, white arm and hand. On the same plate, a crudely made copper handled knife had been set and it was obvious this knife had been used to slice off slivers of human flesh.

I persuaded the mercenaries to take the cannibal priest outside and guard him so he would not contaminate the crime-scene while Sergeant Mumba helped me with the forensics. We bagged-up the knife and the human arm which in the cold light of day had a grey colour about it. The fingernails were bluish with faint lines showing where the dirt had been finely ingrained. Undoubtedly, this was the Italian priest and to make sure, Mubonda helped me take fingerprints of the hand, with the aid of a large metal spoon which we gently rolled around the stiffened fingers. We were obviously in a very vulnerable situation and I made sure each member of the team was fully armed and had an allotted task. Busike, with his unrivalled knowledge of bush-craft, was detailed to go outside and keep a close watch on the approaches to the Mission from a hidden vantage point. Monga and Charlie's job was to make a thorough search of the building, but I warned them not to touch anything in case any of it had been booby-trapped with explosives.

Sometime later, I went outside to fetch more film for the camera only to be confronted by the body of the cannibal, gently swinging from one of the broken roof trusses. As the mercenaries pointed out, they were living in a country so totally lacking in the provision of justice, that justice needed to be immediate. Soon after this, things started to happen, with Charlie and Monga calling me to look at what they called the killing room, previously a bedroom. The few partition walls still remaining were heavily splattered with blood, with dark blood like a crimson lake on the floor. The awful stench of death filled the place and evil seemed to stalk the dark corridors where ripped and stained clothing lay scattered about as witness to the horrifying and murderous acts that had been carried out there. This was soon followed by the sound of engines from outside and a military convoy of mercenaries swept into the compound to collect their two stranded confrères. Shortly after this, Busike came in to say he felt sure there were 'People who were up to no good' massing on the edge of the forest some 200-300 metres away. We went back to his hidey-hole and in the middle distance, the dense undergrowth on the edge of the forest was being ruffled, even though there was no wind.

The officer commanding the mercenaries told me that various elements of the Congolese army were falling back but there were other militia groups ready to fill the vacuum and he urged us to get out of there as quickly as we could, while they covered our withdrawal. We left, with the cannibal's body still twirling in the wind and the mercenaries setting fire to the remainder of this abhorrent house of murder. I still have the cannibal's knife and sometimes at dinner parties, I bring it out with the cheeseboard and watch my friends faces when I tell them the full story.

After all this excitement, the ensuing days were as dull as ditch-water. Our one saving grace was another plea for help from Farm Patrols, who were still faced with an ever-increasing crime spree aimed at rustling cattle. It was still early morning and we were just about ready to move off, when Brian informed us that we were required to act as a backup in escorting a high-ranking politician from Katanga, who was due to fly from Ndola to Paris to attend a number of important international meetings. We had to be at the bureau in Bancroft by 1530 hrs., that afternoon and a saloon car would be sent from Chingola to provide a more comfortable mode of transport for our special guest. It was further ordered that the squad should be armed and would trail the saloon car until the demarcation border with Kitwe and at that point, another police unit would take over the escort duties.

I felt we had more than sufficient time to revisit the farm of our young German friend and we made excellent time and nearing the farm we came across a wonderful African scene. There was an old man, with grey hair, lying flat out on the grass verge, with his head resting in the lap of an elderly woman who was kneeling just behind him. Their two cycles lay beside them and with the dappled sun highlighting the pair, it came across as a serene moment in our usually turbulent lives. At that point though, it started to rain heavily but the couple didn't move. We stopped and Monga went over to the couple and then started to urgently signal to us. It turned out the old man had died the previous day and by now rigor mortis had set in. We gently placed the old lady in the landrover, wrapped the body in a tarpaulin and put it on the roof-rack, and then we loaded the cycles onto each side of the truck. By now we were well behind schedule and it looked like we would be late in reaching Bancroft, so I had to put my foot down and we banged and jostled our way down dirt roads and along rutted village trackways.

I freely admit we were travelling too fast when we hared onto the gravel entrance to the compound, at just the precise moment the District Officer and the political dignitary with his military aide-de-camp was coming down the office steps. I braked hard and we started to aquaplane, then the tyres suddenly bit into the gravel and we came to a shuddering halt. The cycles fell off the landrover with a terrible clatter and worse still, the body of the deceased shot off the roof-rack, where it seemed to bounce off the bonnet. For only a moment or two, the body stood erect, with both feet on the gravel and then slowly it toppled over onto the ground. I think I must have been in a state of shock, but Charlie seized the initiative, jumping out of the landrover as the alarmed dignitaries approached and standing in front of our man from Katanga, he bowed in the traditional manner and said, 'Bwana I know you are a most powerful leader when even the dead stand up to greet you.' The man from Katanga was none other than President Moise Tsombe, who was probably the best-dressed person I ever met. He was wearing a magnificent charcoal pinstripe suit, a blinding white shirt set off with gold cufflinks, each centred with a shining diamond. President Tsombe couldn't stop himself from laughing and there and then he asked Charlie to accompany him and his head of security on the next phase of the journey. I was relegated to the subservient role of the driver, which seemed to please the President enormously.

The body was placed on a stretcher and the old lady ushered into the main building, with the bicycles. Sergeant Mumba and the others were delegated to handle the paperwork while we were away, although we promised to return as soon as we could. The original driver from Chingola seemed only too pleased to take over the landrover for the next sector of the journey and once the luggage had been transferred, we set off for Kitwe. It was obvious President Tsombe liked Northern Rhodesia, especially as his wife had been born there and was the daughter of a respected tribal chief. In the course of the journey, Charlie told him he was getting married and Tsombe asked him if he had a new suit. Charlie intimated that a new suit was far too expensive, but Tsombe said he would send him a bolt of best quality cloth, with the proviso that he wanted to receive a photograph of Charlie wearing the suit.

It seemed no time at all before we arrived at the next scheduled stop and President Tsombe and his security chief were transferred to the waiting transport. A week or so later, we received a telephone call from the customs post near Bancroft, telling us a parcel had been delivered, on behalf of their President, and needed to be collected straight away. Within an hour or two Charlie was holding his precious bolt of cloth, which had been produced in a silver grey colour. It also had a lovely delicate sheen to it and a week later Charlie appeared wearing the suit and I was badgered into taking a series of coloured photos of him, to be sent off post-haste to President Tsombe, in Katanga.

Late evening, and I was sitting on the stoep at home when I looked up and saw Charlie and a tall man standing in the roadway just outside our apartment. I waved them in, and I soon saw Charlie had the Katanga head of security in tow. I welcomed the major who informed me he had now been promoted to the rank of colonel since last we met. We had a cold beer to celebrate his promotion and the colonel informed us that he had been making certain inquiries in the township and had located the whereabouts of a well-known recidivist, wanted in Katanga for a wide range of crimes including the sale of rhinoceros horn for medical purposes, and he wanted to ship him back to Katanga for trial. He added that there were no political motives involved and he confirmed that he also knew we had been looking for a major criminal who had escaped over the border and he was now proposing a swap. It was certainly true we urgently wanted to get our hands on Filipo N'nyenya but he had proved to be very elusive. I realised I was moving into very difficult territory and I told the Colonel we would have to obtain permission from our Commanding Officer before anything could be agreed.

Next morning, we were all engaged in a lengthy conference with Brian and Jack Gowland, then Special Branch became involved until eventually an agreement was reached. The team would pick up the Katangese recidivist who obviously did not have a permit and had entered the country illegally. We would hold him until we had his written agreement that he wanted to return to Katanga, after which we could deport him. Charlie acted as our go-between with the colonel who identified the man, who was living among some of the refugees in the township. The wanted man seemed only too willing to return home and I always had a nagging doubt about the validity of his confirmation but then I urgently wanted Filipo. Charlie made arrangements for the swap to take place at midnight, on a wooden bridge spanning the two country borders and at the appointed time, we arrived at the bridge and backed the landrover into position. The Katangese contingent was already there waiting and the exchange duly completed in the middle of the bridge. Filipo seemed strangely happy to be back amongst his friends and over the course of the next few days, he pleaded guilty to a whole ream of burglaries and house-breaking cases.

Several months later, and I had just been promoted to the rank of Detective Inspector and transferred back to Chingola District HQ, when at home, late one evening, I heard a voice calling from outside. Alex started to growl and stood by the door with hackles raised and I switched on the outside light. A somewhat hesitant Charlie stood there with our colonel from Katanga, although the colonel was dressed up to look like an impoverished African. Charlie had also been transferred with me and was an indispensable part of the new unit. We sat outside on the veranda with a cold beer, as our man from Katanga told us he had now been made a brigadier and was dealing with a very serious case that could affect all of us in Northern Rhodesia.

His story took some time in the telling but essentially it seemed a group of criminals had raided the old Belgian military airbase at Kamina, in the Congo, and hijacked a heavy machine gun and cannon from an aircraft, with an armoured protective canopy that could be manoeuvred, raised and lowered at will. They then bolted this contraption onto a massive low-loader, covering it with more armour plating and then proceeded to attack various banks and financial institutions throughout the Congo. The modus operandi was simple, in that they would drive up to a selected bank, usually around midnight, aim the cannon at the front doors and then blow the building to pieces. Once they had collected any money or gold, they would escape in the transporter, firing heavy machine-gun bullets at anyone rash enough to chase them. The Brigadier confirmed that certain members of the gang had already visited Chingola and had selected a bank situated on the edge of the town's public gardens. He had no idea as to which route the criminals intended to take once they left Katanga, but he did know the chosen date of the bank raid, which was the next Saturday, after 11pm, when it was thought the inhabitants of the town would be all fast asleep in their beds.

The next day, I talked the whole affair over with Jack Gowland, who in turn referred the substance of the idea to senior officers. It was thought that the information was very circumstantial and yet they ought to be ready, just in case. It was considered a judicious move to have the mobile unit on standby as an insurance policy. As I had been instrumental in providing the information, I was designated as the chief officer on the ground and was authorised to stake out the scene on the forthcoming Saturday evening, using my fully armed unit, backed up by a small detachment of armed riot police. Apart from my .38 revolver, I was issued with a Sterling sub-machine gun and of course, Charlie bagged his favourite shotgun.

Saturday evening and we all assembled at the station and went over in precise detail where everyone was going to be placed and what was expected of them, should the Katangese criminals appear. Then we set off and at the selected spot, everyone took up their allotted positions, concealing themselves behind bushes and hedges. Even Charlie climbed up into the branches of a tall, leafy tree that provided a long-distance view over the approach road. Our vehicles were carefully hidden and camouflaged and we left two of our constables to operate the muted force radio. Then we hunkered down for the next few hours. In an effort to install a measure of calm, one of the riot police sergeants moved quietly from bush to bush to encourage the constables in their lonely vigil.

11pm came and not a sign, then 11.30 and still nothing and gradually the idea began to permeate through the ranks that perhaps this was a false alarm. Midnight and still nothing and after some discussion, we agreed we would hang on for another hour before returning to base. Thirty minutes later, Detective Francis Mkwanda suddenly appeared at my elbow having been sent by Charlie who was still in the upper branches, to tell me he could see vehicle lights heading our way. The tension was almost unbearable when a few minutes later, the headlights of a vehicle swung into the bank's car park. We waited with bated breath, our sweating hands, tightly gripping our weapons. We heard doors open and close and then a weird sort of click-clacking sound of footsteps coming around the side of the building towards our own positions. Suddenly, moonlight broke through and we could see a woman in a long white dress, carrying a basket and a blanket which she proceeded to lay out on the grass. Within minutes she was joined by a male companion and the two of them stretched out and began to engage in an energetic sexual ritual. My reverie was soon disrupted by Francis who appeared at my shoulder and whispered that Charlie wanted to know if this was what the Whities called the missionary position! I waved him away for fear of laughing but he returned only seconds later with the comment that Charlie also wanted to know if all the Whities made love like that!

By now the couple were enjoying a cigarette before rolling up the blanket and click-clacking their way back to their car, providing us with the opportunity to rescue a very shell-shocked young constable from his precarious position from the bush nearest the couple. Mid-morning the next day and the Brigadier appeared with Charlie, to tell me the gang had finally been captured in Katanga the night before and neutralised, although he did not elaborate as to their fate. As an aside, the brigadier told me that Charlie's bolt of cloth had been given to President Tsombe by the CIA and the material contained a very thin sliver of a special material, looking rather like lace, that would reduce the devastating fragmentation effects from a bomb blast or from shattered glass. Charlie and the Brigadier then went happily on their way; however, and I was never to see the brigadier again.

Chapter 13

Hunters and Charcoal Burners

Gradually, though, our detection rate began to improve once again with Charlie leading the way. I was spending a great deal of my time in court, giving evidence in a wide range of complicated cases, and Charlie was particularly concerned that poor old Alex the Doberman would be left at home on his own, so he very kindly offered to take him out for a walk at various times during the day, albeit generally in the late afternoons. I was never sure how he managed to take Alex out and still solve such a high proportion of the cases he was investigating, but anyway he certainly succeeded in his work and I could not ignore the fact our detection rate was once again reaching epic proportions. It was also amazing to see most of those arrested by Charlie seemed very happy and relieved to plead guilty in court. On one day alone, Charlie had something like seven defendants due to appear before Keith Pollock, the resident magistrate, and because I wanted to show solidarity and to encourage the team, I decided I would also attend the court proceedings. The cases were wide ranging and it was certainly a very impressive performance as defendant after defendant stepped forward to plead guilty. The last defendant was a local man called Cosmos, who we always suspected of being a habitual criminal but had never been able to prove his guilt, yet here he was willing to plead guilty. In answer to the indictment and the Magistrate's demand, 'How do you plead, guilty or not guilty?' the answer was surprising, 'Bwana, I am guilty because the dog told me I was.'

Mr Pollock's repost was immediate. 'I will not have any police officer referred to in such derogatory terms in my court and if I had my way, I would sentence you to more time in prison than is presently allowed.' After that, he proceeded to congratulate Charlie for successfully investigating so many cases and the court was then adjourned.

On the way back to the station I was lost in thought because I felt something did not seem quite right- but what was not right? After lunch,

I sat in our garden under the shade of a Frangipani tree, with its delicate wax-like flowers, as I tried to scrutinize the reasons for my doubts. Before I could reach a decision, Charlie arrived to take Alex out once again and I was due back in court to give further evidence, however during the afternoon session, the case proceeded apace but suddenly came to a grinding halt on a matter of legal interpretation and so once again the case was adjourned for the remainder of the day. I returned early to the station and I could see our administrator, Constable Alan Phiri, seemed a little uneasy at my arrival. I didn't have much time to consider this aspect, because almost immediately, barking broke out next door only to be followed by a loud cry that soon turned into a low moan. Somewhat startled, I rushed into the CID team office only to be confronted by an amazing series of images and even today, the impact is still as clear and vivid as it was then all those years ago.

There was a poorly dressed man, who had collapsed on the floor with Charlie standing alongside him but the most impressive sight by far, was that of an alert Alex, sitting on an antelope skin that had been placed on the floor and surrounded by all the witchcraft symbols and impedimenta that we had collected through our investigations over the years. It transpired that Charlie had the thought that most of our criminal acquaintances must have carried out more criminal acts than they would readily admit to in normal circumstances and if he could trade on the rumours which suggested Alex was a witchdoctor, then this power could be translated into numerous admissions of guilt. To make the idea more plausible, he had visited Emmanuel our friendly witchdoctor and purloined a whole box full of witchcraft items guaranteed to frighten anyone out of his wits.

In addition, Charlie knew, as did the team, about some of Alex's various party tricks, especially the one where if you bent down and quietly growled in Alex's ear he would start barking. Charlie's ingenious plan was to work in conjunction with Detective Constable Monga. They would bring a suspect to the station and keep him waiting in the charge office while they prepared Alex for the meeting. Then, when all was ready, they would bring the poor unfortunate in and make him sit on the floor, just a little way from Alex. Charlie would tell the man he felt sure he was a thief who had committed many crimes but there was no need to deny this as the dog who was really a witchdoctor who had transformed himself into a dog to smell out the evildoers in Chiwempala would soon confirm if he was innocent or not. If the man was innocent, the dog would simply lie down and go to sleep but if he was guilty the dog would speak up and tell him.

Charlie would then kneel down in front of Alex and then bowing down before him, he would call on the Great Witchdoctor Dog to speak out if the man was guilty or to lie down if he was innocent. As Charlie bowed down for the third time, he would utter a very low growl and right on cue, Alex would start barking. Usually within seconds, the unfortunate suspect would start confessing to various crimes and of course, many of them had never been reported. Monga would cycle to the victim's hut or shop, returning later to report a criminal act and the fact a certain person had been arrested. Although the prospect of so many cases being reported and then solved had many pleasing aspects it could not go on and reluctantly, I had to curtail this particular arrangement. The team took it all in good part, mainly because we had recouped our position at the top of the Divisional detection leader-board.

One morning the team entered my office, with Charlie announcing in a loud voice, 'Bwana, we are not happy at all again.'

'OK, so what's the problem this time?'

'Well it is difficult for us all because we work so very hard but once again, we have too much month left at the end of our money!' Mumba picked up the argument by saying, 'Bwana, it is true because at this time we have no money to buy enough meat to even feed our starving children.'

I thought about it for some time and then answered them by suggesting that perhaps, we should all take some time out to go hunting once again and then hold one of our big parties one evening for all the team and their families. Suddenly the smiles returned and animated discussions started to erupt as everyone wanted to have their say and of course, all at the same time. I talked it over with Brian Thomas; always a stickler for the rules, he pointed out we could not use force transport purely for personal pleasure. The team took this dictate fairly well and Monga, always full of bright ideas, suggested that maybe we could sort out some of the illegal trespassers, hunters and charcoal burners on the edge of the Nchanga Aero Club, after which, we could then go hunting for rabbits providing Alex the Doberman could come along to help us.

Brian approved the plan with the proviso that I should be in my working uniform so that police authority would be visible at all times. We made an exuberant, early start the next morning and at 8am I was standing alongside the chief flying instructor at the aero-club, who I knew well from the few times he had flown me out over the bush on search and rescue missions for lost or stranded hunters. First of all, he welcomed our idea, as the area was under severe threat from both charcoal burners and illegal hunters and their removal would be much appreciated. The club runways and land were also overrun with rabbits but this was a very busy time for the club with many incoming and departing private aircraft so firearms could not be used. I saw this as a terrible blow but the team were not at all disheartened. Monga expounded his theory that we could take the doors off the landrover, as usual, and chase the rabbits until they became exhausted and then he would lean out of the truck and wallop them on the back of the head, with a long-baton. So be it, but first we had to deal with the 'illegals'.

The charcoal burners came first, primarily because we could see the curling wisps of smoke on the far side of the airport and as we were downwind, we could easily detect the cloying smell of baking charcoal. We caught them all by surprise, but they soon rallied and took to their heels down an open long grass avenue between the tall trees and dense bushes on either side. The team took off after them at a fast pace, and I was just about to follow when Sergeant Mumba signalled me to stop and to follow him with Alex. It was more of a gentle stroll than anything else and lacking in any form of urgency until we reached the end of the pathway. I had seen the fleeing charcoal burners turn to the right just before they disappeared from view, but Mumba took the left side and stood looking down a slight incline. He stood there with hands on his hips and shouted out 'We are the police, you can come out now or I will send the dog in to find you and he has big crocodile teeth.'

There was no response to this overture, so he repeated it again and suddenly the grass seemed to move and gradually two forms appeared, who it turned out were the ring-leaders. The team returned, having caught up with their quarries and we soon had them all manacled together by the side of the landrover, with a wealth of spears, clubs, axes and machetes. As the ringleaders said, 'Why us, when the illegal hunters are everywhere?' Then they quite cheerfully directed us towards the hunter's hidden encampment, although we left Mubonda and the sergeant to guard our prisoners and take their statements.

MURDER, WITCHCRAFT AND THE KILLING OF WILDLIFE

We caught the sleeping hunters completely unaware and snoring away after a long night's hunting and later, some serious beer drinking. There were some five or six of them plus a few women and they gave in quietly and without any fuss except for one who took off with some alacrity carrying an ancient rifle and as I was nearest to him I gave chase. In the beginning, he was fleet of foot and outpaced me, but my endurance was greater and gradually I began to gain on him. Almost as a last gasp effort to get away, he burst through some of the dense undergrowth and I went in after him. All I can recall is a deafening explosion, the shredding of leaves and branches and my bush hat being ripped from my head and then before I knew it, I was wrestling the man to the ground. I finally overwhelmed the man who I later came to know as Mutembo Musebo, arrested him and took possession of his ancient rifle as an exhibit. This meant we now had many more prisoners and a much greater quantity of evil-looking weapons, leading everyone to pitch in with the cataloguing as we wanted to move on as quickly as we could to the main event – hunting for rabbits.

Midway through the exercise, we heard the drone of aircraft engines and within minutes, a twin-engine aeroplane, sporting RAF roundels, landed and taxied to a halt not too far away from us. At the same time, a large black Cadillac-style car with darkened windows drove up and parked alongside. The doors of the aircraft opened and steps were gently lowered so that a very imposing gentleman could descend and get into the car, which then drove off at speed. A short time later, a uniformed air-force officer, who I took to be the pilot, ambled over to us and started to inspect our motley collection of prisoners. We must have presented a starling image with the filthy prisoners shackled together, a vast collection of weapons which now included several firearms and of course by now the doors had been taken off the landrover and were lying on the grass verge and although I was not aware of it at that moment, I had blood coursing down my forehead, where I had been creased by a nail as part of a motley concoction fired from Mutembo's rifle.

Once he had taken in the scene, the RAF officer said, 'How did you know we were coming as it has been a very closely guarded secret up to this point in time?'

It didn't take a genius to know they were on a secret mission of some sort, which involved the mine senior management, so I merely said, 'I didn't know anything about it as I was just instructed to arrive here and make the area safe.'

As it turned out, this secret visit had been undertaken by an official from the British Colonial Office to hold private talks with the mine management to cover the eventual independence of the country and the proposed move towards total African rule. Once the pilot returned to his aircraft, I notified the operations room, who in turn notified our chain-of-command. Shortly afterwards the civilian official returned and the aircraft became airborne, allowing us to finally get on with our long overdue hunting expedition.

I took Monga, Busike and Charlie and left Mumba and Mubonda still taking statements from the chained prisoners. With the vehicle doors having been removed, the idea was for me to drive out the rabbits from the long grass onto the shorter cut verge where we could wear them down to the point Monga would hang out from the passenger side with his long-baton and dispatch them quickly with a well-placed, solid blow. In practice, we nearly lost Monga several times, who leant too far out, but more importantly each time he aimed a blow at a rabbit the animal immediately veered off to the left causing Monga to flounder. It was a complete disaster, emphasised by Alex, who barked continuously throughout the exercise to show his absolute frustration at our futile efforts. Half an hour into the hunt and no rabbits and I was becoming anxious to ensure the prisoners could be safely delivered to the prison. We held a council of war, where Charlie suggested we should continue along the same lines but instead of hitting the rabbit on the head, we should let Alex loose to finish the job off for us as he had done previously with excellent results.

So the occupants of the front seats were me, as the driver, then Charlie who was holding a tight rein on Alex, who in turn was sitting in the passenger seat. It worked like a dream, because it was easy to flush out the rabbits from the long grass, then a brief chase along the verge until at a perfectly judged moment, an exhilarated Alex was released to dive out of the landrover. A few short bounds from Alex and a rabbit was tossed high into the air only to fall back to earth stone dead.

As the morning drew to a close, we had an exhausted but happy Alex and some fourteen rabbits. We called up a troop carrier to take our prisoners off to the local gaol and then we returned back to the station where the rabbits were taken off to be skinned and dressed by the team, who shortly afterwards put them into cold storage at a local store. After lunch, we all assembled back in the office to plan the party stage. Sitali and Phiri were given the jobs of providing and placing tables and chairs. The sergeant would be in charge of sourcing cooking pots and Mubonda was given the task of making sure we had enough firewood. Busike and Monga would organise the African mowa (maize beer) and Charlie would scout the area and select the best place to hold the party just on the edge of the parade ground. Then we came, somewhat hesitantly I thought, to my job or jobs.

It was assumed that I would provide all the rice and the saffron which was required to make the rice turn a delicious golden-yellow. I was also deputised to provide an abundance of curry powder to give the rabbit stew a bit of a kick and it would be appreciated if I could provide a number of potatoes, carrots and onions to make it all go a little further. Then it was also to be my duty to provide a sufficiency of cold Castle beer in bottles, to be drunk only by the team members. Finally, could I ensure Willy would attend and cook for everyone, even though they realised it would take up most of the day? It was also deemed a good idea for all their wives and families to attend and then, of course, they also wanted to invite the Officer-in-Charge, Brian Thomas. Phiri had already written out an invitation card in his immaculate handwriting and I was allocated the task of delivering it personally. Later in the afternoon, I handed Brian his invitation and he sat at his desk looking down at it for quite some time and when he finally looked up at me, I could see his eyes had watered and he told me this invitation was one of the most precious things that he had ever received during the whole of the time he had spent in Africa.

Once Willy knew he, Serafina and his son Joseph were invited to the party and there would be free food and beer he was more than happy to do the cooking. All the wives were out scavenging for wood and I paid out to have all the ingredients for the meal delivered, including the extremely large quantities of beer, although Monga had negotiated a good rate for me with one of the local Indian stores, on a sale-or-return basis. We duly assembled at 6pm and the cooking pots seemed enormous and were bubbling away and giving off a wonderful smell. The seating had been arranged rather like a dancer's fan, with Brian Thomas and me being given pride of place at a small square table covered by a cloth with bowls, knives forks and glasses. Chairs were arranged in a semi-circle, for each member of the team and behind each chair, the wives and children sat just to the rear of their particular husband. The one incongruous item I noticed though, was a stretcher which had been carefully laid out behind Mubonda's chair.

Everyone stood to attention when Brian came along and he was warmly welcomed by Sergeant Mumba. Brian said he was proud to have been invited and he would stay only for a drink, but it was a CID party and he wanted them all to enjoy it. Monga acted as a barman for the evening and soon we all had a cold Castle to drink although the families were given nothing and just sat there on the ground in mute anticipation. After finishing his beer, Brian left and then the curried rabbit stew was served and I have to say it tasted utterly wonderful. I think this must have been one of our happiest of moments in Africa, as night had fallen and the flames from the fire shone out on so many animated, and happy smiling faces. Once the team had eaten their fill, it then became the turn of the wives and children who went at it with great gusto and much shouting. As fast as their pots were emptied Willy seemed to be refilling them up again and again until the point was reached when everyone had eaten all they could manage. At this juncture, each family produced some of their own large cooking pots and Mumba took charge of the fair distribution of any of the leftover food for each family and when that had been completed, we all got down to the serious matter of drinking the rest of the beer.

In the early hours of the morning, I could see there would be nothing left to return to the Indian store, but I was consoled by the fact we had enjoyed a marvellous evening. I think Mubonda summed it up that night when he finally managed to stagger to his feet, and swaying from side to side, said he would always remember these times and when he was very old, he would sit around the village fires and regale the elders with this tale. Then he drew himself up to his full height – which wasn't much, came to attention and saluted. Then he looked at me and said, 'I think Queenie 'Lizabeth is a very excellent Queenie,' and with those final words he toppled over and lay prone on the grass, while still in a salute mode. With one big whoop, his whole family descended on him and placed him gently on the stretcher before carrying him off home. There were to be quite a few times at Chiwempala police station when there was too much month left at the end of their money, but I think this one was the best one of all, where we were all strengthened and united by true bonds of service, loyalty and friendship.

Mutembo Musebo duly appeared in Court to answer a number of charges related to firearm offences and illegal hunting and he was given a fairly long custodial sentence. In answer to his question of, 'Who will now feed my starving family?' the magistrate replied, 'You should have thought about that before you committed all these serious offences.' I took charge of his ancient firearm because I had seen an armourer's mark on the barrel and I wanted time to try and trace its origins. I wrote down all the details and information I could gather and sent it off to Force Headquarters. After several weeks, I received a reply from a British Regimental Museum in the United Kingdom that had identified the rifle and traced the name of the sergeant armourer who had last worked on the gun in 1897 in South Africa. That in itself was amazing, but the real question was how had this gun, still in some form of working order made the several thousand-mile journeys from South Africa to Northern Rhodesia.

I think Busike had great respect for Mutembo, who he thought was a special spirit who inhabited the vast bush country of Africa and as such he had kept in touch with him, giving me updates as time went by. Busike felt that such a free spirit should not be locked away as it could destroy him but what could I do? Then one day, the daughter of a business contractor from Chingola reported that her father had gone hunting several days before but had not returned and she felt greatly worried for his safety. The problem was, she had no idea in which area he had gone hunting. A brief search of the bush around Chingola had revealed nothing, so the matter was passed on to us to follow up. The daughter gave us several favourite haunts her father used and the fact he was driving a bright yellow pick- up truck. Operations told me a police flight from Kitwe was visiting Chingola and perhaps we could use it in the search. Brian obtained the necessary permissions and soon I was sitting in a police Auster single-engine aircraft with a large-scale map on my knee, as we travelled along major roads and railway lines in ever-widening search patterns.

In time we flew along the main dirt road from Chingola to Solwezi, a route I knew well. We crisscrossed the area in well-established search patterns and even overflew a large herd of elephants on their annual journey towards Solwezi. We noticed there were some track signs of vehicles having been driven through the bush, but there was no sign whatsoever of the yellow pick-up truck. We were coming to the end of this flight as we needed to return to Nchanga to refuel when the pilot said he thought he had just seen something glinting in the sunlight. Because the hunter may have decided to go out on foot, he would normally have parked his vehicle under a large tree to avoid the boiling sun, but this would make it difficult to spot from the air, so we dropped down to tree-top height. I have to say that this white-knuckle procedure is not one that I would recommend to anyone, but on the last pass, we saw the yellow truck. I marked it on the map and we headed off back to the airport, I radioed in and asked the operations room to contact the team and book the hunter Mutembo Musebo out of the local prison and then meet me at the Nchanga Aero Club.

We had only just landed when Busike and the team arrived with Mutembo in tow, and in answer to the question whether he would help us he said, 'I am dying in that awful prison, and because this missing man is also a hunter of animals I will help.'

We drove on out onto the main Solwezi dirt road and at the point I had marked on the map, we left the roadway and took off into the bush. Shortly before we reached the point where the yellow truck should have been, Mutembo asked us to stop. He told us all to stand back and not trample any signs into the dirt and off he set, although I confess I was more concerned he would make a run for it and escape, but Busike told me once a hunter gave his word of honour, he would always fulfil his promise. After some time, Mutembo came back looking very dejected. He told me he had found the hunter's tracks but the man was stumbling and was not well and besides that, he had obviously tried to return to his vehicle but had failed to see it even though he was so very near. He indicated the man's progress and we set off together walking just behind Mutembo, who from time to time signalled where he thought the man had staggered off to the side whilst looking for his truck. After nearly an hour or so, we came towards a large tree in the centre of the grassland and we could now see a still figure lying underneath the branches and down amongst the very roots of the tree. It was our missing hunter, who failed to rouse himself at our shouting until, as we drew near, we saw he was dead and must have been so for quite some time.

I went back for the landrover and we carefully wrapped up the body in a tarpaulin and placed it on the roof rack. Mutembo had stood by quietly all this time, saying nothing but just looking on when he approached me and said, 'If the hunter died because he had no water it is very sad because water is here.' He pointed down on the ground but all I could see was what looked like a large dark leaved plant and without a word he took one of the metal tools from the landrover and started digging all around the plant. About 12 inches down he came across the large bulb of the plant which he said contained water. He dug it out, cut it open and started to drink the liquid and after a while, he passed it on for me to try. The taste was absolutely disgusting, but Mutembo just laughed and said at least I was alive and would stay alive if I was ever lost. The autopsy, however, proved that the hunter had a weak heart and had failed to take his medication with him and probably through hysteria and panic at losing his way had suffered a major cardiac arrest. Following this episode, Busike pressurised me into taking action on Mutembo's behalf and at the inquest, I explained to the magistrate, Mr Pollock what Mutembo had done to help us and he promised to make certain recommendations on his behalf.

Within weeks, Mutembo was free. I returned his rifle after he turned down an offer to sell it to the military museum, He told us he was leaving this place and he would never again come near the large towns of the whites and the blacks ever again. He was not greedy and he only killed enough meat for his family to live. He would now take his family to reside with the free spirits of the animals in the far off country until he would finally return to the earth from whence he came. In the intervening years, I have often thought about Mutembo and hoped he eventually found the spiritual peace he was so desperately searching for.

The next day, during one of our regular briefings, Monga and Busike mentioned that they had information that a well-known criminal recently released from prison in Ndola, had been seen in the township on weekends, which coincided with a number of high profile burglaries where expensive clothes and money had been stolen. Their informants had told them the man, Aubrey Sichoni, was living quite some way away in a village with other thieves and the place was difficult to penetrate as everyone there was suspicious of strangers. I had been listening intently to their story and I mooted the idea that perhaps two domestic merchants, selling a wide range of household goods, would not create any suspicion and as such could get right in amongst the villagers. Monga had missed the point completely when he asked where would we find two merchants, and anyway, they would not have the courage or the authority to make an arrest.

I agreed but qualified it by saying the two executives I had in mind were called Monga and Busike! I went on to say perhaps our local Jewish shopkeeper would provide us with some items at cost price and on a sale or return basis once again and if we purloined some cycles from lost property, the two of them would be able to go undercover and track down our burglar. There were murmurs of agreement from the team and Monga said he only had one question, which was could they keep any profit they made? Our friendly shopkeeper came up with a good package of basic goods, Brian dibbed up the cash for the bus tickets and Sekondwe found two reasonable cycles from the lost property section, which he proceeded to recondition. The lost property section also came up with two large suitcases, and by the next evening, our two stalwarts were ready to leave.

We took them as near to the coach station as we dared and later Constable Sitali, who had stayed nearby, confirmed all their gear had been stowed away onboard and the bus had left on time. We heard nothing for several days and I was just about thinking of going out to look for them when I received a telephone call from one of the South African farmers who owned a farm way out in the bush country. It wasn't just the farmer's accent that was difficult to understand but the fact that he couldn't stop laughing. He told me in between fits of laughter that a little while ago, two really scruffy individuals had arrived at his farm, pulling along an African who had been handcuffed to one of their cycles. They announced with great aplomb, that they were not really merchants at all but police officers and that they had arrested a burglar that Bwana Matthews wanted to get his hands on.

When I confirmed the story, the farmer said, 'OK, man, now look we are coming into Chingola in a few minutes to pick up supplies so we will bring this bunch in with us, but it is going to cost you a few beers at Bert Gaffney's Nchanga Hotel.'

In the final telling, Monga and Busike had been able to make some good sales and had gained entry into the heart of the village. They found the hut belonging to Aubrey Sichoni and late one night they raided it, where they found Aubrey and some of his stolen loot whereupon they arrested him and then high-tailed it out of the village as fast as they could go, taking Aubrey with them. In the final analysis, they were allowed to keep their profit after the shopkeeper had been reimbursed but they kindly bought beers for the whole team out of the proceeds and life returned to some form of normality once again.

Chapter 14

To Kill a Witch

All the same, there was still an important job of work to be done and daylight was still a long way off when I quietly slipped from under the cotton bed-sheet and made my way to the bathroom. It was going to be another hectic day and I needed to be in the office early to make sure every one of our case notes was all up-to-date and ready for inspection. I was in the midst of shaving when the telephone rang. A sleepy-eyed wife appeared around the side of the bathroom door to wearily announce Charlie had telephoned, yet once again to say a body had been found, and then she added, 'I can't understand why he still asks if you are in the shower, as this joke is beginning to wear a little thin.'

As always, the team was ready to move out when I arrived, leaving Mubonda and Sitali to cope with an influx of work while we were away. When we arrived at the scene in the half-light, we knew straight away from our previous experiences that this was going to be a very difficult situation because the gathering crowd was standing in a wide semi-circle although well away from the epicentre. In many ways, this was a good thing because it had preserved and protected the murder site. One of our constables had already taken control and cleared a pathway through the sullen crowd and a quick examination of the area revealed the true extent of the horror and carnage. Patches of daylight slowly moved across the open land, enabling us to see a body stretched out on the edge of a storm drain, with legs dangling over the side. These storm drains were designed to carry the heavy monsoon rains and flash floods away from the township, and they were very wide and deep in order to cope with vast quantities of rainwater.

We walked gingerly around the concrete edge of the storm drain and the ghastly scene facing us was the most gruesome I had witnessed during my time in Africa and my goodness me, I have seen some! Halfway along the ditch towards the inert body, the team became wild-eyed and tense until eventually Charlie called a halt and expostulated that we were in the presence of great evil and surely faced the prospect of demoniacal witchcraft. As he put it, 'Bwana, we are mostly afraid but if you really want, we will go with you because we know you will protect your boys with your strong medicine.' There was blood everywhere and I saw what looked like several lengths of human intestines arranged in ritual displays on either side of the body. Sympathising with their fears, I sent them back to form a line and start a minute ground search from the edge of the crowd, then working inwards towards the body.

I could see that the body was that of an old woman and I photographed the gruesome aspect including the displayed intestines. I was just in the process of examining the blood-soaked ditch, when the body suddenly sat straight up, right in front of me, bloodstained eyes opened, followed by the eruption of a low moan. At the same time, the watching crowd panicked at the horrendous sight taking place, and took to their heels, running off pell-mell in every direction, screaming out in terror that once again that the white policeman was speaking with the spirit of the dead.

The team reacted well and Monga quickly retrieved a blanket from the landrover, hurried over, and handed it to me, although making sure he didn't venture too close to the victim. I clambered out of the ditch, wrapped the blanket around the nearly naked body and gently lowered the woman back onto the ground. We had previously made a request by radio for an ambulance to take a body away, but now the poor driver was faced instead with having to transport a living soul to the hospital. I took time out to report in by radio, and the Ops Room, in turn, notified the hospital to be ready to receive what I had termed a mortally injured patient.

Busike accompanied the victim, under instructions to record anything the woman might say, and the rest of us started to collect and log some of the exceptionally gruesome forensic evidence. Apart from the intestines, there was a long blood-stained stick with a forked end, where a blood-soaked piece of cloth had been fastened around the two prongs. At the same time, there were various leaves and grasses intertwined and adhering to the cloth. The search continued and revealed assorted items of clothing and a few torn and blood-stained papers listing several names and part of an address. All the body parts were placed in our scene of crime containers to be taken to the hospital, mainly to preserve them in their cold storage facility, but also to have them ready for detailed forensic examination later on.

Minutes later, I was called to the hospital and Charlie accompanied me. The unfortunate victim had already been taken to the operating theatre but Dr Caiger told me, 'This was such a despicable and horrendous attack, we can really do nothing more for the poor woman, and it is only going to be a question of time before she dies.' One of the torn pieces of paper contained a hut number and while Busike waited for the woman to regain consciousness if she ever would, Charlie and I went off to investigate. We found a group of people sitting on the ground outside the hut and they told us they were the family of the occupier, Nkwanda Chumbu, who had gone to the beer-hall the previous evening but had not yet returned. A younger woman came forward and identified herself as Musa Lungu, the daughter, and I explained what had happened. She readily agreed to come with us to the hospital, although I noted she did not seem overly concerned or surprised at the news. Before leaving, I radioed in for another team to be sent to the house to secure it and to keep all the people secured as witnesses.

The police landrover duly arrived with Mubonda, and Phiri and they got down to work straight away, leaving us to return to the hospital. Busike had remained sitting at the bedside but confirmed the woman had not regained consciousness. Musa Lungu looked intently at the woman's face and identified her as her mother. Musa told us that she and all the family had gone to the beer-hall the previous evening but after some time, Nkwanda had ambled off to talk to other people and the party left a little later to return home without her. They were not unduly concerned when she failed to arrive home, because she was well known to carry on like this and often stayed away for several days at a time. Dr Caiger had organised some food for Busike as we waited for Nkwanda to regain consciousness and gradually she began to stir, slowly moving her head and taking her time to look carefully at each of us in turn and then she closed her eyes again.

Busike knew her tribe and asked in her own language who had done this evil thing to her, the eyes flickered and a hoarse but strong voice uttered the words, 'Musa knows all about these things.' Dr Caiger had already told me he didn't know why Nkwanda was still alive but she did not have much longer to live and ideally I wanted to take a statement called a dying deposition, regarded by the courts as being sacrosanct evidence. With a little prompting from Busike and in answer to the same question, all Nkwanda would say once again was, 'Musa knows who has done this thing to me,' then the eyes closed and she drifted off into a coma. Nkwanda held on to life until the late evening when she finally slipped away from the painful bonds of earth, but without saying anything else. I spoke with Jack Gowland and we agreed we should do nothing more until we had conducted a post-mortem, which was scheduled for early the next day. Meanwhile, back at Nkwanda's house, Mubonda had searched the property and found some washed clothes in a bucket that looked to hold faint traces of blood which he bagged up and logged as exhibits.

In the meantime, rumour and counter-rumour spread through the town, emphasising two main issues, one being I had yet again displayed an ability to speak with the dead spirits, and the other more disturbing message to the effect that Nkwanda was a well-known evil witch and her death had been brought about by a rival sorcerer, seeking to usurp her place. Early the next morning, the team collected all members of the family who had been at the house, separated them into different and isolated areas in the police station quadrangle and started to interrogate them. Charlie and I took Nkwanda's daughter, Musa, to the mortuary where we met up again with Dr Caiger. At the outset, Musa officially identified her mother, then voluntarily gave a blood sample before being ushered out of the building into Charlie's care. The injuries suffered by Nkwanda were simply horrifying and Dr Caiger could not explain how she had been able to live for so long. The long stick with the forked end had been inserted into her living body, then the grass and leaves had been dislodged as the stick was twirled backwards and forwards until the intestines had been trapped, and gradually significant lengths were pulled out and left lying on the ground in ritualistic patterns. The pain brought about by this violent assault must have been harrowing and excruciating and I fervently hoped Nkwanda had passed out during this ferocious attack.

Later, it was found the washing discovered by Mubonda did contain blood stains and the blood analysis matched Nkwanda's but not Musa's blood group. One certainty though was the post-mortem, which seemed to confirm some of the rumours that this was a witchcraft murder. However, before long, Force Headquarters asked me to look urgently into the hypothesis this could have been a Mau Mau style murder, as witnessed some years before in Kenya, with the prospect of similar cases spreading throughout our territory. It seemed obvious that we had a number of frightening scenarios to contend with but very little real evidence to go on, especially as it was clear the witnesses were simply too terrified to speak.

In another part of our district, Emmanuel Muleya lived as a respected white witchdoctor, meaning that he specialised in a wide range of herbal remedies and had nothing to do with virulent spells or anything involving black magic. He had helped us previously in solving several witchcraft cases and we knew that he had been well educated, reaching standard six at school, with a good command of English. Before creating a herbalist practice, he had worked in an office in the industrial zone. However, Emmanuel, like most witchdoctors, lived far away from civilisation, where he could practice in peace and comparative safety. As he surveyed his rocky outcrop and the sunburnt grass, he was not a happy man, mainly because he had too many animals, including chickens and goats. His real problem was his clients generally paid for their treatments with livestock or produce, leaving him having to find sufficient land and food to keep the animals.

His daydreams were interrupted by the appearance of a man on a bicycle, labouring up the hill. After some time, he recognised Detective Constable 'Charlie' Nhliziyo from the nearby police station. Charlie greeted him and then went on to say he thought Emmanuel might be able to help the police in solving a very difficult witchcraft murder. Emmanuel was intrigued by the story and readily agreed to help. Nearly an hour later, he arrived at the police station with all his equipment and paraphernalia tied up on his rickety old bicycle and he was quickly shown into our office. I was pleased to see him once again and I carefully explained the case, adding that I had the idea that, if I could understand the tribal methods of killing, then I would have a much better idea who had actually perpetrated this crime. If Nkwanda had really been a witch, we were surely going to need someone extra special, whose spiritual power was far greater than the murderers, in order to break the impasse.

Emmanuel asked for the names of the witnesses and their tribes, besides specific details of the murder, after which he went outside into the quadrangle and laid out all his equipment on the ground. These items included a leopard skin, conch shells, slivers of dark coloured mirrors, part of an elephant tail, hunter's arrows, various red and black bead necklaces and finally, a small parcel of white bones. The family were gathered together in the quadrangle and made to sit on the ground in front of Emmanuel, who it has to be said appeared to relish this challenge. I had taken an instant liking to Emmanuel, who came across as an articulate person of real character, and I could see straight away that he was also a consummate actor, holding his audience in the palm of his hand and as I watched I could already see the family members were becoming increasingly agitated.

Emmanuel made a great play by putting the conch shells to his ear, then nodding his head from time to time as if agreeing with something he had heard. A little later, he threw several bones down onto the ground and looked closely at the pattern, then he lit incense sticks, wafting the spiralling smoke towards the family and finally, taking the elephant tail, he flailed it about him, before jumping high in the air and pointing it directly at Musa Lungu. The family were led away once more to be searched and for further statements to be taken. One of the family suspects was found to have several silver sewing needles inserted under his skin, designed to ward off evil spirits.

Emmanuel followed me back into the office, and I felt sure he already knew the facts of this murder before he had arrived at the police station but as he explained, 'I know Nkwanda Chumbu was a very bad witch, but she was getting too old and feeble and her main rival was her own daughter Musa, who wanted to take over, but her mother refused to leave her high place of office.' He believed Musa had called a meeting of all the family members who were themselves entirely involved in many aspects of evil witchcraft, and they had been ultimately summoned to attend on the day of the murder. Nkwanda would not be present at this meeting, where her murder would have been carefully planned. The killing would have to be carried out by Musa personally, aided by several family members, but it needed to be witnessed by the complete family. The family were all descended from a tribe established near the Congo border, who were well known for hunting elephants, and the murder of Nkwanda was a traditional ritual way to kill witches and the means of killing Nkwanda were also the same traditional methods used in the killing elephants where removing the animal's intestines was intended to release the evil spirits from the body so they would not return to haunt the killers. This was exactly the same sort of ritual I had witnessed several years before on the border with the Congo and in the same area when a wounded elephant has been killed.

Although we were relieved to be able to corroborate that there was no Mau Mau involvement, we were likewise well aware that the main evidence was purely circumstantial. Before progressing any further, it was thought advisable to seek prosecuting counsel's opinion, to see if we had enough evidence to arrest Musa Lungu and certain members of her family for the murder. In the meantime, we had to release Musa and her family on bail, with the warning they would be required to attend an inquest at a later date. Within a few days, we were notified that in spite of the case not being very strong, there was sufficient evidence to arrest Musa Lungu but not other members of the family who would be regarded as hostile witnesses. We decided Busike would make the arrest because he could speak and write in the suspect's tribal language, although making an arrest was easier said than done.

Apart from Busike, there was Charlie, Monga, Sergeant Mumba, and me, and I had brought Alex along to give him a good run out, although, on our arrival, we found Musa's house was deserted and locked. Frustrated, we began to trawl around the bars and shops but without result, at which point Sergeant Mumba expressed the one thought we had all been considering, which was perhaps that Musa had run away to hide in the bush country near her ancestral home. Even so, and just to make sure, we continued to make inquiries at the coach and railway stations although, again without result, and it was an investigation team in very low spirits that started the return journey to the police station.

Driving back, we saw several people walking along the side of the dirt road and suddenly we spotted Musa hurriedly striding out in front. We overtook her, stopping the landrover some thirty yards further along the road. Alex jumped down first and ambled over towards Musa stopping just in front of her, with the rest of us arriving only seconds later. The case may have been brought to a swift conclusion, but there was still one unexpected outcome because rumour spread throughout the township like wildfire to the effect that the government had once again hired the same paramount witchdoctor to turn himself into a large brown dog, to smell out evil witches in the township. Woman Assistant Inspector Betti Jones from Chingola Central Police Station conducted a detailed personal search of Musa and in doing so found several silver darning needles inserted under her skin, in a line across the shoulder blades. Emmanuel confirmed later that this had been done to keep the evil spirits at bay and once again, I could see a direct correlation between African witchcraft and European sorcery.

The next morning, Emmanuel sat on the large stone boulder, alongside his hut, where he thought yesterday had been quite an extraordinary day. Now though, he had more important things to worry about because, on his return home, he had found two of his valuable goats were missing, which meant a significant financial loss. Perhaps he should go and speak with the policemen back at the station and ask for help, because they seemed to be clever and intelligent people. It was strange, he mused that the one called Charlie was a Sezulu who, before the arrival of the British in olden days, would have been a tribal enemy waging war and yet here he was, contemplating going to see Charlie and beg for his help. Yes, that was exactly the right thing to do and without further hesitation, he wheeled his old cycle out and set off for the police station.

At the station, Charlie was very keen to help and Emmanuel soon found himself standing before Sergeant Mumba and explaining his pressing predicament. Once he had recounted the difficulties he faced with all the animals given to him in payment for his spells, everyone started to speak at once, ideas were floated and contrary advice bandied about but it all seemed such a tangled mess. Emmanuel was seriously disappointed, realising not a single workable idea had been put forward. Sergeant Mumba had said nothing but after a while, he raised his hand to silence the others saying, 'This is a very serious matter and we do not have enough knowledge to put you right but I think we should go and speak to our father about this.' Emmanuel couldn't understand why he would need to go and talk to Mumba's father and he said so. Mumba smiled broadly and said 'No! Not my real father but the mzungu next door who is our father on this station. He may be young, but he is much older than his years, and he will surely know all about these things.'

It was mid-morning and Willy had just brought in my coffee when I heard excited voices from next door. Phiri knew exactly what was required and he went off to see what was going on, returning a few moments later with a broad grin on his face to say the team would like to see me. Almost at the same time, the whole squad trudged in with Emmanuel Muleya in tow and I could see he was wearing his best clothes and as he crouched down, in a traditional sign of greeting, Sergeant Mumba outlined some of Emmanuel's concerns.

It was certainly an intriguing dialogue especially when Mumba finished his speech with the telling words, 'I have just told this man that you, my father, will find all the right answers for him.' Somewhat nonplussed, I asked a few personal questions about Emmanuel, his levels of education, his business experiences, his language and writing abilities. Mubonda rolled his eyes as if to say this was all a complete waste of time and the rest shuffled their feet together to show that my questions were not what they had expected. Only Sergeant Mumba smiled and gently suggested we should all come together at Emmanuel's home on the morrow, just to see for ourselves what the real problems were.

During the evening, I began to consider the concept of changing the cost of spells and moving away from the provision of animals and produce, to one of a cash basis only. It would be conditional though on Emmanuel having a very basic knowledge of bookkeeping but if not, perhaps I could give him some training. We would also need to have a much better idea of the range of his spells and then translate his present charges into the cash equivalent. I also had the idea of combining an elementary cash-book and sales-book together, but would Emmanuel go along with this radical new concept?

The next morning, we drove up the long incline towards Emmanuel's isolated shanty and we could instantly see the extent of all his troubles. There were goats everywhere, one or two lambs, and a host of different chickens and cockerels. They covered one side of the hill and in between, a horde of African wild-dogs were harrying and panicking these precious animals. At the team's insistence, we had brought along a bright-eyed and excited Alex and with our exhortations ringing in his ears, Alex was soon leaping into the midst of the wild-dogs who seemed incapable of putting up any resistance. Within minutes, these marauding dogs wanted nothing more to do with this unequal conflict and soon fled the scene. In the process, Alex had totally ignored all of Emmanuel's animals and it always amazed me that without any training, Alex knew exactly what was required of him. We all grouped ourselves around the front of the landrover, while I explained the concept to Emmanuel, who listened without interruption until I had finished, then came the questions.

'Bwana, how will I know what to charge in money from this moment?'

'If you come to the police station tomorrow morning, we will all sit down together and work it out with you.'

'How will I know how to keep the records?'

'I will show you.'

During the previous evening, I had doodled some basic ideas on paper and had brought them with me. I laid them out on the bonnet of the truck and after some further discussion, Emmanuel walked off towards a small promontory and stood there for several minutes, starring out into the far distance, deep in thought. Slowly he turned and said with a deep sigh, 'OK, Bwana, I will do this thing and come to the police station tomorrow to see you all.'

The next morning I was confronted by a table and chairs, placed in the shade of the open quadrangle of the station, where I had a designated place at the head of the table, with my name written clearly on a piece of paper, with Sergeant Mumba alongside me and the others spread out all around and gradually everyone appeared and took up their allotted positions. It was genuinely a dreamlike picture that was compounded when Brian Thomas came along to see what we were doing. When I told him our purpose and introduced Emmanuel the witchdoctor, Brian raised his arms to heaven and said, 'Oh My God, please, don't tell me any more, I just can't cope with it!' Once Brian had left, we settled down and focussed on the business in hand, and even today, thinking back to those far off times, the questions and answers still seem manifestly bizarre.

I started the ball rolling by saying, 'OK Emmanuel, let us begin by finding out what are the most important spells, or illnesses you cure, and what herbs you use and how much do they all cost.'

'Well Bwana, I have many spells to make people fall in love, I have herbs to make people have babies and herbs to stop babies, I have medicines to stop dysentery and also I have herbs to make them shit properly.'

I duly compiled a list until we reached a pivotal point where Emmanuel had a reasonably good spread of cures. 'Right, so how much do all these cures cost your patients? '

'Well, to make people fall in love, or to stop a rival in love, costs one chicken for one time. But to make them have babies or to stop them having them, costs two chickens. For my normal medicines for good health, two to three chickens but for really good fortune for a couple's good health and to foretell a happy marriage will cost them at least one goat.'

I interjected by saying, 'Well, now all we have to do is work out how much a chicken or a goat would cost us in the marketplace.'

After a great deal of discussion where everyone participated and all at the same time, we finally agreed on a minimum price for a good size chicken, which was three shillings and for a scrawny native goat two pounds ten shillings I explained the format to Emmanuel and how I would make him a special journal in which he must write down all the names of his customers, the spells he used and the amount of money he received and if he came to see me again the next afternoon I would show him how to make it all work. The next day, and well before Emmanuel arrived, I visited one of the Indian stores and bought a simple cash-book, and later back at the station, I started to make the headings, much to the wonderment of the squad. Even Phiri became involved in producing a neat handwritten price list of all the available spells and medicines and I think he summed up all our feelings when he said, 'You know, Bwana, when I joined the police force, I never thought I would one day be helping a witchdoctor make much more money than I could ever earn.'

Emmanuel arrived and once again the team became engrossed in setting up the cash-book. He soon developed a sound grasp of what was required, however after a little while he became very quiet and thoughtful and in answer to our questions, he came clean and said he was frightened by how much money he would need to pay us. Once I said everything was going to be free because he had helped us so much, he brightened up considerably and told us he would always be available to help at any time. As it would turn out, we would rely on his knowledge and advice many times in the following years. True to his word, Emmanuel visited us on a regular basis over the next few months. He successfully sold off his extraneous animals and his book-keeping accomplishments were soon evident, because his cash-based business went from strength to strength and he began to make so much money, it became necessary to keep it in a suitcase under his bed. Eventually, I introduced him to the local bank manager, enabling him to open a bank account and ever so gradually, Emmanuel became a businessman of some substance and respect in the township.

Days later, I had an early morning visit from my friend Assistant Inspector John Maxwell, who asked if I could help him the next morning, because the stump of his leg had become red raw with chafing and the hospital decided he had to go in for more treatment, but John was nervous and wanted some moral support. At 9 the next morning, we walked up the few steps of the hospital together to be met by the sister-in-charge, who informed us they were very short of bed-space at the moment and John would have to stay for a little while in the ward known colloquially as the Dying Room. John gave a little shudder, and then he braced himself and stomped off after the sister. On entering the ward, he looked calmly at the long line of patients and then in a loud voice which seemed to echo throughout the ward, 'Let's all just get one thing straight shall we? We all know this is called the Dying Room and I have been here before, so while I am staying here no-one is going to die – got it?'

And no-one did die.

Chapter 15

The Wild Geese Mercenaries

I firmly believe it was the result of several events all coming together in such quick succession that started it all. We had recently received information one of our most wanted criminals was holed up in an isolated village, near the border with Katanga, where it was effortless for him to cross over into another country if he thought we were coming after him. I knew exactly where the village was, because only a few weeks after I had been posted to Chingola, the farm police officer, and poet, David Lewis, invited me and Betti Jones to accompany him on a trip to see some of the beautiful bush country. I was driving the landrover when David told me to turn off to the left and after only several hundred yards, the tall grass in front suddenly parted and we very nearly drove straight down into the river. Nevertheless, we became stuck in the mud and finding it impossible to extricate ourselves, I volunteered to set off on foot and seek help, leaving Betti and David with our only bottle of orange juice and no other sustenance, for what was going to be an inordinately cold night.

I walked along endless winding tracks for the rest of the morning and most of the afternoon until finally, by late evening, feeling parched and hungry, I fetched up at a large village where I was warmly welcomed by the headman. He invited me to sit under a gigantic tree and a wizened old lady brought me a welcome drink of cool water. The headman lent me an old bicycle without a saddle and with only minimum air in the tyres and after resting for some time I set off once again, standing up on the pedals, and bumping my way down long, winding tracks. Later that evening, with the moon high in the night sky, I was forced to rest once more and it was only some ten minutes later that I heard a loud crashing sound several hundred yards away, followed by the terrifying roar of an angry animal. Without wasting precious time, I jumped on the old bicycle and pedalled off as fast as I could go until about one o'clock in the morning when I tumbled out onto the main dirt road. At last, I now knew where I was and decided to take another much-needed rest and simply wait for any passing vehicle to pick me up.

An hour or so later, I heard a vehicle coming from the direction of Solwezi and seeing the headlights I realised the truck was travelling at some speed. Stepping out into the roadway I began waving my arms, as the truck bore down and then I had to jump for my life as it was pretty evident the driver was not going to stop. Luckily for me, I was in uniform and the light beige colour finally registered with the driver, who slammed on his brakes and came to a grinding halt several hundred yards further on. Another hour later, I was dropped off at the Chingola Police Station, with the bicycle, where preparations were already well underway for a search party to be sent out to look for us.

It was decided the rescue party would set off at first light and we eventually towed David and Betti out of the mire with heavy long ropes and on the way back, I stopped off at the village to return the bicycle and there I learned that the old lady had to walk nearly two miles each day to the nearest well to collect water. I made the villagers bring as many containers as they could and I drove a few of them to the well, giving them an opportunity to replenish their stocks. On the return journey, I noticed silent tears of gratitude flowing down the old lady's face. Much later, I stopped at the spot where I had heard the crashing sounds during the night, only to discover that it had been caused by an irate bull elephant who had come across a hunter, out searching for wild honey and in the ensuing mêlée, both man and cycle had been trampled into the dust.

Sometime later, on a particularly hot and sultry morning, I visited colleagues in the Operations Room who asked, if we were going up to the border in the near future, could we pick up some Katangese Simba beer for John Maxwell. John was languishing in hospital once more and crying out for his favourite tipple. I readily agreed and then I was asked if I could think of a way of smuggling the beer into the hospital for John, as the matron was so vehemently opposed to any alcohol being brought in that she regularly mounted a campaign aimed at banning the total consumption of beer in her hospital.

By late morning we reached the African village, but in spite of an apparently very concerned village headman, our target could not be found, although I strongly suspected hidden eyes watched our every movement. Notwithstanding, we decided to push on and a few miles further, we crossed over into Katanga via a narrow village track and drove on for quite a few leagues until we came to a sizeable compound which housed a local trading store and a significant number of village huts. We purchased a crate or two the beer for John, at which point, the store owner, Joseph Andoula, asked if we had come to see the crashed Belgian military aircraft complete with its machine guns. Once he understood we knew nothing about it, he offered to show us the way. We set off, driving behind Joseph, who led in his battered old 2CV that had most of the bodywork removed for extra storage and with wooden box seats installed that allowed the diminutive, almost pygmy-like, trader to just about see over the top of the dashboard.

At the crash site, we saw the aircraft was a single engine trainer previously used by the Belgian military, which had ploughed into the ground nose first and partly onto its right side. The propeller had been destroyed on impact but there were no bullet holes in the bodywork and no debris lying about. There had been no fire and an examination of the cockpit revealed no sign of the pilot. Under questioning from Busike, the trader feigned no knowledge of the pilot's condition or of his present whereabouts although the team felt strongly that he was lying through his back teeth.

There were two machine guns fixed on either side of the wings and although one had been bent on the impact, the other still seemed to be in a reasonable working condition. I would have dearly liked to have removed these two machine guns but we just didn't have the right tools for the job and besides, the trader was becoming very nervous and agitated because distant village talking-drums had begun beating out a resonant message. In a matter of a few minutes, the trader had set off back to his store at a goodly pace followed by billowing clouds of dust and we continued on our way in the opposite direction. A few miles further on and a new, heavy sound of drumming started up as if following our route and I could feel the team becoming anxious, especially as the beat seemed to be coming much louder over on our nearby right-hand side.

Busike was our drum man and it was said he could understand and read most of the signals being emitted. I asked him what it all meant and he replied by saying he was somewhat confused because the main message appeared to be calling for everyone to 'come and join the party celebrations'. This didn't seem at all logical and we all retreated into our own little world, as we tried to make sense of the message until the penny finally dropped and we realised it meant 'come and join us in preparing an ambush.' The hair was beginning to rise on the back of my neck, and I immediately took the next left-hand dirt road and high-tailed it out of there at great speed. Only a few miles down the dirt roadway, we saw a mixed convoy of camouflaged military vehicles intermingled with a variety of coloured domestic cars and vans. I flashed our headlights several times in quick succession and we were soon surrounded by a large group of armed mercenaries, who were mostly white. At first, they were not at all friendly, until one of them, a South African called Dirk pushed forward to say he had seen us some time ago at the Mission Station where a priest had been killed and we were friendly. After this exchange, the mood totally changed and we told them about the drums, which we could still hear thumping away in the distance and at that point, the mercenaries came to the firm conclusion that the ambush was being prepared for them.

We delivered the beer to the Operations Room the next day and I told them I had been working on a strategy for John, which just might work, but probably only once. The idea was for a party of us to appear at the hospital at normal visiting times, in our tracksuits and trainers and with rolled up towels under our arms which in turn would contain a hidden bottle or two of beer. The next day, a very smart band of officers resplendent in their navy-blue tracksuits marched into the wards and closely grouped themselves around John's bed. One by one, the beer bottles were surreptitiously removed from the towels and safely stored at the back of his bedside cabinet. We had only just finished when the ward sister came in to say the matron wanted to see us all. In fear and trepidation, we entered Matron's office, where she began to berate us in no uncertain terms for our callous and insensitive treatment of one of our most courageous colleagues, by showing off our athletic abilities, which he could never emulate again. We endured this verbal assault in total silence until we were brusquely ushered out; still, after all that, John was a very happy man.

Two weeks later, I received in the post an envelope bearing a Katangese postal mark and containing a gilt-edged invitation card headed The Wild Geese, which requested the pleasure of my company at a regimental dinner being held by the mercenaries in Katanga, as a measure of their thanks for my recent actions taken on their behalf and the card added the dress code for the evening was to be formal regimental mess uniform. The invitation was discussed with Brian, Special Branch and the C.O. and it was eventually decided I should go and obtain as much information about the mercenaries as possible. On the appointed evening, I drove up to the border post with Charlie and Busike and I left them to guard the landrover. Smartly dressed but incongruous in my police mess uniform, I walked over to the Katanga side where the border guards all came to attention and saluted. There to meet me was Dirk, who ushered me over to his transport, which was a bright yellow Volkswagen Beetle he had bought on his way from South Africa to join the mercenaries.

The dinner was held well over several hour's drive from the border and only some two or three hundred yards from their supposed front-line, where I could see European and African soldiers in camouflaged uniforms patrolling up and down their lines. I was introduced to a Belgian captain commanding this detachment, who explained the Wild Geese were originally mercenaries who had previously been members of the Irish Jacobean army forced to decamp to France. They were then under the command of Patrick Sarsfield and they often had to make their escape in the large wicker baskets used to transport wild geese to market. This name had eventually become synonymous for mercenary soldiers, between the sixteenth and eighteenth centuries.

All the mercenaries attending the dinner were of fair skin and dressed in varying styles of camouflage uniforms. I could see the gleaming regimental silver on the table, included such items as chalices and bowls, looted from churches and other establishments. The commanding officer, noting my interest in the silverware, told me they had once gone to rescue a party of European nuns at a convent, only they had arrived too late and had to take down the body of a nun who had been crucified upside down on a wooden door. They had taken the silver items deliberately so they would never forget this abominable atrocity.

The table settings sparkled in the candlelight and the meal was delicious, accompanied by a selection of delectable South African wines. Afterwards, the C.O. made a short speech of welcome and in recognition of my help, handed me a plain cardboard shoe box tied up with a red ribbon. On opening it up, I could see it contained many documents and photographs which the C.O. pointed out identified gun-runners, illegal wild-life hunters, diamond smugglers and political collaborators, all from Northern Rhodesia. He felt sure the authorities would be very interested and following the final regimental toast, Dirk drove me back to the border, where I arrived in the early hours of the morning.

The shoebox caused quite a stir in official circles once it had been squirrelled away by Special Branch and later, I heard unofficially, it had trapped a number of collaborators including one police officer and several other government officials, although I was never privy to the full story. Four or five weeks later, when I was out with most of the team and driving along the Chingola-Solwezi road, we could see in the distance a massive cloud of dust rushing towards us at quite an alarming speed. Within seconds, we saw a yellow car moving at an incredible pace and sliding from side to side all over the dirt roadway, to the point it only just missed hitting us as it flew by. We were completely enveloped in a cloud of thick choking dust as I turned the landrover around and started off in hot pursuit.

With flashing lights and siren blaring I tried desperately to close the gap between us, with everyone on board holding on for grim death and after ten minutes of fast and dangerous driving, the yellow car finally skidded off the road and into a ditch. The driver, who was dressed in military camouflage fatigues, jumped out, and ran, helter-skelter into the nearby bushes carrying an assault rifle. We too had parked nearby and took refuge behind our own vehicle. I drew my .38 revolver and called out for the driver to give himself up and, after what seemed like a lifetime of waiting, the man finally appeared from the tall grass by the side of the road. His whole body was shaking with fear and it was only then I recognised Dirk, one of the Wild Geese mercenaries.

He told us he was deserting, because the stress of being shot at by an unseen enemy was just too much to take any more, and he hadn't even realised he had crossed over into Northern Rhodesia. As he spoke, I noticed his eyes were dilated and he carried a small wicker pouch attached to one of his shoulder straps that contained a quantity of Dagga. I was well aware that Dagga is a dangerous form of cannabis, leading inevitably to serious psychological defects. Even so, his vehicle was badly damaged and it was at this point I ascertained there were several artillery shells lying higgledy-piggledy on the back seat. The Operations Room dutifully notified the local Rhodesia Regimental HQ who sent out a bomb disposal expert, who discovered the artillery shells were primed and ready for use and he estimated that if they had exploded on contact during Dirk's mad rush to defect, a large chunk of Chingola Municipality would have been totally destroyed – and what about us?

MURDER, WITCHCRAFT AND THE KILLING OF WILDLIFE

Once we had returned home with the twins, my wife had settled down into a routine with the girls, enabling me to go out at night with the team, scouting through the township, looking for signs of trouble. On this one particular evening, I left her sitting in front of the television, doing her knitting, while the twins were lying in their carry-cots, fast asleep at her feet. She asked me to take Alex with me as he had been such an annoying pest, moping up and down the apartment in a restless state all day, which was beginning to drive her mad. I called out to Alex and he immediately jumped up ready to go, then he stopped, looked at me, then at the twins and gradually he sank to the floor and buried his head in his paws and refused to move.

We had just about reached the market place, when there was a radio message, telling me to get back to the station as quickly as possible as there was a big ndaba (trouble) at my home. Hell! Did we move, with the siren going and dust billowing up behind us in one gigantic cloud. I drove straight through the station yard and on to the apartment. We jumped out, to find a man lying partly on the stoep and partly on the dirt pathway and a very angry Alex sitting on his chest with his jaws firmly clamped around the man's throat. I checked first, on my wife, who seemed totally in control of her emotions and she told me, that not long after I had left, the door suddenly opened and standing in the doorway, was an evil looking man holding a large wooden club in his right hand.

She went on to say that the man had only taken one step into the room, when as she put it, 'Alex just seemed to rise up as if he was floating – and hit the man hard in the chest, sending him flying out of the door.' She had quickly locked the door and telephoned the station and it was only a few minutes later that Sekondwe and Charlie arrived, hot foot. Sekondwe and Charlie were sitting alongside the prostrate form, calmly regarding the antics of Alex, who was still throttling the man and periodically making deep growling noises. I asked Charlie, why they had left the man in this state, and he replied, 'Well, Bwana, we thought Alex, our colleague and our best friend, was doing such a wonderful job for us, we would just leave him to it!' The man had a broken leg and severe bites to the throat and face which required stitches later at the clinic and eventually our investigations showed that he had a serious criminal record and was wanted in the Northern Province for cases of arson and robbery with violence. Nevertheless, we all thought the real hero of the hour was my boy, Alex.

It was at some point that my wife mentioned to me that Willy seemed very distant and quiet, and I put it down to possible stress between him and his third wife Serafina, who would invariably spend some time in the early evenings arguing. The time came when it seemed expedient to say something and the opportunity presented itself just after one lunchtime when I found Willy sitting on the back-door steps. I asked him what the trouble was and after a moment's hesitation he said he wanted to change his arrangement with us but didn't want to make us angry. He had noticed the meat allowance he received each week was not the same good quality as the meat we bought for Alex. I felt terrible hearing this and both of us went inside to look at the meat and it was instantly apparent there was a marked discrepancy in quality between the two packages. I told Willy I would certainly get him the better quality of meat and because I was so angry, I would go straight away and speak with the butcher about it. This butcher had only lately bought the shop having recently arrived from Kenya. He was a South African called Johannes Coetzee and I was already well aware that he made incredibly good sausages, called boerewors, to a special Afrikaans recipe. Still, I tackled him about the quality of the meat and he readily agreed, stating, that when he was a butcher in Kenya, at the time of the Mau Mau uprising, the well-fed guard-dogs of his customers invariably chased the guerrillas away. I told him I was not very happy about his treatment of our people but as he said, 'Well, man, that's your problem, not mine. I just sell the stuff.'

Sometime later, I received information that Johannes was engaged in conducting well organised and illegal hunting expeditions and gradually these rumours spread to the point I knew I had to do something about it. It was Mubonda who first found out a little more about our man and the fact he generally used the weekends to go hunting along the Kafue River with some of his employees, using a large wagon to transport the carcasses back to his butchery. Mubonda continued his investigations and eventually came across a disgruntled ex-employee who said he had been fired without due cause and had not been paid his rightful wages. As a result, he would be only too happy to show us where Johannes normally camped each night. He confirmed our suspicions that Johannes would usually hunt for leopards, civet cats, antelope and even zebras.

Late on Saturday night, we assembled at the station including a uniformed Phiri. I also wore my police working uniform and made sure I was carrying my .38 Smith & Wesson revolver. I issued two .303 rifles and ammunition and of course, Charlie wanted his beloved Greener shotgun. We drove for over an hour until finally our informant told us we should stop because the hunters would soon be able to hear our vehicle engine. We alighted and swiftly moved off on foot but we needn't have worried because we could hear them making such an infernal noise with their singing. This was soon followed by the smell of meat cooking on a griddle and within minutes we could see the flames from their campfire. Signalling for the team to spread out and stay hidden, I stepped out silently into the camp firelight. The singing stopped abruptly and everyone slowly rose to their feet. Johannes came forward holding his hunting rifle in front of him and laughing, 'Not such a smart move, man, coming here to try and trap me. I wonder what would happen if they found your body lying in the bush tomorrow; in all probability they would think you had been ambushed by poachers.' I told him I was not alone and called for Charlie to step forward and then I called the others out into the open. I thought for a brief moment Johannes was contemplating making a fight of it but when he saw we were all well-armed, he capitulated at once. We wrapped it all up fairly quickly, taking the skins of two duikers (a small antelope) and one bushbuck (a larger brown antelope) as evidence together with a large quantity of meat being prepared for making spicy, dried biltong.

Later, a search of his premises revealed several leopard skins, together with the skins of an otter and a civet cat. Johannes showed no remorse whatsoever and later appeared before the magistrates and pleaded guilty to various offences. He received a hefty fine, the confiscation of his vehicle, guns, traps and hunting equipment and afterwards, he decided it was time for him to move on towards South Africa.

Chapter 16

Machine Guns and Black Mamba Snakes

It was just at this point that some senior police officer at Force HQ discovered our station CID establishment was registered only for a Detective Assistant Inspector and not a full-blown Inspector. My transfer came through within days to Chingola District HQ and there was nothing any of us could do about it. Willy coped with the packing by himself, leaving us to grapple with the logistics of babies, carry-cots and Alex. It had all happened so quickly. I wanted to say goodbye to the team in a proper fashion over a few beers late one evening but my replacement, who had suddenly appeared, would have nothing to do with it, leaving me to say goodbye with only a well-meant and sincere handshake. It was all so very sad and probably had I known of this beforehand, I would have turned down the offer of promotion; the really depressing thing was I would never see most of them again. The troop-carrier duly arrived and with our crates loaded on board, we all set off for pastures new.

These were the days when paternity leave had not yet been invented and the move had proceeded with no personal allowances being made. Chief Inspector Jack Gowland softened the blow somewhat by having Charlie transferred with me as well, although Investigation Dockets seemed to come at me from all directions until eventually, Jack Gowland came in with one file of great importance. 'I think this one has your name emblazoned all over it,' he said. It was a report from Special Branch highlighting recent information received from a fairly reliable source to the effect one of my old adversaries, Richard Bwalya, had been running guns and ammunition across the border from Katanga with the aim of using them against the police at some point to ensure independence could be more speedily achieved. The real, worrying aspect was the codicil to the report, which stated Richard had recently acquired several machine-guns in working condition, ammunition and a few grenades together with explosive materials.

This began to resonate with me and I started to think back to my previous visit to the crash site in Katanga and the meeting with the African trader. We put a plain-clothes tail on Richard Bwalya and soon found him settled comfortably in Bancroft, one of the smaller copper mining towns situated right on our side of the border with Katanga. This all began to make so much sense and I suggested to Jack that we should illicitly cross over the border and mount a midnight raid on Joseph Andoula's compound in an attempt to secure some firm evidence. As Jack said, 'Well, it sounds fine, but I don't want to know anything about it until afterwards and whatever you do, for God's sake don't tell anyone else about it.'

I decided to go that night and I took Charlie, who could be relied upon and also a new member of our team called, Detective Constable Hatchikabonta (rechristened Hatch by us) who was one of the real old school of courageous and exceptionally loyal police officers.

Late at night, we crossed into Katanga without any difficulty and after several hours driving arrived at Joseph Andula's compound. I had my .38 revolver and Charlie had his favourite Greener shotgun with him, but we wanted to ensure we would take everyone by surprise. I drove at full speed into the compound, only skidding and sliding to a halt a few yards from the main doorway to his hut, with the truck engine still running and the headlights on full beam. Charlie mounted guard with the shotgun, leaving Hatch and me to rush the door and barge our way in. Joseph Andoula may well have been shocked by our sudden arrival, but he said nothing and he knew nothing; well, that was until we told him he would have to come with us to be interrogated further. Perhaps seeing our weapons, he felt this was going to be his last day on earth until suddenly, he decided he did know something after all.

He told us he had removed the two machine guns and several belts of ammunition from the crashed plane himself because no-one else seemed to want them. He continued, 'Then one day, our village headman came into the store with some people from Bancroft who were visiting him. We then all sat around drinking until I mentioned I had some guns. One man who came from Chingola said he would like to see them, so I took him to my car where I had them hidden under some blankets. He said he would buy them from me, so we took the guns and went back inside to drink some more beer. It was dark when we finally settled the price and I helped them load the guns into their white car, and then they left. I do not know their names but one of them was a Sezulu from Southern Rhodesia, and that is all I know.'

In the meantime, Hatch had conducted a quick search of the store and found a large storeroom, at the rear of the premises, containing vast numbers of stacked elephant tusks. Joseph said they did not belong to him but had been brought in by numerous members of the United Nations Peacekeeping Force, who had killed so many elephants with their machine guns and wanted him to sell the ivory for them on a personal basis. I was well aware the UN forces had a terrible reputation at that time, but regretfully there was nothing much I could do about the appalling slaughter for the moment. We left as quickly as we had come and scooted back to Bancroft where we knew Richard Bwalya was staying, although we did not have his full address. We telephoned Detective Francis Mkwanda who had been out gleaning information on Bwalya, and he was able to give us Bwalya's current address.

Richard Bwalya had enjoyed a relaxing evening in Bancroft the night before. He had done well for himself and his elders certainly respected him, even though he was only just 19 years old and they had all bought him drinks at the dance in the Welfare Hall. He was sitting on a chair just outside his hut when a police landrover drew up and two uniformed officers got out and told him he was wanted at the local police station. He was stunned for a moment and demanded to know why he was wanted. The officers were very polite but extremely blunt, telling him he could either come with them voluntarily or under arrest but one thing was for sure, he was coming with them. On the way to the station, they told Richard there was a mzungu Detective Inspector from Chingola who had travelled over to Bancroft especially to see him and at this, Richard's heart sank.

His mood did not improve when he realised it was me, his old adversary, together with Detective Constable Nhliziyo, one of his own tribe, who were waiting for him.

I started on him straight away by saying, 'Richard, I think you have been a very naughty boy once again, because we know you have been buying guns in Katanga and then smuggling them back across the border, so I want to give you a chance now to come clean about it.'

Richard could see he was facing an abyss and his mind was in turmoil. What did we know? How could we know anything? So he decided the best way was for him to brazen it out. 'You have no right to bring me here and I know nothing about guns or any such thing, and I want to see my lawyer.'

I merely replied, 'I am really sorry to hear you say that, Richard, because only recently I was speaking to Mr Joseph Andoula in Katanga, who has told me all about you and your white car and I know one of the machine guns has a bent barrel, because I saw it myself some time ago.'

At this point, Richard realised the game was up and he needed to get out of the mess as best as he could. He simply said, 'OK', and at a signal from me, Charlie looked at him and said in his own language, 'Richard Bwalya, you are warned the police are making inquiries into a case of being found in possession of a Browning machine gun, ammunition and grenades. You are not obliged to say anything unless you wish to do so but whatever you do say will be taken down in writing and may be given in evidence.'

Richard's statement ran on for four long pages of close writing. He implicated other people known to us, but he also confirmed that he and someone else had taken the guns and ammunition, and hidden them inside the cemetery in Chiwempala location. Later in the day, we took Richard to visit the cemetery but in spite of Richard showing us the exact place where he had hidden the firearms, the hidey-hole was empty and a full-scale search of the whole area failed to reveal anything. As Jack put it so succinctly, 'We know he did it, and he knows we know he did it, but at the moment we have no witnesses – and all the evidence is merely circumstantial, so let's keep him locked up for a little while we look around for some solid facts.'

A day later and still nothing and I knew we would have to let Richard go very soon. Even so, I had other things on my mind, because it had been widely reported that Jonas Ngoma, my first adversary who had absconded to Moscow, had been killed in a road accident in the Southern District of Northern Rhodesia and his funeral was being held later that afternoon in his home town of Chiwempala. I thought it only right and proper I should pay my respects and with Charlie in attendance, I parked a little way away from the large, jostling crowd. It made a strange sight, with fine dust clouds hanging in the sultry afternoon air, because it is a sign of African respect, where the deceased is regarded as now being on a much higher plane than mere mortals, while the mourners remain down here on the earth. Therefore, in order to display true esteem, the mourners often throw dust up into the air to show they are now of a much lower standing than the dear departed. I wondered too if there would be any animosity shown towards me as a policeman and the only European attending but no, I was warmly welcomed throughout the ceremony and I began to relax a little.

The coffin was solemnly carried to the graveside by a phalanx of young men and gently lowered into the open grave. As I glanced up and only for a split second I was astounded to catch a glimpse through the haze, and the dust, of the face of the supposedly deceased Jonas Ngoma. At the end of the ceremony, I hurried back to the landrover and drove off as quickly as we could to make my report. Senior officers were very circumspect, could I have been wrong? Yes, I could have. What did I think was in the grave? I thought the cemetery was too convenient a place in relation to the rumours about hidden firearms and explosives and in the end, they took what I thought was a very courageous decision and ordered me to obtain an exhumation order from the local magistrate. In the meantime, a discreet watch was to be mounted on the cemetery just to ensure that the grave was not violated before we had a chance to exhume the body and this vitally important job was entrusted to both Hatch and Charlie.

It was a tradition for any exhumations to be carried out at midnight and we duly assembled at the allotted time at the graveside. The cemetery was ringed by an armed platoon of riot police in full gear and a specially detailed squad of uniformed police started the process of exhumation, with the grave eerily illuminated by several kerosene storm-lamps. After some twenty minutes of huffing and puffing, a heavy coffin was finally retrieved and laid out on the cemetery pathway. The lid was eventually removed and by the light of one of the Tilly lamps, I looked inside, with some trepidation, and gently peeling back the dirty linen shroud, I fully expected to see a repulsive and decomposing body.

Nevertheless, there was no body, but only a selection of packages carefully wrapped up in brown, grease-proof paper. There were two machine guns, one with the bent barrel, that I remembered, and two belts of ammunition destined for the same machine guns. There were also several hand-grenades and a quantity of miscellaneous ammunition for both rifles and pistols. It was a good thing the stash had been wrapped so carefully because the packaging had safeguarded the integrity of the fingerprints which revealed a whole host of known political activists had been involved in this Machiavellian scheme. Richard Bwalya's fingerprints were clearly identified and with the addition of his previous, detailed police statement, the final nails were driven securely into his own coffin! Case solved.

Days later and a laughing Jack Gowland came into my office followed by a phalanx of orderlies, each carrying large and heavy cardboard boxes. Jack explained, Nchanga Mine had installed a massive new IBM Computer which occupied several large buildings, where it was essential the temperature should remain absolutely constant. Mine Security was now having difficulty in investigating what would appear to be a serious, but not a massive deficiency in the accounts, which they had marked down as potential fraud. Jack had volunteered our assistance, especially as this would be the country's first ever computer fraud and these boxes, soon to be known as elephant's toilet rolls, contained the entire mine's computer printouts for the last few months.

Mine Security had spent hours examining the records and invoices without result and I felt we should leave this aspect alone for the moment. Jack and I talked about the case over several cold beers in the police club after work and came to the conclusion that we would be better employed looking at people and wages first. In between my other pressing cases, I periodically took time out to look at personnel records and the expenditure incurred on wages and salaries, although this was extremely time-consuming. Previously having worked in London, I was well aware I had the really infuriating ability to analyse pages of statements and be able to pick out an item or two which appeared correct on paper but inevitably turned out to be problematic and so it proved in this case. After many days of careful study, I finally came to a combined printout showing all the mine administrative employees in alphabetical order and I soon spotted a number of glaring entries. There was A. Mwanzacombe and B. Mwanzacombe in Personnel, Then C. and D. Mwanzacombe in Accounts and so on.

Jack and I asked Mine Security to surreptitiously pull the files of A, B, C and D, so we could have a good look and get a positive feeling for what was going on. B. Mwanzacombe was just a lowly paid clerk but A was a high-grade employee in personnel, who was authorised to employ African staff, although only up to a certain grade of work. We obtained a copy of his photograph and arranged for Charlie and Francis to be on standby on payday, just outside the mine offices. They didn't have long to wait, because right on lunchtime, A. came out into the bright sunlight and scurried away towards the town. The detectives followed at a respectable distance and noticed he entered one bank for about 20 minutes then another bank for another 20 minutes until he finally met up with a man at Bert Gaffney's Nchanga Hotel and they watched our target pass on a large brown envelope. After half an hour or so, A. Mwanzacombe left the hotel and walked quickly back to his office at the mine.

The two detectives, sensing something was radically wrong, telephoned me and within minutes, we were sitting in the first bank manager's office. I showed him the photo of A. who had been in the bank only several hours previously and he went off to find details of any transaction. He returned to say, unfortunately, we had a made a dreadful mistake because the man was one B. Mwanzacombe, and he had merely paid in his wages as he did every week and although they did have an A, Mwanzacombe on their books, his salary was paid directly into his bank account on a monthly basis by Nchanga Mine. It was the same story at the next bank although this time our man had appeared as C. and once again, he had paid his wages into the account he was purported to hold there.

Jack and I decided on a blitzkrieg approach and while he had Mine Security procure the files of all the Mwanzacombes, I sauntered off to the magistrate's office to swear out a number of search warrants for various homes in the Nchanga Mine Township. The moment A. Mwanzacombe appeared at his office early the next morning, Charlie and I swooped and at the same time detectives burst into a number of huts in Nchanga, with search warrants in hand. By the time we had cautioned A. about our investigations into sustained fraud, written his lengthy denial and eventually returned with him to the police station, you should have seen his face when we entered the charge office and he saw all the other Mwanzacombes standing in line. We dealt with A, last of all, because his numerous minions took little time in coming clean and blaming the whole exercise on him. Finally, we dealt with A, showing him the paper trail, bank documents and signed statements, whereupon, realising the futility of further denial he confessed to this large-scale scam.

On this beautiful morning, just after our breakfast and once the girls had been fed, I took their carry cots out onto the patio and laid, them side by side on top of two occasional tables, and then I walked on down through the police lines to the station. An hour or so later I was ploughing through the previous night's report of crimes in Chingola when my telephone rang. I answered only to hear my hysterical wife, saying that Alex had gone completely mad and was foaming at the mouth. Whenever she had tried to go out of the back door, Alex had thrown himself against the door to stop her and when she moved to the front door, Alex had run around the house and was growling and menacing. As she cried, 'I simply can't reach the babies on the patio. So DO something and NOW.' I told her to stay put and that I was coming back to the house straight away.

The words 'foaming at the mouth' usually meant the onset of rabies, a really horrific disease and the words filled my heart with dread, even though I knew Alex had been given his anti-rabies injections every year since we had him as a puppy. I grabbed the keys to the landrover, then I ran over to the armoury, which was open with the Armoury Sergeant checking various records, I could only stutter out the words that I had a big problem with my dog at home, picked up a shotgun and some cartridges and said I would book it all out later! Then I was gone.

I drove like a wild thing out onto the main road then along to our apartment, screeching to a halt, in a cloud of dust, alongside our building. Alex was standing by the back door with hackles raised. I could also see through the glass panelled door that my wife was in a very distressed state and when she saw me she opened it, whereupon Alex barked and immediately launched himself hard against the door. I started to climb out of the landrover, but Alex saw me as well and came on growling and foaming at the mouth, I had no alternative but to retreat back into the cab and at that point, I knew this whole matter was extremely serious. In the meantime, my wife shouted out to me, 'What about the babies?' and I had seen them still resting on the occasional tables when I had driven in. I realised this situation could not go on for very much longer and with shaking hands, I loaded the shotgun and tried to line up Alex in the sights, however, it was impossible to find a safe line of fire. I told Wendy to get back and right away from the door, but this did not make it any easier because the metal security grilles on the landrover stopped me from drawing a straight bead on the dog.

Alex was working himself into a frazzle and circling the truck one minute then racing back to the back door, then running around to the front door once again. This could not go indefinitely and the only alternative

I could see was for me to jump out of the landrover and shoot the dog as he came for me. I took a deep breath, reached for the door lever and just at that very moment, there was a sharp movement from the direction of the drainpipe that ran under the steps leading up to our back door, and I watched fascinated as a black mamba snake suddenly emerged into the daylight. The black mamba is one of the deadliest snakes in Africa and it had been Alex who had spotted it and tried to save his family, even though we had failed miserably to realise his courageous intentions.

Nonetheless, I was now faced with an even worst state of affairs because the snake was moving rapidly towards the patio where the girls were sleeping. I didn't hesitate for a moment, but jumped out of the cab, ready with the shotgun, but once again, Alex was one move ahead of me and with one mighty bound he pounced on top of the snake and a real battle ensued, to the point it was impossible to see what was happening or even who was winning. There was so much dust being thrown up into the air, it became a complete blur, a thrashing snake intermingled with a large, snarling brown dog until finally Alex must have bitten the snake's head off and he threw the still quivering body high into the air. While all this was going on, my wife had bravely left the apartment by the front door and safely retrieved the babies. Eventually, Willy appeared from the sanctuary of his hut with a spade and just to make sure, he started to beat the head and the body of the snake and thereafter buried it in the far reaches of the garden.

Alex too was completely exhausted. We put a blanket out for him on the patio and provided a bowl of cooling water, which he drank almost in one go. We followed this up by giving him a large juicy bone as a reward for his courage and dedication. All the same, there was a marked change in Alex afterwards because I believe he now considered us to be very poor quality parents indeed and it would be that much better for everyone if he took full responsibility for looking after the twins. From that moment on, he stayed by their side, and never again appeared at the station, which allowed him to devote all his time and energy to looking after his own precious litter.

It had only been a very short time since black and white television programmes were available on the Copperbelt and because of the transient nature of my job we had decided to hire a set and not buy one. Initially, the reaction from Alex had been hilarious, because he kept rushing from the front screen of the TV, around to the back of the set, looking for the mystical actors. Still, we enjoyed the programmes especially the various crime series where the handsome detectives always caught their man, in spite of the criminal's clever tricks in perpetrating their crimes.

I have no idea where we had been but we were obviously in a pretty good mood when Charlie pointed out the comical procession of several young boys and youths ambling along the roadside, crocodile style, with each one carrying a small cardboard box in front of him and where they seemed to be grouped in a line according to age and height, as we swept by. We were just coming down the hill towards the police station when our reverie was interrupted by the sight of a police constable standing alongside a brown saloon car, and anxiously waving us down. We parked in front of the saloon car, occupied by two men and when we got out, I saw the constable had once been a member of my old shift from years before. He told me he was very concerned because he thought these people in the car were criminals but he didn't know why! The two men were staring straight ahead with the windows firmly closed and with the engine of the car still running and they totally ignored my order to switch off the engine and then open the windows.

Charlie's answer to all of this, as usual, was unequivocal action, for when they failed to acknowledge my commands given in the Bantu language, he took one step forward, smashed the driver's side, window, with his baton, reached in and removed the keys from the ignition. In the meantime, I walked all around the car and then I couldn't stop laughing. Charlie followed me around and then he couldn't stop laughing either. We eventually pulled ourselves together and asked the driver for his driving licence and insurance details. He explained to Charlie in the vernacular that this was not his car but it belonged to his brother and he had merely borrowed it for a day or two to collect some goods from Chiwempala and all the paperwork was in his hut, although he was quite prepared to go and get it and come back to the police station afterwards. As Charlie said 'Bwana, I think this man is either a stupid dreaming idiot or a drunk,' and with that, he hauled him out of the car and handcuffed him. His accomplice put up no resistance, only saying he was a passenger and knew nothing about anything. The constable was still a little confused until we pointed out the number plates had not only been changed but the front plates showed a completely different set of numbers to the rear plates! However, this did show the power of television because it had only been a week or two previously when one of the crime stories on TV showed a criminal changing the number plates on a stolen vehicle.

No sooner had we taken the accused pair into custody and delivered them at the police station than we were requested by police radio to attend a recent housebreaking case, just along the road we had passed, only an hour or so ago. We drove up to the house and in spite of the fact I must have driven by many times, I had never noticed this property before. It was almost hidden behind tall trees and a high, flowering hibiscus hedge running the full length of the garden and with a stately pair of heavy, wrought iron gates. The house was a modern bungalow, set apart in its own extensive grounds with a garage capable of taking two cars and a substantial outbuilding which looked like even more accommodation. We drove in and parked on the gravel pathway, ensuring we closed the gates behind us but before we could jump out of the landrover we were met by a very well dressed man who introduced himself as Moses.

Moses said he was employed by the owners and he had been out buying groceries at the local stores. When he returned, he had noticed the gates were slightly ajar and on entering the house, he observed that some of the furniture had been moved and a few small personal items belonging to the owners seemed to be missing. He stated he had not touched anything and had locked the house after he left and telephoned the police from his own quarters. I was becoming quite intrigued, because I had never known a house-boy to be so well dressed and have his own accommodation (much better than mine) and with his own private telephone.

It was then Moses said he had a major problem, because the owners were an elderly couple who did not like the police at all and wanted nothing to do with them. They had been very angry with him for reporting the case, while they were away from the house, and they had subsequently retired to their bedroom and would stay there until we had all left. This just wasn't on, in anyone's language and Moses was dispatched to notify the owners it was imperative they emerge and talk to us. After a few minutes, Moses returned to say the owners were in shock and too afraid to come out. He went on to explain both husband and wife were Jews and during the last war, they had barely escaped the German Gestapo and virtual annihilation, through the help of an under-ground movement that had eventually secreted them out of Berlin. They had been totally traumatised by this experience and the whole episode had left them with an in-built dread and fear of the police.

This left me with something of a dilemma and we took time to sit down on the patio to talk it through. I told Moses that he needed to go back and tell the owners that we were not like the Gestapo, and in fact when I was very young, during the last war, the Germans had invaded my island of Guernsey and taken my parents and me to a number of concentration camps in Germany where I had come into contact with many Jews. Moses went off again to speak with the owners and in the meantime, I had the team make a detailed examination of the exterior of the building. It wasn't long before they found a very small side window had been broken but as Charlie said, only a midget could have got through there. He also dusted the window for prints and soon lifted a set of very small finger marks which could only have come from a dwarf or a very tiny person. There were also two varying sets of footprints in the flower border showing, two much larger people had stood there and only recently. Francis started mixing the plaster-of-Paris in preparation to lift the footprints when Moses returned and said the couple would reluctantly speak with me, but only me.

Moses came with me and we waited in the lounge until finally a very subdued couple came in and introduced themselves as Reuben and Rachel, who had retired and lived peacefully in the house now for a great number of years. They were still hesitant and fearful, so I told them a story that I had endured being incarcerated by the Germans in a concentration camp in Germany when some of the prisoners had been detailed to walk to the railway station under armed guard and meet some new arrivals. The story went something like this.' After a long wait and in the gloom of late winter's afternoon, the train steamed into the Biberach railway station and everyone including the German guards were horrified to see the pathetic and bedraggled mass of humanity alighting from the carriages. I saw ill clothed walking skeletons and a nearby German guard was being violently sick by the side of the railway tracks as he witnessed the appalling state of these people.

All I could see was their skin, the colour of old parchment, tightly stretched across protruding bones and then they were gone. At that moment my father began to worry if on their return there would be chaos and trouble over ownership of the various piles of clothing, yet on their return, everyone went quietly to their own pile of wretched belongings and stood waiting patiently for their next orders.'

When I had finished, Reuben and Rachel were holding hands together with tears running down their faces, and very gradually I was able to steer the conversation around to the break-in proper, although we soon hit another snag when I said it was normal police procedure to carry out a search of the exterior buildings. Realising this would include Moses's adjacent accommodation, they objected immediately with some strength of feeling and Reuben went on to say they regarded Moses and his wife as being part of their own family as they had no other kith or kin. They had drawn up a legally binding will, which stated on their deaths that Moses was to inherit all their property, money and personal effects but in return and until the time of their deaths Moses had pledged to look after them and safeguard them from any political interference and harm. Moses saved the situation by immediately volunteering his property for the search as he realised an impasse such as this would seriously hinder the investigation.

The stolen objects were all small but of high value besides being easy to transport and even easier to sell and it was then my mind went back to the comical line of youths we had laughed at as they had made their way along the highway in crocodile file. I reckoned they were heading for Chiwempala and I used Reuben's telephone to ring my old CID office and I was pleasantly surprised to hear Alan Phiri, my ex-administration clerk's voice answer. I told him I anticipated this gang would be somewhere in the Township and probably near the market if he could get someone to track them down while we made our way to join them. Phiri asked me to wait for a little and I could hear various mumblings until Phiri came back on again and said they were unable to help as they were far too busy with their own cases. I asked Phiri if this was his new CID boss speaking and he answered me in a faraway voice, 'Yes, that's right, Bwana, sorry we couldn't help you this time.' I took my leave from Reuben and Rachel and told Moses we had an idea where we might find the criminals and we would soon be back in touch, and then we were off again heading for Chiwempala Township.

We were just passing the municipal offices when we were waved down by a smiling Constable Monga, who told us Phiri had mentioned our plight and he and Busike had decided to help without anyone in authority knowing anything about it. Unrecognised, the two of them had followed the gang from the market place to a clear spot, just outside the beer-hall, where they had commenced unpacking their cardboard boxes and setting out their proceeds ready for sale by the side of the road. At this point, Monga had left Busike on watch and had come directly to meet us and redirect us to the beer-hall. We drove up in a cloud of dust and before the gang could move, the team ably assisted by Monga and Busike were right in amongst them and had them restrained with the proceeds of their crime safely back in our hands. We summoned up additional transport from Chingola and conveyed the whole caboodle back to be charged and for the stolen items to be logged in as exhibits. In the meantime, I took some of the stolen items around to show Reuben and Rachel and they immediately identified the pieces as being theirs. Once the case had been successfully finalised in court, I was able to return all the stolen artefacts to Reuben and Rachel, after which I kept in touch with them and Moses and I always received a very warm welcome until I left Chingola to go on leave. In the intervening years, I have always thought about them and I hope everything worked out well for them and for Moses during their remaining twilight years in Chingola.

Chapter 17

Murder by Black Magic and the Birth of a Son

My early promotion was eventually followed by six months leave, on the tranquil and beautiful Channel Island of Guernsey and afterwards, on my return, I was transferred to Lusaka Divisional HQ and attached to the Criminal Investigation Department. This group was commanded by Senior Superintendent 'Lofty' Blackwell and my immediate superior, Superintendent Don Bruce, where both officers gave me every encouragement. I was given a few days grace to sort myself out and leaving my wife and baby twin daughters with Superintendent Chris Thorne, another of my old college friends, while I travelled the several hundred miles back to Chingola, to collect my car, and our much-loved Alex from the kennels. Alex may have been the runt of the litter, but he had developed into a magnificent animal, highly intelligent totally loyal and manifestly courageous. He was exceptionally large too for a Doberman and I could see since our time on leave, he had developed even further, and there was a dog at the top of his form, compact, muscular and exceptionally powerful.

Alex and I next moved on to rural Kapiri Mposhi to pick up Willy, who had been staying happily in his own village. Originally, I had been posted to Fort Rosebery, where Brian Thomas was now the Officer in Charge having been promoted to Assistant Superintendent and I had looked forward enormously to our reunion, but alas this was never going to happen. I could see the hand of Chris Thorne in all of this, because he was aware that my wife was once again expecting a baby and he knew the medical facilities in Fort Rosebery probably lacked sufficient expertise to cope, bearing in mind our previous medical history.

First of all, I called in at the Kapiri Mposhi police station to thank the officer-in-charge for his help in keeping a watchful eye on Willy during my time on leave and in paying out his monthly wages and meat allowance. Willy seemed very happy to travel to Lusaka, but first, we had to take, his third wife Serafina and his eldest son Joseph, to catch the train. Willy too had enjoyed six months leave on full pay plus his regular allowances and all he had to do was visit the police station, once a month for his money. Willy had thoroughly relished entertaining his friends, socialising and drinking large quantities of beer but he had soon found the constant nagging of his four wives very wearing and by the time Alex and I arrived, he was more than ready to go back to work.

In Lusaka, our wooden crates containing our personal possessions had duly arrived from the police stores and Willy started to unpack everything. We had been allotted one of the older Colonial type bungalows, which had an obsolete firewood cooking range, so it was back to our own two-plate electric cooker. We had three bedrooms, a large lounge-diner and an extensive covered veranda with orange flowering bougainvillea growing right over the roof. The front of the bungalow looked directly over an old parade ground, partially covered by grass but in order to create a modicum of privacy, we built ourselves a rockery surrounded by a large woven reed fence, which gave us a wide circular driveway. Under Willy's careful ministrations, the house was soon looking spick and span and Alex had been enthusiastically reunited with every member of his family to the point he refused to leave our sides, probably in case he thought we would suddenly disappear and leave him behind once more.

Two days into our house moving and a neighbour's house-servant appeared at the back door one lunchtime to say his Bwana, Inspector Peter Jordan, who occupied one of the new bungalows just opposite ours, wanted to see me urgently after lunch. I walked over to his bungalow and found Peter sitting in his wired-in garden with his pet baboon. Peter was fairly tall and of a stocky build but with a very engaging smile. He said that everyone in the camp knew I had a spectacular Doberman, regarded by many as a powerful witchdoctor. He had found out that one of the African officers, who regarded himself as a paramount witchdoctor, planned to subjugate Alex and bring him totally under his personal control by carrying out a devil dance ritual at our bungalow, at about 2 o'clock that same afternoon.

It was already five minutes to the appointed hour when we made our way back in order to watch the impending confrontation between man and dog. We could see Annette and Karen sitting in their plastic paddling pool in the shade of the veranda, splashing water not only on themselves but also all over Alex, who was quietly lying alongside. Within minutes, the devil dancer suddenly appeared on his bicycle, pedalling ferociously down a slight incline to build up speed. It was a dreamlike sight with this apparition clad in clumps of straw from top to toe, apart from a grotesque and fearsome mask. His first pass in front of the veranda created no reaction from Alex; in fact, it almost produced the opposite result. Alex appeared to be completely bored by the whole procedure, and Peter started to laugh and said a little incredulously, 'My God, you know it is working, this devil dance really is working.' The second pass produced exactly the same result, as the devil dancer slipped by once again, without interruption. Tears of laughter were rolling down Peter's cheeks, but what the devil dancer had failed to notice was that when he disappeared from view behind the fencing, Alex had imperceptibly inched nearer to the edge of the veranda.

On the third pass, the devil dancer, imbued with clear visions of glory and final victory, started to chant and whoop as he approached and at that precise moment, Alex exploded into action, leaping high into the air and landing right on top of the devil cyclist. Alex fixed his strong rear legs firmly into the man's back, with his rigid front paws digging painfully into his neck and inevitably, under this additional weight, the devil dancer started to wobble. Meanwhile, Alex was busily chewing and slicing large swathes of straw from the man's body until eventually the devil dancer gave up the unequal fight and, leaping from his bicycle, took to his heels at Olympic speed, closely followed by Alex who was now treating this episode as an entirely new and wonderful game. A few minutes later, Alex returned, still spitting out shards of straw and took up his accustomed position alongside his beloved twins. I left the cycle propped up against the rockery and on checking much later in the evening, I saw it had vanished.

I took to Peter immediately and recognised him as a warm-hearted and generous man who would be a true friend for life. Unfortunately, this concept did not last, because several weeks later Peter was seconded to serve in Chinsali, in the troublesome Northern Province where his patrol was ambushed in an attack instigated by a disaffected religious sect under the control of the prophetess, Alice Lenshina, who I had met a year or so before. During this brief incursion, Peter was tragically killed, leaving behind a lovely young widow to give birth to a daughter, Zoe, who he would never see, hold or love.

I was now back in the harsh real world with a vengeance and with a whole new team of detectives. Busike had been replaced by Detective Constable Bukhama and as such, he took over the heavy mantle of being the team's conscience. Still, this time the team knew exactly what they were getting with my arrival. The African bush-telegraph was noted for being both speedy and efficient in operation and it was a long-standing tradition for our African colleagues to give all of their officers two names. One name would be a total distraction, acting as a sop in case it was ever discovered, whereas the other was a cold clinical appraisal of one's character, warts and all, and an assessment you would never, ever come to know. My good name was described as being 'He who likes people to be happy.' but only God and Africa knew what my nom de guerre really was!

Meanwhile, outrageous events were already taking place in rural Northern Rhodesia only a few scant miles from Lusaka, but they might as well have been committed at the very dawn of civilisation. In one of the villages, Margaret Masupa was not a happy woman, which was a great pity because this was going to be another fine day, not too hot and not too cold and no blustering wind to contend with. She lived a reasonably comfortable life in the thatched village hut, with her husband of five years and the only trouble facing them had been their inability to conceive. The couple had frequently visited local witchdoctors and herbalists, dutifully drinking various expensive and foul-tasting concoctions and potions but without the desired result. However, the main source of her present dissatisfaction was the recent surprise visit of her husband's parents and from the time of their arrival some ten days before, they had made her life a total misery, with a constant barrage of complaints and criticism aimed directly at her. The food was either poorly cooked or the hut had not been cleaned properly and worst still in their eyes, her husband's clothes needed urgent repairs. The litany of her faults was legion, although Margaret knew the real reason for their dissatisfaction was the fact she was barren and because of this, they now blamed her for last year's poor maize harvest.

Margaret cheered up when she remembered she would be free of them for the whole day, because she had to spend time working in the family plot down by the river, tilling the land, hoeing the weeds and bringing up water for the parched maize plants. The maize crop was growing well but urgently required water, as did the watermelons she had planted in the shade in between the maize. She said goodbye to her husband and set off, walking hurriedly out of the village and as she went, Margaret resolved to go scavenging for copious amounts of firewood and maybe, just maybe, that might stop the in-laws from harping on about her many imperfections, although inwardly she doubted if this would ever happen.

At the river bank, she started collecting water in two old plastic buckets which she hung at either end of a long wooden pole, rather like a yoke, and with this, she carried the heavy water to the fields. It may have been very time-consuming work, but she found it most rewarding. There had been recent talk amongst the villagers about seeing more crocodiles than usual along the reaches of the river, so she moved very slowly and carefully along the river bank. On her third journey, she was surprised to see the diminutive approaching figure of one of the most recent witchdoctors the couple had consulted. He was clad in a long and flowing white robe, with a gourd tied at his waist and he was holding a knobkerrie in his left hand. As he approached her, he made the stooped traditional greeting by tapping his left wrist with his right hand and she politely responded. Momentarily she saw a billowing white cloud, the bright flash of a silver blade, and then a blood-red mist flooded her mind before finally, a terrible blackness enveloped her whole being as the spirit left her body.

Early the next morning, when she had still not returned home, her desperate husband organised most of his village neighbours into a search party, in spite of his parents hopefully suggesting that she might have run away with another man. It did not take long before the body was found and because they were so horrified by what they saw, the villagers did not dare to approach too closely because it was obvious to them that evil spirits had walked abroad. A village runner was quickly sent to report the matter to the nearest District Commissioner's office and later that day a police contingent arrived post-haste from Lusaka.

I led the police team and we were taken some two miles along a well-worn cart-track, meandering out from the village and down towards the banks of the river. The poor girl was lying on her back with her blood-stained clothes in some disarray and it was patently clear her throat had been cut. There were also deep cuts on both her wrists and worst still; both her eyes had been gouged out. Part of Margaret's skull also looked as if it had been fractured during what must have been a frenzied and violent attack. As usual, I stood back a little way and carefully studied all aspects in the greatest detail, although the team would invariably confide to the watchers that I was speaking directly to the spirits of the dead. This murder had been a vicious frontal attack and the victim obviously knew her attacker, enabling him or her to get so close. There were bare footprints near the body, which did not belong to the victim, requiring plaster-casts to be made. Some of the team conducted a detailed search of the area looking for the murder weapon, which was never found, although they did retrieve a small enamel beaker nearby, stained with blood. A forensic examination later confirmed it had contained the victim's blood which had been drunk, although curiously enough there were no fingerprints found on the cup. The spilt blood of the victim covered such a large area and it seemed to us that the murderer must also be contaminated. Detailed photographs were taken before the body was finally removed and sent under escort to the Lusaka mortuary, pending a later post-mortem examination.

It was late evening when we returned to the village to find the husband in a distraught state, although we noticed the in-laws did not appear to be too upset over the events of the last twenty-four hours. Some of the detectives moved from hut to hut in the village, carefully taking statements and asking questions and soon elicited the fact the husband and wife were a happy and hard-working couple who both longed to have children. Everyone in the village knew the couple had consulted witchdoctors to remedy the situation but so far without success. It was also said the village community disliked the in-laws intensely because they had continuously blamed the wife for the failure of last year's maize crop and also for the fact she was barren.

An exhaustive search of the family hut revealed nothing of any real importance, although we decided to take the husband into custody to help us with our inquiries. The next morning back in Lusaka Divisional HQ, we held a debriefing session with Don Bruce and the whole team, where we realised the gouging out of the victim's eyes was significant, because from my previous studies at the Police Training School, I was aware that in 1927 in England, there had been a similar case involving a Police Constable Gutheridge, who had been on duty in London early one morning when he stopped a car driven by Frederick George Browne with a passenger William Henry Kennedy. PC Gutheridge knew both these criminals and in fact the car had only just been stolen. Without hesitation, Browne wound down the window and shot the police officer twice and then he got out of the car, walked to the body and blew both eyes out with the revolver, because of the myth which expounded the theory that the last sight a man witnessed would be photographically imprinted on the retina of both eyes. It is strange, but not for the first time I had found strains of European sorcery resonating with African black-magic.

The team set about the investigation, with the perception the victim was almost certainly likely to have known her murderer. The early results were in from the post-mortem and revealed Margaret Masupa had died almost instantaneously once her throat had been cut. Her wrists had also been deeply scored and used to drain some of the blood, which had then been collected in the enamel beaker. It was also confirmed she had been raped when dead, and finally, her head had been battered in by a heavy blunt instrument, as part of a diabolical ritual killing.

The husband's alibi that he was visiting the co-operative stores, many miles away to buy produce and seeds, stood up to detailed scrutiny and we soon had the addresses of the two witchdoctors and several of the herbalists who had been consulted by the couple. The herbalists were speedily exonerated and the first witchdoctor also turned out to be more of a herbalist himself, enjoying a good reputation in the community whereas the other witchdoctor lived much further afield on the outskirts of Lusaka, where he was generally regarded as being wholly evil. Bukhama and another constable took the landrover and visited the deceased's village once again to ascertain if anyone not previously interviewed by the police had seen the white-robed witchdoctor and sure enough they eventually found one man who declared he had seen the suspect visiting the couple's home during the morning of the murder. Our witness also confirmed he last saw the man leaving the unoccupied hut and walking off down the cart-track towards the river. Now, finally, we could place a possible suspect at the scene of the crime and very near the time of the murder.

We obtained the suspect's name and address and set off to apprehend him for further questioning. He lived in total isolation, in a large thatched hut on the edge of one of the Lusaka suburbs and as we drew near to his address, we suddenly saw this diminutive figure emerge from one of the rundown Indian stores. He was dressed in a long white robe and carrying a small bag. However, in the blinking of an eye, he saw us too and dropping the bag, he started to career off across the dirt roadway.

Just at that precise moment, a large low-loader truck slowly overtook us, fully laden with five or six massive tree trunks of exotic wood, destined for the nearby sawmills. Without a moment's hesitation, the man threw himself onto the low-loader and started to clamber up and over the tree trunks until he was standing astride the very top one, with his long white robe billowing out behind him in the wind.

We started to give chase, with our headlights blazing on and off to attract the attention of the driver and with our shrill police siren blaring out. The heavy vehicle began to sway from side to side and every time we tried to overtake it would crowd us out to the verge of the dirt road. The dust rose up and enveloped us like a sandstorm, impeding our visibility, but we pressed on. The driver had become totally panic-stricken, particularly as he could see the imposing witchdoctor in his rear-view mirror. The witchdoctor was urging the driver ever onwards, with one hand raised high in the air and yelling obscenities at us, as he exhorted him to produce even more speed. The driver continued to throw his heavy cargo of tree trunks from side to side until he finally hit a monumental hump in the middle of the dirt road and suddenly the vehicle lurched dramatically to the right with several of the vehicle's enormous wheels lifting clear off the ground. Inescapably, the force of this upheaval was so great that one of the links in the chain holding the tree trunks together broke and the trees started to topple over, and one by one, they slowly cascaded down in a terrifying scything motion, taking the screaming witchdoctor along with them.

The vehicle came to a shuddering halt and the driver abandoned his cab and ran off into the surrounding properties at full pelt. As the dust settled, we saw the witchdoctor had been crushed to death, although eerily his eyes were still wide open and he appeared to have the beginning of an enigmatic smile. Mysteriously, although he was dead there were no wounds or contusions on his body and subsequently we found some of the blood stains on his robe matched the same blood group Margaret Masupa. Besides this damming evidence, the plaster-cast footprints taken at the scene also matched the witchdoctor's feet. At our case review, the whole team felt we had caught the murderer but had not apprehended the person or persons who had commissioned the witchdoctor to commit this atrocity. It seemed clear the husband was not involved, although our suspicions fell on the in-laws. Despite our sustained and robust questioning of the terrified in-laws, we failed to move the story forward and not for the first time, I realised the power of ever-present evil witchcraft overrode everything else in the native psyche. With no other corroborative evidence to support us, this tragic story ended in the blood and dust of an African trackway.

At home, Alex continued his guardian angel duties with the twins, while fussing over them at every given opportunity, but here again, I think he realised my wife was once again expecting another baby and decided he would certainly be on hand to look after and protect the new arrival. As my wife grew in size, one of her best friends in the UK, Ruth Henderson decided she would come out to Northern Rhodesia and help take care of the twins during this difficult time. I think this was a magnificent gesture and one I don't think I ever gave sufficient thanks for. Later Ruth would go on to marry Inspector Roger Knight, my original shift leader in Chingola. We soon settled into a blissful routine until one day when I came home, my wife told me Willy wanted to see me urgently. I said I hoped it was not for more money as we were living on the absolute edge at that time, but she said Willy had been very difficult in recent days and only that morning he had put a broom handle through a pane of glass and he had also burnt the dinner. I found Willy sitting outside under one of the tall and leafy trees and when approached him I could see he had been crying.

When I inquired about what was troubling him it all came out in a flurry of words as he said, 'Bwana, I am your boy Willy and I have worked hard for you for many years now and I thought I was your trusted man. Now you have brought another woman into your house and yet you have not told me who is the number one wife!' I was so taken aback, I told him people from England did not have more than one wife at any one time and that there was only one Donna (head of the house) and the other lady was only a friend who had come to help us when the new baby was born. Willy immediately broke into a smile and trotted off back to work as if nothing had ever happened.

Life in Lusaka was hectic and acted as a hub for riotous behaviour on the part of various political factions and my new team and I were constantly being dragged away from criminal investigations to assist in putting downs these riots and so it was on one of these occasions when I received a radio message to disengage myself from such strife and get down to the Lusaka hospital as quickly as possible as my wife had gone into labour. Some thirty minutes later, I was charging through the main lobby of the hospital when I was brought to a shuddering halt by the strident voice of the senior nurse on duty. 'Right, now, my lad, and where do you think you are going?' she demanded. I replied that I was in a hurry to be with my wife who was already in labour but she interrupted me by saying, 'Well, let me tell you, you are certainly not going anywhere near that poor girl, in that disgraceful state,' and it was only then I realised I was still carrying my side-arm and when she indicated one of the mirrors I saw my face was covered in streaks of blood and dirt. After I had washed and then wrapped up and concealed my revolver I was allowed to go into the delivery room but I knew even as I approached I was too late as I could hear my newborn son's strident voice that sounded exactly like the same tone of his twin sisters when they had been born a year before.

Days later when mother and son returned home, our guardian angel in the form of Alex, refused to leave Andrew's side, the name we had given to our newborn son. Alex spent many hours lying alongside the crib on the stoep, whenever Andrew was put out there to sleep. Alex almost became neurotic if Andrew ever cried and he would rush in to let us know in no uncertain terms that something was amiss. He hated anyone peering over the crib and once again he was known to pick up and then drop the handset of the telephone if he thought the ringing bell was going to disturb the baby. As Andrew grew in stature, his faithful friend was always there beside him and if ever Andrew became fractious, which certainly wasn't very often, Alex would suddenly appear with the favourite toy of the moment and drop it carefully into Andrew's cot for him to play with.

One bright sunny morning, Mr Harry Nkumbula, leader of the African National Congress telephoned me at work to say he would like to come along and discuss a number of various important matters with me. I readily agreed and we confirmed a time just before lunch on the same day. I notified Don Bruce and within twenty minutes or so a delegation appeared, headed by officers from Special Branch who started to install a tape-recorder under my desk. Although I was not overly impressed, I was told in typically blunt fashion that I would once again have to do as I was bloody-well told and I should not, on any account, argue with my superiors.

At the appointed hour, a constable from the charge office knocked on my door and told me Mr Nkumbula was downstairs to see me but that he did not want to come up and speak to me in my office. I went downstairs and greeted Mr Nkumbula, whose immediate response was, 'No! Please just call me Harry, everyone else does.' And Harry he became. He carried on by saying, 'I think it is far better for us to speak outside like this as you never know who might be listening, as even you British say walls have ears, especially police ones!' Harry went on to say he would like me to come to his house later that evening if I could manage it, for a beer, as there was something very important he wanted to discuss with me, but he also wanted me to bring Alex along as well.

I notified my superiors and flatly refused any more clandestine tape recorders or other surveillance equipment being placed upon my person and at about 8pm, I duly appeared at Harry's house with Alex in tow. It turned out Harry also had a liver and tan bitch Doberman, and after hearing the stirring stories that abounded about Alex and his mystical powers, Harry thought a union between both dogs would produce puppies guaranteed to keep him safe from harm. However, during this very evening when he explained to some of his advisers what he planned to do, they were aghast at the idea, for they could see the public would regard any union as the subjugation of his dog by a hated European animal, so regretfully he would now have to forgo that idea. I was not particularly concerned about this new state of affairs because it was fairly evident to me that Alex had expressed no desire or interest whatsoever in Harry's pride and joy.

I have to say I liked Harry Nkumbula enormously, although I think by the time I came to know him, he had finally realised he was not going to win any election campaign against Dr Kenneth Kaunda. Harry had been born in 1916 and had received his early education at several Methodist Missionary schools in Northern Rhodesia, where later he became a teacher. He worked for a while in London but returned to Northern Rhodesia in 1950, where he soon became a nationalist political leader. He was elected President of the Northern Rhodesia African Congress in the following year, although this organisation was soon renamed the African National Congress. In 1955, Harry and Kenneth Kaunda were both sentenced to two months' imprisonment and eventually, Kenneth Kaunda broke away from Harry's organisation to form his own political party. Sadly, Harry Nkumbula died in 1983.

No sooner had I arrived home, late as usual, when my wife told me that Alex had been a real pain all evening, padding up and down and refusing to settle, although the children had already been bathed and were safely tucked up in bed asleep. At this period in the season, the nights were exceedingly humid and heavy and we were not blessed with any form of air-conditioning in the old bungalow, so I usually slept naked, covered only by a cool, cotton bedsheet. Because of the sometimes difficult political state of the country, it had become the habit for Alex to sleep on his rug, by my side of the bed, so he could react quickly and warn me if anything untoward should happen during the night.

It seemed to me that no sooner had I fallen asleep than I woke up with a start to find Alex gently prodding me in the chest and growling in a very low voice. Then, I heard it myself, the slow rasp of metal on metal and I realised it was the mosquito netting of one of the lounge windows being gently raised. I slid cautiously out of bed, grabbing my long-baton and with Alex alongside I reached the bedroom door. Very quietly, I eased the door handle and by now I could see it was a perfect night and the moon was shining almost as bright as the daylight. Then, when I reckoned our burglar was just about inside the bungalow, I opened the door wide and rushed out, hotly followed by Alex. Thinking about it afterwards, I wondered if this was my first mistake because the momentum of my rushed entrance failed to take note of any of the children's toys which were unusually strewn all over the dining room and I had to cross both dining room and lounge to get at the burglar. First of all, I inadvertently placed my feet on some of the twin's wooden building blocks which very nearly crippled me and threw me completely off course. Unsteady and still reeling I was having the greatest difficulty in keeping my balance and slowly but surely, I toppled over.

Worse was yet to follow because, in falling, I landed heavily on one of the girl's wooden clacking toy ducks and with this toy duck fixed firmly between my buttocks, I quacked my way across the floor, until I fetched up against the far wall with a great thump, and just for a brief second, I saw a frightened face looking down at me as I was looking up at him, and then he was gone. Alex arrived almost at the same time and appeared to be totally nonplussed and I am sure he must have wondered just what the devil I was up to. Over the years, I have consoled myself in thinking back over this event and although I agree this was not one of my best efforts, I have come to the definite conclusion, that somewhere in the darkest realms of Africa, and huddled around a blazing communal fire with a group of village elders, my man will be telling them all in hushed tones how he once discovered the true secret of the white man's success, because when the going gets really tough, wild ducks fly out of the white man's backside!

Chapter 18

Looking For an Idiot

One fine morning, Superintendent Don Bruce told me he had been called to Force Headquarters to discuss a rather sensitive matter, and when an hour or two later I heard him coming up the long stone staircase to our offices singing, I knew by experience I was in for more trouble. He told me that Force H.Q. was looking for an idiot and I had been unanimously nominated for the job! He continued by saying there had been several serious political uprisings on the borders with Mozambique and Southern Rhodesia at a place called Feira. The army had been sent in to deal with the problem, but the insurgents had merely taken to their boats and dugouts and paddled across the Zambezi, to the Mozambique side, only returning once the army had left. Don continued, 'Their Lordships at Force HQ have decided in their wisdom they need a snatch team, led by an idiot, to travel there incognito and seize one or two of the main trouble makers and then get the hell out of the area, and you have been given the job.'

He went on to say that I was required to prepare a basic plan of action, to be discussed first with him and then to be detailed at a later meeting at Force HQ. It didn't take long to formulate a fundamental strategy and a day or two later, Don and I sat in conference at Force HQ with a group of senior officers. We worked through the concept, point by point, starting with the cover story, which was that I had been authorised by the Commissioner of Police to lead an armed anti-poaching patrol through various wildlife parks and game reserves in the Luangwa Valley area. The Assistant Commissioner CID, Denis Brockwell stated the success of this venture hinged on the tightest security and it should be left completely me, as the officer on the ground, to organise. The transport officer pre-empted my next item by telling me he had reserved a long-wheel-based landrover complete with tools, ropes, roof-rack external petrol cans and water carriers and being grey in colour he thought it would fit in neatly with the idea of an anti-poaching patrol. In addition, the normal police radio had been replaced with another powerful version tuned directly into the Force HQ frequency, but that radio silence would be essential at all times. The question of arms and ammunition involving a shotgun and three rifles were quickly agreed and the admin officer, not to be outdone, soon chipped in with a selection of government maps, fuel and food vouchers and a stores list for a more extensive first aid kit and basic medicines.

Special Branch confirmed the names and last known addresses of the two main activists and probably the most vital piece of information was the name of our contact who we would meet in a true cloak and dagger fashion at a certain signpost on the Feira road, at 1930 hrs., in two days' time! The plan was approved and I was pleasantly surprised by the understanding and invaluable help I had received. My last order was to look out for a mission station and two Polish Jesuit priests who had last been heard of in 1956 and with a few good luck and be careful comments, I was left to get on with it. The agreed cover story was also the one I gave to the team and those selected to go on this foray were looking forward to an exciting change in their circumstances, especially where they would live out in the open and sleep under the stars. They all set to with a will and with all the equipment loaded, we set off at daybreak the next day. There was very little traffic on the roads leading out of Lusaka, allowing us to make good progress in covering the 350 km or so to Feira.

We were nearing our next watering hole, which was a petrol station cum restaurant and bar run by a European couple who we had been warned by Special Branch had more than a sympathetic leaning towards one of the main political parties. Just before we arrived, I pulled over and gave the team the next part of the plan which was going to be play acting and they all had a major part. We went over the cover story several times which was, that we were going into various game parks to investigate the poaching of wild animals, especially elephants and leopards. Then, when we had filled up with petrol, Bukhama was to make sure the truck had sufficient oil and water and the tyres were at the right pressure. I would be leaving them and going into the bar and appear to drink copious amounts of beer and I would completely ignore them. I was going to give them money before I left, enabling them to buy their own drinks and food, but they needed to be careful not to get drunk.

This was all in preparation for the next act of misinformation, because we needed to catch the last evening ferry just a few miles distant from the service station. Timing was going to be critical, because there were two main roads after the ferry crossing, one going towards the game parks and Mozambique, the other towards Feira. It was important our journey to Feira was kept a secret for as long as possible and I didn't want any travellers coming from the direction of the game parks to say they had not seen us or even worse, travellers from Feira saying they had passed us on the road. If we caught the very last ferry, anyone passing us once we had landed on the other side would have to wait until the next day before continuing their journey and by then, the planned operation should have been accomplished.

We drove in and refuelled, leaving me to enter the bar and order a cold beer. The bar was full and being the only European there, it didn't take long for the woman owner to come over to my table to welcome me and not too subtly question me on my presence and my destination. I ordered some roast chicken for me and had some plates made up and sent out to the team. Periodically, I walked out onto the decking where I could see the team sitting in the shade alongside the vehicle and from time to time, various men would come up and engage them in conversation; so far so good. Surreptitiously, I poured most of my beer down the gaps in-between the decking and then reordered, giving all and sundry the impression I was a heavy drinker.

At the prescribed moment, Bukhama came to the outside decking and made a point of letting me know in a rather dissatisfied voice that unless we got on with it, we would miss the ferry crossing. Reluctantly, I left my glass of beer and with a cheery wave of the hand to the watching drinkers, we wove our way out of the car park at which point everyone in the team broke into fits of laughter and giggling, as they started to recount how everyone had asked them questions about the purpose of our visit. As we neared the embarkation point, we passed one or two vehicles travelling the other way which meant they must have just left the ferry and sure enough when we came over the next rise, we could see one or two vehicles beginning to drive on board and within minutes we were the last to board. It was a short journey, across a quiet stretch of the river and soon we were being waved off on the other side. There were no other cars waiting for the next day and we simply let the other passengers speed away into the distance. We carried on slowly for quite some time along the strip road until we reached the Feira turn-off, where I pulled over, giving us enough time to prepare for the next phase of the operation, where weapons were issued and loaded, torches were made ready and I warned everyone they should be extremely vigilant because we were now entering dangerous, enemy territory.

An hour or so later and the sun was beginning to dip a little and we had just breasted a small hillock, when the sergeant, who was sitting in the passenger seat suddenly yelled out 'Enemy in front.' I slammed on the brakes and we all piled out of the landrover. The sergeant headed off into the bush, just in front of me and I followed on, with my .38 revolver in hand and within seconds he had tackled a struggling man to the ground and I joined in, adding my weight to help pinion the man. It was evident he was a lookout, although, once he had recovered his equilibrium, he refused to answer any of our questions. The man had been hiding out at the crossroads and had neatly removed all the signposts leaving them in a heap by the side of the track, although he supposedly indicated the proper road to Feira.

I doubted this was correct and testing the wind direction, it was evident he was intent on sending us on a route where any potential ambushers would easily hear us approaching. I told the team we would be going via a circular route to overcome this threat, whereby, the sergeant was so incensed, he took the man's spear, pushed him hard against the trunk of a nearby tree and began to bend the spear tightly around the man's throat and thence around the tree. It was impossible for the man to move and when the sergeant told him we might come back for him the man started to wail about being eaten by wild animals. As the sergeant said, 'That is your penalty for telling lies to the police.'

Armed and with fingers on safety catches, we slowly moved off down the right-hand track which dropped away into a narrow valley. It was at times like these I missed having Alex along with me but he was on baby-watch, back in Lusaka. I had a distinctly uneasy feeling in the pit of my stomach and then we saw it, a heavy-duty rope hanging from the top branches of a tall tree and tied to what looked like a horizontal branch a little lower down. These partisans had picked a perfect ambush position, more especially if we had come the other way. If we had swung around this sharp bend, we would have driven right into a strong rope mesh hanging from a large horizontal tree branch, which was designed to collapse on top of a vehicle, enveloping everyone inside. We found that the rope was in turn holding a large part of a sawn-off tree trunk, which on being cut would have careered forward and deliberately smashed into our cab. While we cut down this battering ram and the interwoven mesh rope, each of us knew it had been a very lucky escape. We drove back to the crossroads to see if our man was still pinioned to the tree, but our bird had already flown, probably freed by some of his compatriots.

The light was beginning to fade, giving us little time to reach the prerequisite milestone rendezvous and it was already dark when we reasoned we must be somewhere near our meeting point and it was only then we saw a flickering torchlight in front of us. The glare from the headlights revealed a district messenger in full uniform, with a sergeant's stripes on his arm. He stepped forward to introduce himself and told us there was some good news because the two main targets were closeted together in one hut but he did not know if there were any other criminals in the hovel. The place was some five clicks away and I seemed to remember a click was a slang term for a kilometre. Before leaving, I wanted to obtain some more information from our worthy sergeant who I noticed was wearing the 8th Army war ribbons, amongst others on his tunic, and without fail, any ex-soldier wearing this ribbon invariably turned out to be an exceptional character, courageous and principled. The sergeant said he would come with us and point out the building, but he warned us that there were a number of other huts nearby and he didn't know if all the occupants were friendly or not.

The sergeant's bicycle was loaded onto the truck and we continued until we breasted a small knoll and could see several huts outlined in the moonlight. Switching off the headlights, we coasted down the short incline, stopping a little distance away from this modest village. Careful not to create any noise, we started out on foot with the sergeant leading the way and with the team being armed. Having indicated the hut, which had only one doorway, we kicked in the puny entrance without hesitation and swarmed in with our torches illuminating the interior of the hut. There were only two occupants lying under several dirty blankets and our arrival was a complete surprise. They readily confirmed their names and were duly arrested and handcuffed. The ringleader, who had identified himself as Mateous Lubimba, suddenly became belligerent and asked to see my identification. However, instead, I showed him the arrest warrant I had already sworn out in Lusaka.

He looked at it for some time and then said, 'So who are you to come here in the night to cause me troubles?' Before I could reply, Bukhama cut in to answer Mateous by announcing, somewhat theatrically I thought, 'This is my Bwana who is a great Mfiti [Witch] who you will know speaks with the dead spirits. Be very careful otherwise, a great tragedy will fall on you.' At this dire pronouncement, Mateous suddenly collapsed in a heap on the hut floor and within a second or two his companion Elias Muchos, likewise keeled over. Bukhama looked at me a little sheepishly and said with a nonchalant wave of his hand, 'Well Bwana I did warn them all about that.'

At this juncture, we had no idea if their collapse was serious or mere play-acting, but just to make sure, we handcuffed them both and carried them bodily to the landrover. Our messenger friend confirmed there were a few vacant cells at the nearby Native Court and we could then ask one of the nuns from the hospital to visit, just to make sure. It was only a twenty-minute journey before the two unconscious prisoners were deposited on rough beds in the cells, allowing the messenger and Bukhama to set off for the hospital. It was well over two hours before they returned with a nun who briskly examined the prisoners and stated as far as she could ascertain they were suffering from debilitating bouts of malaria and should be transferred to the local hospital, run by her religious order.

I wasn't too happy about this, because I still wasn't sure if Mateous and Elias were putting on an act, but eventually, the nun told us they could be treated on site, with medicine which she would give us when we returned her to the hospital. My next problem was how to get these two miscreants back to Lusaka but our messenger friend had the smart answer. He suggested we could bring them before the Native Courts, where the chiefs would hear the case and justice would be swift and much more harrowing than would be meted out in Lusaka. He went on to say these two misfits had greatly offended their chiefs and had tried to usurp the power of the Native Courts in conjunction with their cronies, so retribution would be both painful and very personal. However, as I would not be permitted to appear before the Native Court, our detective sergeant was given the job. The messenger told us our captives would almost certainly end up wearing the dirty, grey linen garb of prisoners and would be breaking up stones in the local quarry for many months to come.

On his return, Bukhama said there was a group of Mateous's friends stopping people from entering the hospital, if they were not of the same political persuasion, unless they made hefty contributions to their funds and I resolved, when we had cleared up this little matter, we would go and visit the hospital and see what we could do to help. It was well past midnight when we decided to go and look for a campsite for the remainder of the night and the messenger said he would show us a good spot. At the appointed place, I kept the engine going and we used the searchlight to give us sufficient light so we could search for firewood. We soon had a blazing fire going, and it was at this point we realised how hungry we were and with Bukhama having been elected cook for the night, a nourishing meal was produced in double quick time.

Guards were posted, with me taking the first shift, and when I finally lay down on my camp-bed, it seemed no sooner had I shut my eyes than it was daybreak and the pots and pans were rattling away again over a red-hot fire. The early morning light gradually spread and colour began to fill the land and we could see the district messenger had brought us to a special spot, not too far away from the banks of the majestic Zambezi. The river bank right in front of us formed part of Northern Rhodesia territory, whereas the bank to our immediate right was the land of Southern Rhodesia and the bank on our left-hand side belonged to Mozambique. This time, breakfast included bacon and fried potatoes, with a mug of hot coffee and a shot of cognac to ward off the cold morning air.

We broke camp and started back to the Native Courts to deposit both our messenger friend and our detective sergeant in readiness for the anticipated court case. Having set up our man with all the necessary legal paperwork, I notified HQ in Lusaka, using our adapted radio that the operation had been successful and the targets were sick with malaria but would be sentenced at the Native Courts. I received only a terse acknowledgement, which left us free to investigate the difficulties at the hospital. I had previously asked our local friend about a particular Mission Station manned by two Polish priests who had not been heard of for several years and he confirmed the Mission was still operating and doing a really great job in the community and it would be probably much easier to call in at the Mission first, before moving on to the nearby hospital.

Bukhama seemed to know exactly where he was going because after an hour or so, we drove into the courtyard of a brick building with a few lopsided wooden outer structures, where various youths were engaged in some form of carpentry work. A wizened and diminutive European, wearing a battered old bush-hat, came out of one of the buildings and walked over towards us. He introduced himself as being Polish and one of the brothers running the Mission Station called Katondwe. I introduced myself and he told me Europeans in this part of the world were very few and far between and the last hunting party had passed through some seven years before. He invited me to meet the other brother and the team, in our time-honoured fashion, went off to make general inquiries and find out the lie of the land for future reference, while I went inside.

The brothers made a spectacular sight; the one I had met outside was probably about 5ft 2in, whereas the other must have been at least 6ft 2in. Over coffee, they told me how as young men in their seminary back in Poland, they had decided to come to Africa and serve God in any way he wanted. The shorter brother then left us, to continue his work and the taller of the two started to talk about their history. Brother John Waligora had been born in Poland in 1890 and the two of them had arrived in South Africa in about 1927 and immediately bought a covered wagon and several oxen and then set off into the hinterland. They arrived at this present site in 1929, having spent several years endeavouring to negotiate some of the most difficult terrain and turbulent rivers. Their primary objectives were threefold, where the first thing was to bring Christianity to a land beset by witchcraft and they realised it was no good saying that in God's eyes everyone is equal when it was patently obvious this was not the case, but the lives of Africans could surely be improved immeasurably if they had a good trade and education behind them.

The final and most urgent requirement was to fight against the iniquitous spread of sleeping sickness brought about by the tsetse fly, which was invariably fatal. This was a time when they had nothing except the use of their hands and labour and they struggled in the oppressive heat to improve the lot of their flock. They worked hard to try and eradicate the tsetse fly habitat through land clearing, which involved the removal of brush and vegetation along river banks, swamps and around nearby villages. They knew their methods were crude, but they had no other weapons in their armoury to combat the onward march of this exhausting enemy, except God and their own sweat.

The Mission work continued apace until at some point in the late 1940s, they were faced with such a massive onslaught of sleeping sickness they were unable to cope and in sheer desperation they prayed continually for several days and nights, promising their God if he would spare the villages surrounding the Mission, they would build a church to honour Mary, the mother of Jesus. After several weeks, it became clear the outbreak had miraculously bypassed them. Now, to fulfil their promise, and they were soon made aware that there was an old military style Bailey bridge that had been thrown up over a river tributary during the last war and which was no longer being used. Taking the Mission oxen and carts and helped by a phalanx of loyal villagers they travelled many miles to dismantle it and bring it back to the Mission.

Long before this, they had decided to build a chapel high on a hilltop very near the Mission and the brother invited me to join him to pray in this chapel dedicated to Our Lady. We walked slowly up the incline and entered the building and I could see various parts of the demounted bridge had been incorporated into the fabric of the sanctuary, where metal plates had been used to create a pathway along the floor and struts provided a spectacular altar rail. After praying together for some time, the brother said he wanted to show me something rather special. After leaving the chapel, we continued along the ridgeway until we came to a clearing on the edge of an escarpment that had an awe-inspiring vista, not only down the several hundred feet into the valley below but also giving unrestricted views right across the African plains, with herds of zebras, giraffes and antelope moving ever so slowly over the land.

We moved to a promontory where Brother John pointed out several small rectangular holes that had been hacked out of the side of the escarpment. He explained that, every so often, when he found life too difficult to bear, he would have his flock bring up several heavy wooden beams which would be lowered over the side, and inserted into the openings, then a pre-built wooden floor would be lowered and fixed on top of the beams. Finally, he would be let down by rope, where he would spend many long hours in prayer and meditation. His only concession was the provision of an awning to reduce the burning heat of the day and the devastating cold of the nights. He revelled in the sunrise and the deep colours of sunsets and he relished looking at the herds of wild animals moving far below him. Food and drink would be lowered down to him once a day and his assistants would regularly make sure all was well.

I then had to reluctantly leave the brothers and move on, to check out the nuns at the hospital and for the life of me, I cannot remember exactly how far away the hospital was, although I sense it was only nearby. It was certainly not long before I met up with the Mother Superior, who, in spite of being oppressed by gangs of men sitting outside, felt that her God would protect her and her nuns throughout these difficult times. Our friendly messenger intimated that these groups were not averse to charging patients arriving at the hospital, depending upon which political party they supported and I resolved to stop this activity once and for all.

My first meeting with one of the larger group of men who supported Dr Kenneth Kaunda was confrontational, aggressive and showed little promise of improvement. It started badly, with their leader stating that this was their country and I could do nothing about it and it would be far better if I left right away. In reply, I pointed out they were committing a number of criminal acts, including threatening behaviour, obtaining money by false pretences, where all of these cases carried lengthy prison sentences with hard labour. I went on to tell them I personally knew President Elect Kenneth Kaunda, who was a committed Christian and had been educated at a Mission Station and I knew he would be very angry when he heard how his followers were treating the nuns so badly at this hospital. This last remark clearly unsettled them, and I took advantage, by asking Bukhama to place a large watermelon on top of a nearby grassy bank. Then I had him put an old hat on the top of the melon and told the mystified crowd, this represented a human head and I would show them what could happen to them if they persisted with their criminal acts.

I took my Remington hunting rifle, and inserted a dumdum bullet into the breach, took aim at the melon and fired. There was a short pause then a voice muttered something and everyone began to fall about laughing. Their leader murmured, 'I think Mr White policeman you have been very silly, because you have missed hitting even a large melon with your little pop-gun.' I led him over towards the melon because I could see a small hole in the front of the melon, leaching a dribble of juice where the bullet had struck and when I moved the melon, part of the back had exploded and a large chunk of fruit had fallen away.

The leader was left in a state of shock and I followed this up by telling them we now had to leave and go to the Native Courts; however, I would inform the Native Chiefs of what was going on here and I would be returning the next morning to continue my investigations. When we arrived back at the Native Courts, there was a mood of jubilation because both Mateous and Elias had not only been given long prison sentences with hard labour but they had also been cringingly ridiculed by their chiefs. Their reign of terror was over and their many victims took the opportunity of heaping insults on them both, whereupon the duo hastily informed our detective sergeant they would publicly renounce their actions if the white policeman would remove his evil spell from their bodies!

Chapter 19

Zambezi Moonlighters

Another night camping out in the bush near Feira and another BBQ to savour, alongside our flaming campfire; such wonderful times indeed. We had invited our district messenger friend to join us and he, in turn, asked us if he could come along with us the next day when we returned to the hospital. Sitting around the fire, watching the leaping flames and the sparks flying ever upwards, the messenger said that it had been an idea by one of his chiefs to clear a strip of land near the hospital, that could be used as a landing place for a small aircraft during any medical emergencies. We talked late into the night and in looking at a bright, star-filled sky, I began to develop the germ of an idea.

After a bright and early start the next morning, we arrived at the hospital to find a significant reduction in the number of men sitting around the main entrance. I went to check with the Mother Superior, leaving the sergeant and district messenger to speak with the crowd and when I returned, the messenger was laughing as he said the leader of the group wanted to talk with me on rather an urgent matter. The man came over and for once, gave me the traditional tribal greeting, and then he went on to say he very much regretted his actions and rudeness the previous day. He went on to say, 'Dear, sir, I did not know you were the one who casts spells and can speak with the spirits of the dead, and if you leave us completely alone and do not tell Mr Kaunda we will be very good guys from now on.'

In reply, I told him it was all very difficult, because they had all been very bad and had angered the spirits, therefore, the only way forward was for them to do some good, so the spirits would be pleased. I thought I might be able to help because one of their own chiefs had suggested they could clear a strip of land by cutting down the tall grass so an aeroplane could land, in any medical emergency. In this way, they would be helping all their people and besides, Mr Kaunda would be very happy to hear about their good work, when I returned to Lusaka.

It only took a few minutes discussion within the group for an agreement to be secured and it quickly became a hive of activity with some of them being sent off to pressgang others to fetch hoes and machetes. Leaving Bukhama to guard the landrover, we did our part too, in marking out the airstrip and then walking the ground and removing any large stones and boulders, besides identifying any large bumps in the ground that needed flattening. Soon lines of men and women began scything their way through the tall grass, and there is something magical in hearing harmonious African voices raised in singing some of their ancient tribal songs. By late afternoon, the job had been completed and lines of men and women were busy collecting the cut grass to use as fodder or bedding for their animals. I promised I would send them a windsock which could be attached to a tall wooden pole to show any incoming pilot the way the wind was blowing, and that was that, well at least I thought it was until our messenger said he wanted to speak to me privately.

'Bwana, I have such a big problem, but I do not know how to settle the matter. You see, there is a man I suspect of stealing here in Feira, then taking the goods by boat over to the Mozambique side of the Zambezi river for sale. Then he steals once more in Mozambique, comes back to Feira and sells those stolen things here, – but how can I catch him?'

I asked him where the man was now and he told me he was away in Mozambique at the moment but would probably be back on our side of the Zambezi later that night. He then threw me another curve ball, when he added a few more salient facts by telling me the suspect was often seen in the company of another criminal who had previously been convicted for poaching and the illegal possession of ivory and in gun running and he thought these two criminals might well be working closely together.

I could see the chance of an early return to Lusaka the next morning was fading fast, in spite of the fact further questioning revealed that apart from suspicions, we were going to be sorely pressed to provide meat on the bones, with any hard evidence. Our worthy messenger did not know the man's name or his exact address and furthermore, he did not know at what time he was likely to arrive or even where he would land along the river bank. I talked it over with the team who took the view that without the district messenger's help we would never have succeeded in achieving any of our objectives, consequently the very least we could do was to stay and try to help him out.

We drove back to the river bank well before the light faded and selected an area not too far away from civilisation where the messenger told us most of the burglaries had taken place. We walked the bank, ostensibly to fish, but in reality, looking for signs of activity in the soft river mud. We soon found several deep marks and grooves in the mire which indicated the prow of a small boat had previously been forced into the side of the bank, enabling goods to be offloaded and with no other alternative, we decided to hide out in the surrounding bush and take our chances. We left the area for the moment and organised a scratch meal, while we planned how we would handle the matter. We drove back much later, using only the vehicle sidelights and parked up just in front of our chosen spot, hiding the landrover in the long grass of the river bank, yet giving us an uninterrupted view of the landing place and a stretch of river. The team was issued with loaded firearms as a precaution and Bukhama stayed with the vehicle, where it was his job to use the searchlight to illuminate the scene, whenever I blew three times on my whistle. This would also be the signal for the team to reveal themselves and make sure the two suspects did not escape.

We settled down in our hidey-hole but by 2 o'clock it all started to feel a bit flat, with the team becoming restless, then suddenly we heard the muffled sound of oars, propelling a boat ever forward along the river and within a few minutes, a small craft emerged into the pale moonlight and we could see its two occupants, busily preparing to land alongside the river bank. I waited until the boat was beached and the occupants had started to offload their cargo and at that moment, I gave three short blasts on my whistle and the team sprang into action. Right on cue, Bukhama started the truck engine, to save battery power and switched on the searchlight which cut a swathe of bright light through the darkness. One of the suspects became belligerent and demanded to know why a law-abiding trader was being so badly treated as he went about his lawful business; well, that was until I saw who he was. At that point, I just couldn't stop myself from laughing and this in itself mystified everyone, until I stepped forward and said, 'Ah, Mr Simon Chibwe, at last, we meet once again.' I explained that I knew Simon of old, when after his last conviction in Chingola; I had advised him to get as far away from me as possible and seek alternative employment somewhere else! The boat was full of goods, of small but valuable items and also in the bottom, hidden under a rug we found a loaded .45 automatic pistol.

We then decided to search both the suspects' homes and although both refused to tell us where they lived, the district messenger, had a rough idea and eventually after much searching, we located Simon Chibwe's hut, which revealed a treasure trove of goods, that were unlikely to have been bought by an impoverished man. We left one of the detectives to record all the items and then we moved off towards the nearby home of the other suspect, Joli Ntemba. Ntemba lived a little away from the main group of houses and in far greater splendour than poor Simon. There were two large, thatched roof huts standing near each other, with a much smaller hut situated some way behind these two units. This was often the traditional way of handling several wives at any one time. Joli would live in one hut with his chosen wife of the moment and his other wife or wives would live, harmoniously in the other hut. The small building lying behind the others was called the piccanin kaya, meaning a small place or in more modern parlance, the toilet.

It was obvious that Joli Ntemba had nothing to hide, for he ceremoniously invited us in to search his house, and after about half an hour, we had found nothing. Joli said, 'I did not know that the other man was a thief, all it was, he kindly offered me a ride home in his boat as I had been visiting friends on the other side of the river. So now I want to be left alone in peace.' Unfortunately for Joli, I had some experience in locating poached ivory from previous investigations. I requested Bukhama to back the landrover up nearer the toilet hut and switch on the searchlight. The smell was horrific but we pressed on and in the roof space we found a selection of elephant tusks. Hiding elephant tusks in the conical roof spaces of thatched huts was a time-honoured way of camouflaging the tusks so that Indian traders would not notice molten lead had been inserted into the hollow of the tusk, to increase both weight and the value. The hollow interior of the tusks would then be covered with beeswax and allowed to mature and collect dust for several months. After this, we descended on the hut used by his wives and lo and behold, there were even more tusks hidden in the roof space.

Early the next morning, it was a morose Joli Ntemba and a rather subdued Simon Chibwe who were arraigned before the chiefs at the Native Court and both sentenced to lengthy prison terms with hard labour, followed by deportation to Mozambique to face numerous other cases there. All the illegal game trophies were sequestered and Simon's haul was locked away until victims from Feira and Mozambique could visit and identify the various items. All in all, not a bad outing for an Idiot!

In the intervening months, I kept a watching brief on our friendly district messenger who continued to thrive and also on the Mission and Hospital, which remained trouble-free. We managed to obtain a windsock from the Lusaka Flying Club, that was duly sent on to Feira after our incursion, and there was no further confrontation from this far-flung part of the country.

Our next important criminal investigation began, as is often the way, with rumour and innuendo involving the owner and managing director of an auctioneer and storage company in Lusaka, who was suspected of being involved in various fraudulent dealings. He was invited to attend at the police station in the company of his solicitor and make a voluntary statement under caution, which he did. In his signed statement, he denied any wrongdoing, or the misappropriation of any deceased's personal effects, following which he was released on police bail to appear several weeks later at Lusaka Magistrates Court. The court day arrived and there was a succession of witnesses including his wife, who all testified against the defendant. I seemed to spend an inordinate amount of time in the witness box being cross-examined by defence counsel, who tried unsuccessfully to make me acknowledge this had all been the conspiracy of a malevolent and jealous wife, who was trying to unjustly bankrupt her husband as a marked act of revenge.

When that ploy failed, the solicitor moved onto the asset valuations of various personal effects, asking me how I had the temerity to know what the true valuations were and was I assuming to be a professional witness? In retrospect, I think the solicitor perhaps wished he had never asked that question because the answer scuppered his client once and for all when I replied, 'No I am not a professional witness, because I obtained valuations from two qualified officials of the local Auctioneers and Valuers Association. However, during my business training in London, and before I joined the police force, I had studied for a number of years at St Martin's School of Art, under a diploma scheme that included valuations of second-hand goods, and furthermore I had been employed in the Contract department of Maple and Co Limited, the most reputable retail and second-hand furniture company, certainly in the UK.'

Nonetheless, the case set me thinking and I thought back over the legal proceedings and decided it was questionable the way the defendant had cosied up to various senior staff at the Administrator General's Department, which handled deceased intestate cases. I was authorised to instigate a planned skirmish with some of their senior managers that involved a whole series of lengthy and detailed meetings. Personally, I thought I had been quite gentle and understanding, but apparently not, for later when I returned to my office, I found a message waiting for me and notifying me that I should call a Senior Superintendent at Force HQ, as a matter of some urgency. An hour or so later at Force HQ, I was handed a formal letter of complaint being made against the police, to the effect that my visit had been totally unwarranted, and a direct abuse of police powers. As a form of rebuttal, I launched into an explanation, and at that precise moment, the officer started to laugh and said, 'Look here, both the Assistant commissioner CID and the Commissioner have seen this note. They are real policemen through and through and they sense that you are about to lift the lid on a massive case of fraud.' He then went on to say,' Good luck, but just be very, very careful from now on!'

I started to develop the investigation by establishing the way forward, but first I took the time out to speak about it with the squad of detectives who knew absolutely nothing about fraud or the falsifying of accounts although they were willing to learn. I told them I would have to rely on them in many instances because I would not have the time to run the investigation and do all legwork myself, and not only that but they would certainly find it all very confusing.

Once again, I was called to Force HQ, although this time, I was welcomed with a cup of coffee, a rare treat indeed for such a lowly and junior officer. 'Well!' the officer said. 'You have definitely rung the bell this time and no mistake, and you will be pleased to learn that the Secretary of the Lusaka Riding Club called John Lawson has suddenly absconded with some of their funds and fled to South Africa.' I couldn't see how this affected me until he clarified matters by saying, 'Oh! I forgot to mention that John Lawson is or at least was a senior administrator in the Administrator General's Department. Now, there has been a definite movement to have the case taken away from you and handed to a more senior officer; however you seem to have quite a few friends in this place who have stood up for you and so you will continue to run things for the time being.'

This now gave me direct entrée to the government's AG's Department although it soon became apparent I would be facing a very hostile environment. My answer to all this, was to obtain a fairly wide-ranging search warrant from the High Court which I pointed out I didn't want to execute but I would if they continued to frustrate me and there would surely follow a charge of obstructing a police officer in the execution of his duty. I had John Lawson's office closed as a potential scene of a crime and I also took full possession of all the documents and cases he had been working on during the last six months. In the meantime, the team had an industrious time; filling cardboard boxes with papers and documents and transporting them all back to our Divisional HQ.

Back at our offices, I spent hours poring over mountainous piles of papers and documents, although it all seemed completely watertight. It was evident our man was a consummate con-artist who knew explicitly how to cover his tracks and he had done so extremely carefully, however, it was now our turn to search for the hook that might unravel everything. We tried a number of logical approaches, one was being to locate all the people who had bought or acquired assets from the various deceased estates that John Lawson had been working on, with special reference to auction sales. Within days, we had a very long list of people, all of either European or Indian descent and then we started the process of identification, using telephone directories, civil registers, voting registers and anything else we could think of and to be fair, the team joined in with great enthusiasm. Those purchasers we did find gave us written statements about their acquisitions, including the cost and also their impressions, because it was obvious by now everyone knew what we were after. Then we came to the people who we couldn't trace and I soon realised we had ultimately hit on Lawson's modus operandi in providing false names and vague addresses to hide his misappropriations, so we were gradually getting there, but where had all the money gone?

John Lawson's bank statement had been sequestered from the bank, but it merely showed an account devoid of any cash transactions, but they had only sent me one page and in order to get our hands on all the statements, I was forced to return to the High Court to obtain written authorisation. I thought the bank was being very difficult and obstructive, especially as I had discovered several of the bank staff were very close friends of John Lawson and I told them so, which resulted in another letter of complaint to the Commissioner of Police, who immediately let it be known to all and sundry that he was very pleased with the investigation as it was obviously beginning to produce significant results!

Lawson had been devilishly clever in muddying the waters but now I had all his bank statements and office records, enabling me to unravel and follow the wandering paper trail. I examined one particular file from the AG's department where he had personally authorised a payment to a non-existent person who had made a claim against the estate of an Indian lady who had died intestate. The amount was quite significant for those times in the sum of £150, but at first glance, there was no corresponding entry in Lawson's bank account, until I looked a little further on and a week or so later there was a slightly higher amount paid in. I reasoned, then he had waited a week or so and then added a few pounds to show a totally different amount and then he had paid it all into his personal account. Once I had his methods firmly established it was open season and we began to move quickly through a whole litany of offences.

An appointment was made with the Director of Public Prosecutions, who I had met before and who I believed was a lateral thinker who would not countenance a situation where the South African Government would ever refuse John Lawson's extradition, because he felt they would not want a such a con artist remaining on their turf any longer than was absolutely necessary. The legal proceedings now got underway and all I could do was sit back and wait. Nothing very much happened for several more weeks until one fine day I heard that the South African police had interviewed him in Cape Town, and he had volunteered to return to Northern Rhodesia at his own volition. He arrived at Lusaka airport on 21 July 1964, at which point I met him and took him into our custody on suspicion of various cases of obtaining money by false pretences, forgery and uttering.

John Lawson, who was 41 years of age, was lodged in the Lusaka remand prison for the night and then brought to our offices the next morning with his solicitor. We started with the first six cases of forgery that had been presented to the South African Authorities and in reply, he stated that he fully understood the charges. Against his solicitor's advice, he went on to say as an aside that he wanted to get the whole thing over and done with as he had experienced very little peace of mind, in recent months, and in answer to the charges, he said, 'I admit all.'

As far as I can recollect, Lawson also asked for many more cases to be taken into consideration. I was asked to speak on his behalf which

I did, emphasising the point he had admitted all the charges brought against him and he had not sought to prevaricate in any way. It seems very strange to me now, but I cannot recall what his sentence was, although I strongly suspect it was a fairly long term of imprisonment and I received a commendation from the judge for handling such a very difficult and complicated case of fraud. As a digression, several senior managers at the Administrator General's Department and the bank resigned forthwith and left the country in some haste.

The team had been mesmerised by the entire goings on and it must have been inevitable that word of this spread like wildfire, with the explanation that I was not only a witchdoctor but now I was also a magician, who could conjure up all sorts of evidence from a jumbled heap of papers and make them dance to my tune.

Chapter 20

A Kidnapping, Attempted Assassination and Dag Hammarskjöld Air Crash

Early, Friday evening and the street lamps in downtown Lusaka spread their pale yellow light across roads and pavements. Moffat Kumwenda was on his way home and had just passed one of the political compounds when he heard the squeak of the metal gates opening behind him, but thought nothing more about it until he felt a heavy blow on his left shoulder and at the same time some six or seven men suddenly surrounded him. Then they bundled him the short distance to the main building. Once inside, they began hitting him and when he fell down, a man called James Chipanta kicked him several times in the stomach. They proceeded to drag him into a side room and tied him up to a metal loop hanging from the wall before leaving and slamming the door behind them. How long he was left dangling on the end of the chain he had no idea because he drifted in and out of consciousness, but eventually, they came back and he became aware of a bright light shining in his face. James Chipanta was smiling and seemed very friendly and this time and had even brought in some food and a bowl of water.

Chipanta undid Moffat's chains, and intimated, 'Your uncle will need to pay us much money for us to let you go, probably more than even a hundred pounds.'

'I am sure he does not have any money,' replied Moffat, and in that one split second, the beatings started again, until mercifully he slipped away into unconsciousness once more and when he regained consciousness, the room was in darkness and silence prevailed. He needed to go to the toilet which he reasoned would be a good excuse and with that, he stumbled his way to the front door and discovered it was unlocked. Even though he was badly hurt and dazed he moved furtively alongside one of the back walls of the compound, still keeping well into the shadows and then he escaped. He ran and staggered, lurching from side to side, until finally he ran up the steps of Lusaka police station and collapsed in the entrance, gasping for breath.

By late morning, we had been able to build up a strong case, and it was unmistakable we had a multitude number of felonies to deal with, from kidnapping, assault causing actual bodily harm, to false imprisonment, and I felt sure if I put my mind to it we could come up with quite a few more. Step by step we constructed the offences, covering every aspect and ensuring the whole process would be watertight, an obvious necessity as the waves this case would cause were already beginning to reverberate and create havoc among senior police officers. After lunch, I was stunned to have an apologetic senior officer telephone me from Force HQ, to say two of President-Elect Kaunda's personal entourage wished to review the case for themselves, at Force HQ at 0900 sharp the next morning and, I could easily see if I was not very careful I would be handing vital operational and confidential information to the very people who were of the same political party and ideology as the perpetrators, a totally unacceptable situation as far as I was concerned.

Meanwhile, a few miles away in one of the sprawling suburbs of Lusaka, Petal Musapha was already engaged in the busy routines of a young mother with a two-year-old energetic daughter. Petal was a tall and attractive woman of mixed race, euphemistically categorised in those far off days as being Coloured, a word I detested then and still hate to the present day, and I always found Zambians of mixed race invariably carried themselves with great dignity. Petal had left her daughter playing on the living room floor for only a few moments while she attended to the washing machine but when she returned only a short while later, the child had disappeared.

She ran out into the road, shouting out the name of the child as she ran, while looking into all the other garden plots as she passed by, and at this point, she realised she needed help urgently. She returned to the house, locked it and started running to the nearest police station. She explained the urgency of her plight to the European officer on duty, who sympathised with her, but said he had no transport available and she should go to another suburb police station. Outside she flagged down several cars which failed to stop until an old and decrepit van stopped and agreed to take her to the main Lusaka police station where she arrived in rather a dishevelled state some twenty minutes later.

Bukhama was sitting on one of the benches, downstairs in the charge office, watching and listening to the exhausted woman trying to get the obstinate European police officer to understand her plight, but without success. In total despair, she turned with tears running down her face to be met by Bukhama who introduced himself to her and said she should come upstairs with him and speak to his Bwana. When Bukhama entered the office, I thought this was excellent timing as I was just about ready to leave for the meeting at Force HQ, and I have to say I was not amused to hear what he had to tell me. I told him bluntly that we were already late and perhaps our own jobs depended on the outcome of this meeting when he said something that pulled me up short. 'I would rather lose my job than lose a life, Bwana.' The Conscience had spoken and he was absolutely right, I told Bukhama to bring the poor woman in and sit her down, then to go and find the rest of the team and beg, borrow or steal as many sledgehammers, bolt cutters, crowbars as they could find and be ready to leave after I had telephoned Force HQ, and postponed the meeting.

We set off at a fast pace with Bukhama driving and within 20 minutes or so, we were outside Petal's home. It was already close to 10.30 and we could all feel the heat of the day building up. Everyone had some implement of sorts to use and we agreed we would start at Petal's home and then radiate outwards. It seemed a good idea to pay special attention to any abandoned cars, breaking catches and locks or in forcing open all closed boot-lids and also to make sure the doors of any neglected fridges lying about, were removed and their hinges smashed. Finally, if anyone found the child or if they needed help, they should give three short blasts on their police whistles and we would all converge on that spot.

It was a monumental task as car wrecks and abandoned fridges seemed to lie outside nearly every house or hut, but we all set to with the will to succeed. I suppose it was only right Bukhama should prevail, because at one point he approached an old car and tried to open the boot but without success and he was just about to move on when he remembered his instructions to break the locks and using his heavy crowbar, he forced open the boot. As the lid rose slowly in the air, he saw the sleeping figure of a young child curled up on the floor of the car. He didn't blow his whistle for fear of waking the baby but walked back slowly towards us and

I shall always remember the wonderful sight of Bukhama coming towards us, gently holding a beautiful, sleeping child in his arms.

However, it had not gone unnoticed that we were still in the middle of a very tricky political situation and it would certainly require another miracle for us to survive that one. Back in the office, I started going through the operational file once again, when a lady telephoned to say she was speaking from the offices of the Director of Public Prosecutions. She told me the Director wanted to see me rather urgently and within a few minutes, I was entering the magnificent and spacious office of the DPP. He offered me a cup of tea as he went through the file while making the odd notation on a scrap pad. After ten minutes or so, he laid his pen down and said he thought the cases I had presented looked pretty substantial and he knew I was rightly concerned about unauthorised people gleaning strategic facts from the docket. He proposed keeping it in his own safe overnight and suddenly, I saw people like him holding the scales of justice firmly in their hands, who would not allow them to be subjugated by political pressure from any quarter.

The next day and a smart looking Bukhama drove me to Force HQ where a Senior Superintendent was already waiting for me, although I was still a few minutes early. While we walked the corridors of power, he expounded the thought that the meeting was going to be a little boisterous, but he would do his best to deflect any antagonism. Not a very promising start and certainly not the one I was hoping for. There were two other gazetted officers already present with two very young and well-dressed men, who had chosen to seat themselves at the head of the conference table. The officers introduced themselves, but the two representatives chose to ignore me and weighed in straight away. One of them was wearing a bright red tie and the other a vivid blue one. Red Tie let it be known at outset they both represented the President-Elect, Dr Kenneth Kaunda, and I should look upon this meeting as if I was speaking to him personally. Blue Tie said the delay to the meeting had put them out badly but they fully understood the reasons and he then inquired what tribe the young baby had come from and when I said there was no tribe but the child came from mixed-race parentage, both Red and Blue threw their pens down onto the table and pushed their chairs backwards in exasperation. Then Red Tie uttered the immortal words, 'If you intend staying in the police force after independence you will need to be much more careful in establishing your true priorities with us.'

Blue Tie continued by asking where we were holding the accused and I explained as carefully as I could that we had not made an arrest as yet, because, in my opinion, based on a great deal of experience, the man would not be in residence until the hue and cry had died down. Red Tie then asked sarcastically, 'When in your expert opinion do you think this miracle will come to pass?'

I could sense we were getting near crunch-time and I needed to be very cautious, I replied, 'I would think we could mount an operation early next Sunday morning.'

Blue Tie then chipped in. 'OK, so where is the file of all this for us to see then?'

'I am sorry, but it has already been requisitioned by the Director of Public Prosecutions who is checking it over on the basis UNIP intend instructing a lawyer to defend what appears to be a cast-iron case. However, I have been told to keep you regularly updated and informed as regards events and progress.'

This reply did not go down at all well, and once again pens were thrown down on the table and papers dislodged. Blue Tie's parting shot to me as I left the meeting was to the effect that he hoped I was right; otherwise, we would all be coming together again in the very near future to discuss my status and extremely precarious position within the newly formed Zambian Police Force.

On the way out, the senior superintendent who accompanied me said he was extremely sorry for the outburst and he would tell the commissioner, but I must realise that in giving away the day of the proposed operation, it was inevitable the accused would be informed, and subsequently disappear. When I said I was actually planning to go early on Thursday morning instead, he stopped, dead in his tracks, looked at me and said, 'My God! Your secret is safe with me, but I can think of two well-dressed idiots who will not be very happy about that.'

The resident mobile unit was officered by the remarkable Tim McCoy who had helped me out many times during the troubles and upheavals on the Copperbelt. I went to see him and between us, we carefully arranged the forthcoming operation and in the meantime, my CID watchers confirmed the kidnappers had now returned to their compound. The formal arrest warrant presented no difficulty and in fact knowing we had named the accused and secured an arrest warrant, I could see this would be useful in putting additional pressure on Red and Blue Tie.

I also thought it advisable at the same time, to swear out a search warrant with one of the High Court Judges.

It was 3 o'clock on the Thursday morning, when we arrived shortly after the riot police and just in time to see the man on the main gates refuse to let them in, whereupon on being signalled, the driver of the police troop carrier very neatly drove his truck flat out and adroitly took the gates off their hinges as he swept by. Those of the inmates, who elected to climb over the wall at the rear of the building, were met head-on by a solid body of angry riot-police, who convinced the escapees this had not been a very good idea. Only a few minutes later and we were inside the main building, where the team quickly identified James Chipanta as the ringleader. He was cautioned and handcuffed by my detective sergeant and in reply, stupidly said, 'I am not the one, I will say nothing, but you should not have come here until Sunday morning!'

We walked through each room, photographing the chains and taking samples of blood from the walls. In the final analysis, the blood matched Moffat's type, and his fingerprints appeared on several utensils. We took our accused man back to the station to be formally charged. Under caution and in answer to the charges, James Chipanta stated, 'I know nothing about these things as I was not there, I do not know the person who said he was beaten but I think he was lying, and I am still waiting for my lawyer.'

I retrieved my docket from the DPP, who had informed Red and Blue Tie that if they wanted to defend the accused, they had better go for a QC and not an ordinary lawyer, and bearing in mind the exorbitant costs as opposed to any benefits, they might well want to reconsider their position. He told me he had added the codicil, that it was evident there had been a most serious breach of security, because Chipanta had admitted under caution he knew the raid had been planned for the Sunday morning and as such it had been suggested in other judicial quarters, that both Red and Blue Tie should be summoned to appear at the High Court to give evidence.

Days later, I was informed in writing by the Director of Public Prosecutor's office, the case would no longer be defended and the investigation docket was forthwith returned. James Chipanta was later convicted in the High Court on all charges and sentenced to a hefty term in prison. But as he said as he was leaving the dock, 'It doesn't really matter, because I am Mr Kaunda's boy and I will be set free when Mr Kaunda is made President.' Unfortunately for James, that just didn't happen.

But Red and Blue Tie had not yet finished with me, because a week or so later, a number of police officers were required to mount a tight security cordon around the President-Elect, Dr Kaunda when he made his first public speech at the Horticultural Show Grounds just outside Lusaka. There must have been five or six police teams assembled and gradually each team was called forward by name and issued with details of their respective boundaries. We were the last team, indicated by a mere wave of a hand, no naming ceremony for us and then, to sniggers and broad smiles by the various political entities, we were handed the job of patrolling the rear of the grounds. Red Tie could hardly contain himself from laughing, telling us to make sure we wore waterproof boots because the whole area had been flooded recently and was completely churned up with mud.

If anything, this was a gross understatement because the ground had been turned into a veritable swamp. Bukhama parked our truck on a reasonably higher portion of land which enabled us to get out without our feet sinking into the morass and there we simply stood and waited. Cars and vans slowly came in, trying desperately to avoid becoming bogged down, and I have tried to analyse what happened next, but I still have difficulty in explaining my reaction. A small grey saloon car entered the arena and drove with some difficulty, over to the far side of the mire, to park. We moved towards the car, and we arrived just as the four occupants were alighting. They were all wearing long overcoats and trilby hats and they appeared to me to be a real motley crew.

I identified myself and showed them my warrant card, and my goodness, were they nervous, and I could see one of them was actually shaking. Their main spokesman stepped forward and said they were already late to hear Mr Kaunda and they wanted to get to their seats as quickly as possible, but the man was fidgeting all the time and kept his right hand firmly in one of the overcoat pockets. I could see the coat was bulky and I asked him what he had in the pocket and he said somewhat belligerently, 'Nothing of importance, and certainly nothing to do with you either!'

In response, I said if it was nothing of importance, I should like to see what it was. Once again, the man expostulated to the effect that I had no right to harass a member of the public in this way and he would most certainly report me to my superiors and have me dismissed forthwith from the police force.

He then tried to barge through our ranks, but our tall detective sergeant, who had been standing just behind the man, suddenly moved forward like lightning, and abruptly pinioned his arms tightly to his side and stated he had just seen something metallic peeking out of the coat pocket. Bukhama felt inside the man's pocket and gingerly extracted a loaded .45 automatic pistol, with the safety catch on, complete with a full magazine. By now, I had my .38 Smith & Wesson revolver pressed against the suspect's back as he was handcuffed. He was cautioned and in reply said, 'OK, so I am a senior member of the African National Congress and I wanted to hear what total rubbish this Kaunda person had to say. We were very frightened to come here amongst our enemies but on the way here we stopped in Kafue and I was only relieving myself by the side of the road when I saw this gun lying there and I picked it up. That is all I want to say.' After that, the man was arrested, and I took possession of the firearm.

We later received a radio message ordering us all to report back to the main marquee at the end of Mr Kaunda's speech and an hour or so later and looking more like sodden refugees rather than police officers, we were ushered into the marquee to meet the great man himself.

'Ah! Mr Matthews, so we meet once again.'

'Yes, we do indeed, sir.'

He continued, 'I think I have to thank you for probably saving my life?'

'I am not so sure, sir. On the face of it, I think you may well be right, but the man is an ANC supporter who stated he was terrified of being discovered sitting among your supporters. Against that he states he only found the gun today in Kafue, but I need to clarify this aspect.'

At this Dr Kaunda started to laugh and looking hard at Red and Blue Tie standing nearby, he spoke more to them than me. 'I think some of my boys here have learnt a great lesson today, in that it is much easier to trust an incorruptible man than become involved with many yes men with greasy palms.'

My boss, Superintendent Don Bruce and I had previously talked about the circumstances surrounding the tragic death of the United Nations Secretary-General, Dag Hammarskjöld at Ndola, in Northern Rhodesia, and several years after this fatal air crash, Don asked me to accompany him to Force HQ to view some artefacts from that catastrophe that had previously been salvaged from the crash site. We were shown several items of clothing and equipment but the one item which caught my attention was a printed bright yellow tie, with horse-head motifs surrounded by olive wreaths and a spectacular gold tie pin fixed in the centre, and we were told it had belonged to the American CIA man on board. Closer examination revealed the tie pin was in the form of an ancient blunderbuss and when I knelt down to look at it further, I was astonished to see a miniature, live shell positioned in the barrel – all real James Bond stuff!

Still the whole episode set me back thinking about a night on Sunday 17 September 1961, when, when shortly before midnight, I was given the chilling news by my Officer-in-Charge, that an aircraft on a flight from Elizabethville to Ndola, was overdue and I was asked to mount a search and rescue party, at daybreak. I was ordered to concentrate on the border area near the Congo and towards the Katanga side. I was also informed the Operations room would be telephoning all the outlying farms in the area to see if they had heard or seen anything which might prove helpful.

I organised a scratch team, taking with us, ropes, spades, first aid kits, additional petrol cans and a compass plus several small arms and ammunition. We also took along a radio so we could listen to the Federal Broadcasting News because I knew we would quite likely be out of police transmission range for most of the time. We set off several hours before daybreak to make sure we would be ready to jump off once daylight provided us with suitable visibility. It also needed to be borne in mind that the nearer one gets to the Congo, the denser the vegetation and the wider the top canopy of the trees.

Finally, dawn broke and we drove to the crest of the nearest hill, giving all-round vision and where we faced another obstacle because this was the dry season in Northern Rhodesia, well before the rains were due and the country was simply tinder dry. At this time of the year, fires were a frequent hazard, with some started by villagers using their ancient customs to slash and burn, or through lightning strikes and it didn't take long for us to spot the first fire and smoke. Once we had a compass bearing, we set off, which was easier said than done though, as the journey was difficult in the extreme, forcing us to ford streams, remove fallen trees from disused trackways and at times hack our way through the dense brush. All in all, on that dispiriting day we traced five fires with negative results until finally towards the end of the day when we were tired and hungry, we heard on the Federal News bulletin, that a plane had crashed near Ndola airport, leaving us to return to base completely exhausted. Sometime later, I felt personally slighted by media comments suggesting the police had been tardy in organising a search pattern.

I believed then, as I do now, the Douglas DC 6B operated by Swedish Transair under registration SE-BDY and carrying the United Nations Secretary-General Dag Hammarskjöld and 15 other passengers including the pilots, from Elizabethville via Leopoldville en route to Ndola had crashed through pilot error. I would refute entirely any criticism of the extremely detailed and careful investigation carried out by senior police investigators and I am sure they would not have countenanced any cover-up of their research and probing, under any circumstances.

I obviously read the newspaper reports and eye witness accounts, especially where one said he had heard machine-gun fire as the Hammarskjöld plane flew overhead and I had a distinct feeling then there could well have been trouble with the aircraft engines, back-firing or breaking up. However, I also gave credit at that time, to the report there were a missing two hours or so, where no-one knew where the aircraft or the UN Secretary-General was, or indeed who Dag Hammarskjöld had met en route. There was further confusion over the filing of a false flight plan which has never been satisfactorily explained, and this leads me to believe that renewed theories about conspiracies and the possible shooting down of the aircraft will all come to nothing, and the rumours surrounding these awful events will eventually be resolved satisfactorily.

Chapter 21

Crocodile Skins and an Elephant Tusk

Following action for our investigations in Kafue District in relation to the potential assignation attempt on the life of President-Elect Kaunda, I visited Kafue Police Station, more out of courtesy than anything else, where the Officer-in-Charge told me he had a very difficult case on hand and wondered if I could help him, because although he had received reliable information that a local South African farmer was illegally exporting animal skins and trophies he had slaughtered, he had been unable to prove it. He had been given dates when the goods would be transported but when he lay in wait and made a thorough search of the farmer's convoy, he had found absolutely nothing. He confirmed his scrutiny had been extremely detailed and even included using a dipstick to test the metal drums containing diesel oil. He felt sure his information was correct but how could he prove it? He had stopped the farmer's vehicle twice now and in response, he had received a curt letter from a Lusaka lawyer threatening legal action for such serious and unprovoked police harassment of an innocent and law-abiding member of the public.

I took the complete investigation docket back with me to read through and that evening, over a glass of red wine, I spotted an anomaly, where one report indicated the oil barrels were painted green and another report stated they were blue. I resolved to visit the local Shell Petroleum depot to check and the next day the manager categorically stated all diesel oil drums were in fact black! He examined his records and realised the farmer was one of his clients. He made the point that there would be a specific weight to the barrels if they truly contained only diesel oil and he offered to lend me some industrial scales to prove it. In the meantime, Kafue station notified me they had been informed from their same secret source that the farmer would be moving goods again, shortly after midnight the next night. I agreed to attend with my team and as a precaution, I swore out a search warrant with the local magistrates.

During the interim period, we collected the scales from the Shell depot and arranged that once we stopped the convoy, we would insist on it being brought to the police station, where everything would be carefully examined under the full glare of the police station floodlights.

We set up the roadblock and stopped the convoy just after midnight. The farmer was extremely angry and confrontational, stating our actions were totally illegal and he would make sure we would all lose our jobs and pay a heavy price in compensation. I showed him our search warrant and escorted everyone, including some six or seven labourers, to the station, where, the team led the labourers away for further interrogation, leaving us to start offloading all the goods from the vehicles. There were bags of mealie-meal, tools, timber and then we came to the five or six barrels, reputed to contain diesel oil, although this time they were once again painted blue. A police constable climbed up on the trailer and used a dipstick to check the levels, showing they were full to the brim. At this point, the farmer became even more voluble and kept on saying, 'Well, I told you so, and I now want to telephone my lawyer and start bringing a civil action against the police.' A uniformed sergeant escorted him into the station charge office to make his telephone call and the rest of us brought out the heavy-duty scales. One of the barrels was rolled off the back of the transport onto large rubber tyres and then placed on the scales. Needless to say, the weight did not bear any relationship to the stipulated figures given by Shell Petroleum. When the farmer returned, he was aghast and almost had apoplexy when we began to decant the diesel, and in doing so, we found that there was not even enough oil to fill a bucket and in answer to our questions, the farmer stated he knew nothing whatsoever about it. We finally released him on bail but required him to attend at the police station later that afternoon.

Meanwhile, Shell Petroleum sent along one of their engineers to safely cut and remove all the lids on the barrels and help us solve the deepening mystery and we soon found out that the farmer had been quite adroit in constructing and welding a metal cylinder support inside the barrels, so that they could be filled with diesel oil and give the appearance of being completely full. Then he had jam-packed each barrel with the skins of butchered crocodiles which he had then liberally laced with salt in order to preserve them During their interrogation, the labourers decided to come clean and implicated not only the farmer but also the lawyer from Lusaka, who they said had even brought various clients to the farm in Kafue to negotiate the illegal sale of elephant tusks and leopard skins.

During the afternoon, the farmer returned together with his lawyer, during which time he was formally arrested and admitted his guilt, although this time he was refused bail. His lawyer asked to see me in private where he stated this had all come as such a shock to him and of course, he was not involved. I pointed out the statements provided by the labourers did not agree, and his case and involvement would be submitted later to the Bar Council by the Director of Public Prosecutions, for them to take the necessary disciplinary procedures. Later in court, the farmer was handed a prison term and all his goods, weapons and vehicles were confiscated.

It had been one of those very lazy Sunday afternoons at home and even though I was the CID officer on call, it didn't mean a great deal, as my turn to be on call only came around every five weeks or so and I had as yet never been called out anyway. Willy had prepared one of his amazing curries with the fluffy rice, coloured a beautiful golden yellow with saffron. It may have been one of his signature dishes but we also knew that he would sometimes cook just a little extra, knowing full well my wife would tell him to take the left-overs back to his hut as a treat for his family Still, I was in a very contented mood when the telephone rang, although this state of euphoria did not last very long, when the caller identified himself as the senior officer-on-call at police Force Headquarters. His opening gambit was a little disquieting, as he said, 'So what do you know about explosives?'

'Not very much and only what I have picked up here and there.'

'Well, that's going to have to do, because we have a bit of a flap on here and everyone else is out on other cases right now. The Ridgeway International Hotel has a Jewish trade delegation staying there who are visiting from Israel and at the same time, an Egyptian trade unionist and his party are also staying there, to meet up with various African Trade Union members. The Egyptian delegate was returning to his room this evening to change his clothes when he noticed the door of his room was ajar and he swears that he had locked it before he left at lunchtime. He steadfastly believes the resident Israelis have planted a bomb in his room. Now, I have arranged for a truck to pick you up about now with some of your CID team, so ring me when you get to the hotel. I have also arranged with the hotel management to clear guests from several of the floors and isolate this particular room in question.'

No sooner had I put the telephone down than the truck arrived and I just had time to change, pick up my torch and strap on my pistol. At the hotel, the European manager seemed very calm and relaxed and he told me he had quietly ushered most of the guests into the lounge bar and provided them with a few free drinks while I went up to the first floor to investigate. The door was certainly ajar, and I had a telephone extension led from one of the guest rooms, strung out a safe distance away, which would be used as our command post and communication point and I put the detective sergeant in charge as our contact man. Then, I opened the line to Force Headquarters and my man there started to give me instructions.

'Don't push the door open too wide, and don't put the lights on as everything may be booby-trapped. Feel around the door for wire and if it's all clear give the door a good push and duck! If that's OK, then unscrew all the light bulbs and check the insides for any sign of tampering, then again if all's well put the lights on and run back to the telephone – just in case.'

Heartening words indeed, and I wasn't sure if it was my stomach churning with fear or the after effects of Willy's fabulous curry. The bedroom door flew open on cue and the light bulbs were checked out and the lights switched on, so back to the telephone.

'So far so good, now have you seen anything of a disturbing nature in the room?'

'No, only a pair of very old and long cotton underpants hanging over the bath.'

'Right, now, gently take the toilet cistern apart and then report back.'

I returned after a few minutes ready for my next set of instructions which was quickly forthcoming, and I have to say I was not likely to dance with excitement when he explained the next phase of the operation. 'We are now reaching the most dangerous part of the operation, so be very vigilant as we now need to check the bed. Do not sit on the bed or put any weight on any part of it. First, check out the headboard and then very gently feel under the pillows; if that seems alright, gently remove the pillows and again telephone me back.'

The headboard was fine and the pillows did not present any problems whatsoever and probably imbued with this success, I gently eased the bedspread up and carefully laid it over the eider-down and kneeling down, I peered into the dark depths under the bed, and I would swear later that my heart stopped beating for a few moments at least, because I saw only one white, or rather one bloodshot, unblinking eye, looking back at me and to this day I am not sure who was more frightened; me or the owner of the unblinking eye.

There was a muted, spluttering sound and the bed began to shake and tremble as the body extricated herself from under the bed, and my God! she was enormous and at that point, I realised I had seen her a number of times before in the station charge office having been arrested for soliciting in the Lusaka city centre. Some cruel officer had given her the nickname of Bloody Mary, and I have to say it suited her rather well. The story poured out that she had been recruited (if that was the right word to be used) to act as a companion for the Egyptian trade unionist for the night and she had already been paid for her services. When I reported back to my contact in Force Headquarters, it took quite a few minutes of laughing before the senior police officer could manage to speak properly and sign off.

I went downstairs to find the Arab gentleman who inquired as to whether I was going to arrest anyone in the Israeli delegation and when I told him it was just as likely a person or persons from the trade unions who would be placed under arrest for engaging in illegal prostitution, it was wisely decided he would be more than happy to withdraw any unwarranted allegations against the Israelis. I then went next to both the Israelis and the hotel management and told them it had only been a false alarm and the hotel was now clear. The hotel manager asked me if I could announce it to his guests in an official capacity and as I stood outside on the steps of the hotel in front of a large number of the guests, Bloody Mary, walked by, pushing her bicycle. She stopped just behind the assembled guests to put on her wide-brimmed hat, then she took out a large cigar which she lit and finally, straddling the saddle to such an extent her ample posterior completely overflowed the bicycle seat, she rode off into the dark, warm night with an imperious wave of her hand in my direction.

But it was now time to take my best friend and saviour, Alex the Doberman to the vet for his annual anti-rabies injection. The vet was an old friend and I found him looking very glum and forlorn. He explained he was feeling extremely sad and low because so many Europeans who were now moving back to the UK or going on to South Africa, were bringing in some wonderful and fit dogs to have them put down. I came to the conclusion then, this was soon going to be our problem as well because the day of our intended departure for Guernsey was drawing ever nearer and at a seemingly increasingly fast pace. Still, the visit to the vet niggled me badly and the thought of so many loving and loyal creatures being put down out of hand left me feeling distraught and uneasy. Over lunch, I mentioned my visit to the vet to my wife who said, 'Well, we will have to decide what we are going to do about Alex as well, and very soon too.' Over our lunchtime coffee, it gave me a chance to think it all through once again and I reached the inescapable conclusion that I could not contemplate having Alex put to sleep under any circumstances and certainly not after his constant devotion to me and his whole family. I went through the long list of his high points from saving me from ambush, and attacks, to his defence of the family from a black mamba snake and so forth. No! I rationalised if needs be, I would have to take out a bank loan to pay to have him shipped back to the UK, even though I knew he would have to spend six months there in quarantine.

On 27 August 1964, after much searching, I eventually fetched up at Gaydawn Kennels, of P.O. Box 778, Lusaka owned by the fantastic Hall family and they readily agreed to take Alex in when the time eventually arrived for us to leave Northern Rhodesia. Furthermore, they would look after him and then have him crated up and airlifted to us in Guernsey. I have to say, they did an incredible job and their kind actions certainly gave us peace of mind and I still keep their invoice, in remembrance of such a good deed. Several days before we were due to jet off back to the UK, I delivered a slightly bewildered Doberman to the kennels and took my leave. Fast forward a few weeks, and I was sitting in the family home, back in Guernsey, when I received a telephone call from the States of Guernsey Airport, Animal Handling Section, to the effect they had just received an enormous wooden crate from Africa that contained an angry and wild hyena and no-one there was going to go anywhere near that damn crate until I arrived at the airport to sort it all out for them and in double quick time.

It was probably only 20 minutes later, before I arrived and already, as I approached the animal section, I could hear a ferocious growling and barking. I stood in front of the shaking crate so Alex could have a good view of me and called his name. Well, that certainly stopped him in his tracks and he started sniffing the air and then came up to the wire door of the crate and stood looking at me as if to say, well what the hell took you so long? As the airport staff scrambled out of the area in complete panic, I unlocked the crate and then put a lead on Alex and walked him around a little before giving him a bowl of water and a few meat titbits and after that, all was peace and quiet. The Secretary of the Guernsey Society for the Prevention of Cruelty to Animals soon arrived to transport Alex to the quarantine kennels and then he made a very wise statement. He said, 'Either you leave him alone with us now for the next six months or you must promise to visit him every day.' I elected to visit Alex each day and that was what the whole family did after school or work and at weekends, when we would all troop off to the kennels to encourage our best friend, our loyal and dedicated Alex. But that was still some way away in the future whereas I was honour bound to live in the present African scene.

Over the years, I think it is fair to say, we had all tried to eradicate the trophy slaying of wildlife by inhabitants that embraced many nationalities and with a fair measure of success, and it was therefore with some pride I attended an event organised by various senior members of the Game Department of Northern Rhodesia, soon to be a defunct body at independence. I was told it was to thank a number of people, like myself, for all their endeavours over the years and I would find myself in good company. In actual fact, I didn't know anyone else there, but I think we all enjoyed a glass of wine and a few canapés as the organisers mingled amongst us. Eventually, with much pomp and circumstance, the audience was called to order and the award ceremony got underway, with books, and vellum scrolls being handed out to grateful recipients. When my turn came and I was called up to the rostrum, I was astounded to be handed a single elephant tusk! My award was concerned with the arrest of some 125 Europeans, South Africans, Indians, Portuguese, Greeks and Africans for various poaching activities and for the confiscation of significant amounts of ivory, leopard and zebra skins, vehicles, guns and ammunition. Initially, I thought they must all be mad, but now I think that maybe they knew I would keep this memento as a family heirloom, complete with a metal plate bearing my name, and therefore the tusk would never form part of any illicit sale. Today, it has a place of pride in my house and whenever I look at it, I am once again transported back to the country and the people I had come to love.

One of the hardest things I had to do was to say goodbye to Willy Kabeka, who had looked after us all so well and loyally over the years. On one of our last evenings, I sat down with him and tried to understand what he would do when we had left Africa for good. Did he want to go back to his village? No, he said he would rather stay in Lusaka as the prospect of a job was far greater there. I had previously made out several letters of recommendation he could show any prospective employer, but I also gave him some additional cash, to cover a train journey home for him and his family, just in case he changed his mind about going back. I also handed Willy another six months' salary and covered his meat allowance as well, and then we gave him all our pots, pans, cutlery and linen plus an additional set of uniforms. He had arranged to stay with a tribal brother in Lusaka and I drove him, his wife Serafina and his son Joseph there with all their gear and that had to be one of the saddest times, of saying goodbye to such a wonderful man, because I knew in my heart of hearts, I would never see him again.

My team of detectives and I stipulated that we would never say goodbye and my wife and I held an impromptu drinks party with a few snacks for them in our garden a day or so before we were due to depart. We were a very subdued party, but we all put on a brave face, with them not knowing how independence would affect them and with me unaware how my life would pan out back in Guernsey. A day later, my family and I arrived at Lusaka International Airport to take the mid-morning flight back to London and then onto the Channel Islands, when suddenly we were surrounded by the whole team who had asked permission to see me off, from Superintendent Don Bruce, who had agreed but stipulated that they had to pay their own fares out to the airport. Bukhama said he had come specifically to make me change my mind and stay on with them in the new state of Zambia, although I had to regretfully decline. Then knowing the impossibility of me staying the Sub-Inspector, spoke up to say, 'Bwana, we have all been together for quite some time now and you should stay with us, because once you leave us here, you will never, never be so loved or respected ever again.' Hearing those words, I am not ashamed to say, tears welled up and coursed down my face and I recall precious little of the flight home, but over the years I have remembered his words and just how prophetic they would turn out to be.

ADDENDUM

I have only recently been made aware of a surprising situation that has emerged from the Kruger National Park in South Africa. The reserve is the largest in the whole of Africa and covers some 7,577 square miles and was established in 1926. The game wardens there have been using Doberman dogs and other breeds to track and capture poachers engaged in the merciless slaughter of wildlife throughout the reserve. This operation now accounts for 80 per cent of all arrests made and is some 55 years after my boy Alex and I devised the same scenario in Northern Rhodesia. As Napoleon once said, 'The more things change the more they remain the same.'

Lastly my own Website complete with more information and photographs, which is available for those readers who are curious to learn more.

Stephen R. Matthews. Author

(http://stephen-r-matthews.wix.com/author)

If you have enjoyed reading this book, then I would love to hear from you; by using the Comments Section in my Website. I do appreciate all comments and I reply personally to all messages.